Ways of Knowing in Science Series

RICHARD DUSCHL, SERIES EDITOR

ADVISORY BOARD: Charles W. Anderson, Nancy Brickhouse, Rosalind Driver,
Eleanor Duckworth, Peter Fensham, William Kyle,
Roy Pea, Edward Silver, Russell Yeany

Problems of Meaning in Science Curriculum

EDITED BY

Douglas A. Roberts and Leif Östman

FOREWORD BY F. JAMES RUTHERFORD

Teachers College, Columbia University
New York and London

Published by Teachers College Press, 1234 Amsterdam Avenue, New York, NY 10027

Library of Congress Cataloging-in-Publication Data

Problems of meaning in science curriculum / edited by Douglas A.
Roberts and Leif Östman ; foreword by F. James Rutherford.
      p.   cm. — (Ways of knowing in science series)
    Includes bibliographical references and index.
      ISBN 0-8077-3709-7 (cloth : alk. paper). — ISBN 0-8077-3708-9
(paper : alk. paper)
      1. Science—Study and teaching—Curricula. 2. Meaning
(Philosophy) 3. Science—Study and teaching (Secondary)—North
America. I. Roberts, Douglas A. II. Östman, Leif. III. Series.
Q181.5.P76   1998
507'.1—dc21   97-46462

ISBN 0-8077-3708-9 (paper)
ISBN 0-8077-3709-7 (cloth)

Printed on acid-free paper
Manufactured in the United States of America
05 04 03 02 01 00 99 98   8 7 6 5 4 3 2 1

◯ Contents

◯ Foreword

THE PAPERS IN THIS BOOK are frankly provocative, taking issue with traditional ways of thinking about science curriculum, demanding that we turn away from business as usual. You may not agree with some of the claims made in the papers—I surely do not—but you cannot ignore them, for the claims are as deeply challenging as they are forcefully put. If significant and lasting reform on a grand scale is what we science educators seek, it matters less whether we embrace or reject every one of the many absorbing ideas in these papers than that we understand and respond to them thoughtfully.

Moreover, the papers are of a piece. It is not surprising that these distinguished authors from half a dozen countries would produce captivating papers for this volume, since without exception they are accomplished scholars and activists who have long been known to the science education community through their forward-looking writings. What could not have been predicted, however, even given the strong and deft hands of the editors, is that the set of papers would fit together so well, so harmoniously, to form a coherent whole. Thus, while each chapter is conceptually self-contained and merits close attention to its details, the reader will find, upon stepping back a bit from the details, chapter by chapter, that a story is being told and a shared point of view articulated.

The theme of the story—not to be done justice in a few words—is that a curriculum is not merely a collection of courses and subjects, but something much less concrete, yet far more powerful. A curriculum, according to the view presented by these authors, is an array of *experiences*, which inevitably foster *meanings* that shape the lives of young people. The experiences are more richly complex than can be conveyed by noting which topics are studied in what order using which pedagogical techniques, more deeply human than suggested by data about class size and teacher credentials. And the resulting meanings are more numerous, intimate, and enduring than revealed by official lists of learning goals and objectives.

The moral of the story in this book is that we have to look beyond the obvious in thinking about the curriculum, beyond the usual focus on questions of content and organization and authority. We have instead to examine the very character of the human interactions that are at the heart of the school experience, and we have to consider meanings from many perspectives, above all, from that of the learners themselves. The authors flesh out the story by offering thoughts on what that might entail.

All in all, a challenge well made, a story well told.

For all of that, other readers may, as I did, end up feeling somewhat frustrated. Without exception, every chapter puts forward ideas and claims that, just as the authors intend, invite—no, demand—our personal responses. The volume calls out for debate, for us to refute or extend or modify this claim and that idea, for us to explore the story line from different vantage points, question its premises, and estimate its reach. But alas we cannot talk back, at least not so that the authors can hear us and respond to our responses, or so that we readers can hear and respond to one another. It strikes me, by way of remedy, that this is exactly the kind of publication that should be on Internet. Were that so, we could easily and promptly have lively electronic conferences on each of the chapters, challenging one another worldwide, idea by idea. We could all practice what the authors preach.

F. James Rutherford
American Association for the Advancement of Science

○ Preface

THIS BOOK IS ABOUT curriculum and meaning. As a component of the school curriculum, science has features that are both unique and representative. It is our view, and the view of the other authors in this volume, that making sense of curriculum issues is best undertaken when the specifics of a school subject are close at hand to provide some grounding. We trust that this approach will enable readers with a more general interest, or an interest in other subject areas, to make use of this work by viewing science as a type case. Within science education, we hope that the approach we have taken will help revitalize debate about curriculum *substance*, a matter we believe is in need of serious attention.

We argue, broadly, that the "socialization" of students is not only a matter of their deportment, attitudes, conduct, and so forth, as the term tends to be used, but is also very significantly associated with the *meanings provided* by their educational experiences. Science textbooks, teachers, and classrooms teach a lot more than the scientific meaning of concepts, principles, laws, and theories. Most of the extras are taught implicitly, often by what is *not* stated. Students are taught about power and authority, for example. They are taught what knowledge, and what kind of knowledge, is worth knowing and whether they can master it. They are taught how to regard themselves in relation to both natural and technologically devised objects and events, and with what demeanor to regard those very objects and events. All of these extras we call "companion meanings," and that concept occupies center stage in this volume.

Companion meanings function as both context and subtext for the more obvious subject matter meanings in school subjects. The concept itself is like Dewey's (1938/1963) "collateral learnings" and Schwab's (1962) "meta-learnings," although it is much elaborated and expanded. Both Dewey's concept and Schwab's were meant to suggest unintended learning, companion meanings in curriculum and teaching that go unnoticed and are hidden from rational control and decision making—until, that is, someone calls attention to them. Like the gender bias that goes along with having only males pictured as scientists in a science textbook, such meanings are not hidden any longer once they are conceptualized and exposed. They can be made the subject of analysis, criticism, debate, and curriculum revitalization, and that is where we are headed in this volume.

The concept of companion meaning owes its origins in large part to Roberts's (1982b, 1988) work on "curriculum emphases" in science education, which was an effort to classify and understand differences in broad educational goals as they appeared in different textbooks and curriculum documents for school science. Of course, just classifying educational purposes or goals is not really doing anything new or exciting, especially in a postmodern academic climate, and this volume goes much further. It has been more than two decades since Eisner and Vallance (1974) published their work on "conflicting conceptions" of curriculum, and Lawrence Gabel (1976) produced his massive study classifying the goals of science education in North America since the turn of the century. Classifying is a significant aspect of information processing, to be sure, but there is a danger whenever inventing and refining categories is seen as a suitable and sufficient end in itself.

What is required for any critical edge to flourish is to *interpret* differences among curriculum emphases, conflicting conceptions, or goal clusters, after one ferrets out the broadly differing companion meanings, and to contemplate *action*. Such activity leads to questions with deep moral implications, as developed in Östman's work (e.g., 1994), and provokes other questions with significant theoretical and practical import. What is the qualitative significance of the differences, and what accounts for them? For example, in an epistemological sense what are the "roots" and "traditions"—what might be called the deep-seated meaning makers—of different companion meanings? That is the preoccupation of the five chapters in Part I of this volume, "Back to the Drawing Board." In Part II, "Into the Classroom," four chapters are devoted to understanding practice. How does one recognize, in text and classroom, the different kinds of companion meanings being communicated? Finally, the four chapters of Part III ("Behind the Scenes") take up the perspective of power. Whose interests are being served by having X kind of companion meaning dominate the curriculum, and how was it decided that X gets to be the winner in the curriculum struggle just now, or whenever?

THE NEED FOR DEBATE ABOUT CURRICULUM SUBSTANCE

Being expressions of educational purpose, companion meanings are very much the object of debate about curriculum, sometimes more so than the particulars of subject matter content. Some kinds of companion meanings can provide an answer to the student question, "Why are we learning this stuff?" and of course students have the right to expect that grownups have given this kind of question some serious thought. Yet, consider how hauntingly familiar is the Eisner and Vallance "curriculum as technology" concept (meaning curriculum as value-free instrument), to capture the vulgar but currently fashionable image of students as economic units competing in the global workplace. What a meaning for a student's education. What a vacuous, thoughtless educational purpose for a school system, a state or province, or indeed a country. And yet right now an astounding amount of energy is being put into standardized achievement testing and curriculum "standards" around the world, usually in the service of that view of educating. Where is the debate about that issue?

The view of the student as a pawn in competitive economics is one signal about current trends in educational commitment and preoccupation that has led us to conclude that critical debate about the substance of the curriculum is in serious decline. There is a second, more specific signal. It appears as if there is considerable debate going on just now over what should hold sway in school science. But in large part it is debate in appearance only. Most of it is raw advocacy. Some argue for history and philosophy of science, some for constructivism, yet others for science-technology-society issues, others again for what is being called the content core. The options are advocated as ideological winners and losers, as if one were better than all of the others. In part, this is a problem of how proponents, opponents, and witnesses see the function of these options. We hope to demonstrate that such options are *considerations* for curriculum planners, rather than general and universal solutions to what their proponents perceive to be generally and universally wrong with science education.

THE PROPER CHARACTER OF DEBATE
ABOUT CURRICULUM SUBSTANCE

We do not think proponent–opponent debate is helpful. We are thinking of critical debate that is much more particularized and is much closer to teacher thinking. We seek ways to understand what school science programs are offering to students, especially in the way of companion meanings; to predict the potential consequences for students; and to assess how appropriate those consequences are. This kind of critical debate has the character of inquiry and reflection rather than advocacy and altercation. It goes on in the minds of individual teachers, often with respect to individual students. It is based more in analysis than in testing, seeking to understand in advance what might happen rather than waiting until after the teaching to see what did happen. It depends for its depth and rigor on the quality and appropriateness of the theoretical perspectives used as lenses-for-looking, rather than on grand theoretical formulations intended to dictate what will happen in all classrooms. Finally, it is associated closely with moral and political issues in the societies within which educational systems function.

We submit that this kind of critical debate is vital for anyone who seeks to understand and revitalize science or any other subject in the school curriculum— be they teachers, researchers, policy makers, government officials, students, parents, or critics. We submit also that what passes for critical debate about science or anything else in the school curriculum at this time is not very sophisticated. What one debates with respect to the curriculum is closely dependent on what one sees there, and the seeing is in turn closely dependent on the quality of the looking. We hope this book will make a contribution in that regard.

ACKNOWLEDGMENTS

We acknowledge with gratitude the generous support of the Centre for Didactics and the Department of Education at Uppsala University, the University of Calgary, and the Social Sciences and Humanities Research Council of Canada. We extend special thanks to Marnie and Elisabeth for their unfailing patience and support while this work was completed.

PART I

Back to the Drawing Board

WE ARE CONVINCED THAT understanding and debate about the substance of science curriculum need to be pushed "back to the drawing board." It is time to have another go at things and, in order to do that, one needs to know what one has to work with.

The authors of these five chapters are all trying to "unpack" curricular diversity—what it is and can be, where it does and can come from, and how it is and can be manifest in the educational process. As suggested in the Preface, this venture will draw heavily on the concept of companion meanings.

In Chapter 1, Roberts presents an account of his earlier work on "curriculum emphases" in science education. Curriculum emphases are clustered companion meanings. Each cluster, taken as a whole, provides an answer to the student question, "Why am I learning this stuff?" There are different answers to that question, related directly to broad educational objectives. The diversity being unpacked, then, is at the surface of curriculum, so to speak. The different curriculum emphases function as a classification scheme that permits one to go just a bit below the surface and find out what is different about, say, different textbooks that present the same science content but have a different curricular intention. Roberts then develops the concept of companion meanings as a way to expand the scope of the curriculum emphases concept and establishes a framework for the remainder of the book.

Tomas Englund takes the reader deeper, in Chapter 2, to get beneath the surface manifestations of curricular diversity. He presents a categorization of different ways of approaching educational content generally, in terms that permit one to see how a subject such as science relates to broader educational purposes. The background for his work is an analysis of a distinction developed in Sweden between "narrow" and "broad" didactics, a distinction central in recent work that brings together two strands of research: the German didactic tradition and the North American curriculum tradition. The distinction has been, respectively, instructional (usually with a single subject) and curricular. We can express it, if crudely, by putting a question about student learning in these two ways: "How can we get them to learn this content better?" versus "How can we decide whether this is the content we think is worth learning?" In order to ask the second question, and get anything about which to make a *curricular* choice (rather than an instructional choice), one must "problematize" content, but Englund points out that educational philosophy has shied away from that function in the latter part of this century. He illustrates this problematizing by delving systematically into the deep-seated basis for different conceptions of curriculum content.

Englund's broader educational purposes constitute an example of a category system focused on the *sources* that give rise to different meanings in diverse curricular efforts, even within a single subject area such as science. Such meaning makers are frequently designated by words ending in "-ism" or "-ology," and they usually represent fundamental presuppositions about people and purpose. For example, Eisner (1992) has identified six "curriculum ideologies" that function as "belief systems that provide the value premises from which decisions about practical educational matters are made" (p. 302). Toulmin (1958) distinguished such deep-seated presuppositions as being at the level of "backing" for the warrants that give structure to an argument (in this case an argument for claiming that a curriculum is of one sort rather than another).

In Chapter 3, Brent Kilbourn also takes the reader to a deep-seated level of analysis. He argues that the social reality we construct for ourselves can be seen to have elements of different meaning systems, and he approaches the identification of meaning-makers through exploration of some disturbing everyday issues, each with an aesthetic component. His analysis is based on the "root metaphors" of four different knowledge systems identified by Stephen Pepper—formism, mechanism, contextualism, and organicism. There is a convincing demonstration that basing our meaning creation on a "crude" version of these could account for our increasing tolerance of dehumanizing rhetoric and practice in everyday life. Kilbourn argues for more of the kind of talk in the curriculum that would enable students to have a better metacognitive purchase on how they are being socialized to construct their reality.

Roger Säljö shifts the scene, in Chapter 4, from the *sources* of different meanings behind curricular diversity to the way meaning is created in the classroom. He presents an analysis of the way discourse depends for its meaning on rules that are most usefully seen from a sociocultural perspective. That is, students entering schools or other institutional settings enter a discourse with its specific ways of using language and other tools, which are different from the ones to which they are accustomed in everyday life. The analysis of learning from this point of view is the key to understanding how both scientific meaning and companion meanings are communicated and learned.

In Chapter 5, Leif Östman brings together some of the themes that have been put forward in earlier chapters in this part. He connects to the perspective outlined in Chapter 4 by taking up the matter of how interests, values, and the metaphors described by Kilbourn (Chapter 3) govern language usage in science education, and therefore how communication in text and classroom can express companion meanings. Three ever-present companion meanings in science education are discussed: a view of science as knowledge, a view of nature, and a view of the relationship between human beings and nature. The production of these is illustrated with text excerpts and vignettes of teaching. In order to visualize and systematize the three companion meanings, Östman uses—in addition to the curriculum emphasis categories—two other, complementary categorizations called subject focus and nature language. The chapter thus picks up themes set up by Roberts and foreshadows the next part of the book.

CHAPTER 1

Analyzing School Science Courses: The Concept of Companion Meaning

DOUGLAS A. ROBERTS

To SAY THAT SCHOOL SCIENCE courses exhibit a lot of diversity is to state the obvious. But what is this diversity all about, and why is it there? In their engaging history of biology in the school curriculum, Rosenthal and Bybee (1987) stress a major distinction that can be found in different school biology courses, characterizing it in the following way:

> A major theme throughout the history of biology education has been the continuing debates about its primary goal: whether it should be a science of life and emphasize knowledge or whether it should be a science of living and emphasize the personal needs of students and the social needs of society. (123)

How is it that a school science course could have two such different meanings as "a science of life" and "a science of living"? Surely both courses would have to be based on currently acceptable scientific explanations—what Ziman (1980) called "valid science"—for such phenomena as photosynthesis and the Krebs cycle. Something other than scientific meaning has to differ in the two courses, and the same tension can be found in the history of other sciences in the curriculum. Moreover, the classification of courses as different as these has a fairly respectable history in the literature of curriculum and, to a lesser extent, in science education.

In their classification scheme for "conflicting conceptions of curriculum," Eisner and Vallance (1974) would likely say the first course is devoted to "academic rationalism" and the second to "social relevance and/or reconstruction." I would say that the "curriculum emphasis" (Roberts 1982b, 1988) of the first could be "Correct Explanations" or "Structure of Science," while the other could be "Everyday Applications," "Self as Explainer," or "Science, Technology, and Decisions." In a slightly different take on the matter, Layton (1972) and Goodson (1987) would, I think, classify the two "traditions" represented as "academic" and a mix of "pedagogic" and "utilitarian." Yet again, Fensham (1988) would call the first of these orientations "induction into science" and the second one "learning from science." Östman (1994) would see a different "subject focus" in the two, and a different "nature language" as well. That there is such a "rich repertoire of curricular possibilities" for any subject matter is one of the points Ben-Peretz (1975, p. 155) stressed when she introduced the concept of "curriculum potential."

In this chapter my intent is twofold. First, I will introduce and develop a concept, *companion meaning*, which gives one a basis for grasping the diversity of school science courses. Second, I will use that concept to provide an orientation to the kind of inquiry represented by the other chapters in this volume. I am talking here about what has come to be known as the intended or proposed curriculum. With some modifications, what I have to say would apply also to the taught curriculum. I demur with respect to the learned curriculum, however, for unpacking that would require a different kind of inquiry. That is, a school subject will have as many meanings as the number of individuals studying it; the personal meaning that students make of what they learn is by definition unique to each student. Nevertheless, one matter that is certainly under the control of curriculum policy makers and teachers is the kind of meaning that is *provided* for students, and the more one understands the meanings that are possible, the richer can be the policy-making debate. Let those points provide the focus for what follows.

To accomplish this agenda, the chapter has three major sections. In the first, I review the development and substance of the concept of "curriculum emphases." This concept claims parentage for the idea of companion meanings (developed in the second section), but the companion meaning idea has broader scope. In the last section I link the companion meaning idea to the coming chapters in this volume.

SEVEN CURRICULUM EMPHASES
IN SCIENCE EDUCATION HISTORY

I developed the concept of curriculum emphases in science education as part of a paper for a Festschrift in honor of Fletcher Watson when he retired from Harvard in the late 1970s. Fletcher had become convinced in the early 1960s, as had Gerald Holton and Jim Rutherford, that an alternative high school physics course was needed in the United States to complement the Physical Sciences Study Committee (PSSC) course being developed at the Massachusetts Institute of Technology by Jerrold Zacharias and others.[1] I was a bystander in this process, but it intrigued me that this was more than a Harvard–MIT rivalry. The *intent* and *overall orientation* of the Harvard Project Physics course were quite different from the intent and overall orientation of the PSSC course. This was not simple rivalry; it was the expression of a very different purpose for learning science. Something different was to be emphasized, overall, and to capture what that was, I (Roberts, 1982b) expressed the meaning of a curriculum emphasis as

> a coherent set of messages to the student *about* science (rather than *within* science). Such messages constitute objectives which go beyond learning the facts, principles, laws, and theories of the subject matter itself—objectives which provide an answer to the student question: "Why am I learning this?" (p. 245)

Such messages accompany the teaching of science subject matter and are communicated both explicitly and implicitly, by what is not said as well as what is said.

The PSSC course, with a curriculum emphasis I dubbed Structure of Science, was very much in line with a lot of high school course development in the United States in the late 1950s and 1960s, and not only in science. In fact, Phenix (1964) proposed an organizing structure for the entire curriculum based on an approach of that sort, but broader, when he wrote *Realms of Meaning*. The sense in which he uses "meaning" is the meaning associated with logical features of organized areas of human endeavor—six different types of meaning, more comprehensive than simply the disciplines. While he rejected the latter, more narrow approach advocated, for example, by Paul Hirst, Phenix's sense of the word *meaning* was not at all as broad as the sense in which we are using the term in this volume.

The enchantment of the American science education establishment with the structure of the disciplines approach to curriculum design lasted for quite a long time, very powerfully and generously supported especially by the National Science Foundation. Structure of Science replaced an emphasis in science education I have labeled "Everyday Coping," which was in vogue from about 1910 to 1950 in North America—a curriculum emphasis that related scientific concepts to an understanding of objects and events in students' everyday lives. One of the most commonly used physics textbooks in the United States at that time (I had made use of it, as a teacher) featured an elaborate set of four acetate overlays to be used to show students, in a color-coded schematic, the different types of levers operative in an excavating crane, or steam shovel. I attended a lecture once when Zacharias peremptorily declared, "This isn't physics! It's technology!" The unfortunate object of this derision became known as "steam-shovel physics." Against that, a highly respected physics teacher of my acquaintance in the Boston area commented, when reviewing the first draft of what Zacharias and others produced as the PSSC text, "This isn't physics, it's philosophy!"

How is one to make sense of such judgments? Watson, Holton, and Rutherford adopted the stance that it was important to have a high school physics course with a broader appeal than pssc—one modeled after the general education science courses at Harvard, which presented science essentially as one of the humanities. I have called this a Self as Explainer curriculum emphasis (they did not use that terminology). Zacharias rejected the Everyday Coping emphasis in favor of a Structure of Science emphasis (he did not say so in those words). Clearly, powerful judgments and influences are at work in the approval and disapproval of these orientations to science courses. And these influences and preferences have a great deal to do with how students are to be socialized with regard to the meaning of the subject matter of science.

The "curriculum emphasis" concept captures the point that different broad, overall orientations are given to science courses, indicating what a science course, or program, will emphasize as its intent and orientation—hence the term. In an examination of science education history, which is corroborated by the work of Paul Hurd (1969) especially in the area of biological science, I found seven of these as distinct entities. They are presented below, based on descriptions I have given elsewhere (Roberts, 1982b, 1988).

Everyday Coping

This curriculum emphasis in science education socializes the student to grasp science as a way to make sense of objects and events of fairly obvious everyday importance, and therefore to cope with them better by understanding them scientifically. As suggested before, topics in biology can be organized so that students "see" their instruction as a way to understand the functioning and intelligent care of the human body, to avoid disease, to respect the need for sanitation. Indeed, that is one way to make a biology course teach "a science of living," in the terms used by Rosenthal and Bybee. (As a high school student in 1951, I studied from just such a biology textbook [Baker & Mills, 1943], which I saved, as it happens.) Hurd (1969) referred to this biology orientation as "civic biology," and noted a similar orientation in school chemistry and physics in the United States in the early decades of this century. That is, topics in chemistry can be organized and taught so that students come to know about familiar chemical processes that occur in the automobile, the house, and industry. Physics topics can be embedded in this curriculum emphasis so the student sees how various common home devices—such as the telephone, the furnace, or the electric iron—function and can be maintained.

Structure of Science

In the American (and British) science curriculum reforms of the late 1960s, as suggested earlier, there was a definite orientation of science courses toward understanding how science functions as an intellectual enterprise. Attention was given to such matters as the relationship between evidence and theory, the adequacy of a given model to explain phenomena, the ways in which science as a cumulative body of knowledge is self-correcting, and similar aspects of the growth and appraisal of scientific knowledge. Biology taught as a "science of life" might have such a curriculum emphasis.

Self as Explainer

The Harvard Project Physics course exemplifies this curriculum emphasis. It differs from the Structure of Science in the extent to which it makes links between a particular idea in science and the scientific and cultural framework of the era in which that idea was developed. There is a focus on explaining as a process, on what influences the ways people explain, and on the way the process functions. By concentrating on the "human-ness" of explaining, this emphasis goes far beyond the intellectual gymnastics associated with the Structure of Science. Issues of authority within explanatory systems are readily broached. For that reason one can see this emphasis as a basis for a school science course that could deal with the persistent dilemma of the tension between special creationism and evolution. That is, one has to ask about the process of explanation itself, and the human purposes being served by explaining in different *ways*, to get any kind of reasoned purchase on that debate. Otherwise it is little more than a dead-end discussion of a power struggle.

There are two other points. First, although terms such as constructivism, prior conceptions, and alternative conceptions were not in vogue in the mid-1960s, the significant attention now being paid to *students*' explaining as a human activity in these important areas is similarly a manifestation of the Self as Explainer curriculum emphasis.[2] Second, the extent to which a student develops ownership in the process of explaining by understanding what the process itself is all about, is very much a function of the power politics and style of power distribution in the science classroom. (See Munby & Roberts, Chapter 8 in this volume.)

Scientific Skill Development

The most significant embodiment of this curriculum emphasis in school materials was the "Science—A Process Approach" program developed with support from the American Association for the Advancement of Science. This is an emphasis that says to the student, in essence, that using the right processes (and using them well) inevitably will produce reliable knowledge. It is a highly decontextualized approach to the teaching of science, one in which a noticeable aspect of the materials is that one hops around quite a bit from one subject area to another, so that a cumulative development of propositional knowledge is very much a secondary consideration.

Solid Foundation

Cumulative development of propositional knowledge is front and center in this curriculum emphasis. The message to the student is that one needs to learn this, now, so that one can understand what is coming up in the next science course. This emphasis stresses the need to become increasingly sophisticated as one develops "genuine" or "deep" scientific understanding.

Correct Explanations

Very little explicit communication about "why we're learning this stuff" is provided the student in this curriculum emphasis. The reason for learning science that is communicated implicitly is that science presents a correct interpretation of the world. While I mentioned earlier that the Structure of Science emphasis replaced Everyday Coping, in a number of textbooks used in the late 1950s, the Correct Explanations emphasis also was very noticeable. This was part of the impetus to "get behind" the alleged correctness in order to see why one declared ideas to be correct or incorrect, which was a preoccupation for a lot of the reformers who spawned such emphases as Scientific Skill Development and Structure of Science.

Science, Technology, and Decisions

In the late 1970s, when I did this work originally, there was very little on the scene that embodied this curriculum emphasis, and most of it was going on in England. Currently, science-technology-society (sts) courses flourish all over the world for school science, and the term has many shades of meaning. The sense in which I originally used Science, Technology, and Decisions was to capture the differences between theoretical and practical reasoning, in the Aristotelian sense. That is, scientific knowledge has limitations in the practical arena of trying to make decisions about, say, the placement of a nuclear power plant. The way in which theoretical considerations are blended and woven with values, and how students come to regard the comparative significance of matters theoretic and matters practical, are important components of this curriculum emphasis. (See Geddis, Chapter 9 in this volume.) sts is a much broader, richer, and more widely accepted concept today than the Science, Technology, and Decisions idea I conceptualized 20 years earlier.

EXPANDING THE CURRICULUM EMPHASIS IDEA
TO COMPANION MEANINGS

Most of the curriculum emphases represent coherent clusters of messages about science that are deliberately, intentionally interwoven with science subject matter, in order to socialize students in selected directions. That is, they have been the objects of policy choice. In other words, a Structure of Science curriculum emphasis (for instance) does not appear accidentally or without deliberate purpose.[3] However, the curriculum emphases that tend to be silent about the purpose of learning science—

Solid Foundation and Correct Explanations—may not have been *deliberately* selected, but their message and socializing influence are no less powerful for that.

There is another whole realm of messages that can be communicated by science curriculum and teaching, the ones that are uncovered by inquiry associated with critical theory, poststructural analysis, and a postmodern vantage point. For example, gender bias in science textbooks surely is not a deliberate choice on the part of a textbook writer, but its message is still there if one knows how to look for it. The same is true for messages about what kind of knowledge is good knowledge for explaining the world, about which people have a say on that issue, and about the way the environment should be treated, to name a few more.

When Leif Östman and I began collaborating in the early 1990s, his research on school science textbooks in Sweden was focused not only on curriculum emphases but also on this other realm of messages being provided to students, whether deliberately (i.e., by policy) or not. He had systematized diversity about the kind of language used to talk about nature and about the relationship of human beings to nature (the "nature language" and "subject focus" category schemes, which he discusses in Chapter 5). An overarching concept was needed to bring together the deliberate (policy-driven) and not-so-deliberate (but still very real, as he had found) "extra" meanings that accompany scientific meaning, in curriculum and textbook as well as in teaching. We decided on the idea of companion meanings as a concept with enough scope to satisfy this need.

Once the idea is in place that companion meanings can and do accompany scientific meaning in teaching, text, or curriculum, at least two interesting points arise. First, there is potentially a considerable array of companion meanings, only some of which have received systematic attention; others are relatively unexplored. Second, companion meanings are communicated contextually, which opens a broad avenue of methodological questions about the role of language and discourse conventions in science education.[4] These matters are explored briefly in the final section of this chapter.

THE ANALYTICAL THEMES OF THIS VOLUME

The chapters in this volume are based on the heuristic assumption that companion meanings do indeed accompany scientific meaning in science education, and that these can be either deliberately planned and incorporated in policy (as with curriculum emphases) or "unintentional" (as with gender bias, world view bias, cultural bias, and many others). The four most important analytical themes in the coming chapters are diversity, communication, ideology, and power. To a degree, all of the authors deal with all of these issues, but some are emphasized more than others in individual chapters.

With regard to the first, the diversity of deliberately planned companion meanings (those of the curriculum emphases) makes it clear that the substance of a school science program is a matter of choice, based on justifying the particular directions in which to nudge students' socialization. What seems to be needed to assist in the revitalization of this kind of discussion is a sort of calculus of curriculum thought that distinguishes "curricular conclusions"—"We'll do it this way"—from a "curricular menu"—"What are our choices?" Such matters are explored by Orpwood in Chapter 10, Bybee in Chapter 11, and Solomon in Chapter 12.

Two bases for better understanding the diversity of the science curricular menu are explored in this volume. One is the matter of where some of the choices on the menu come from—instead of what gives rise to them in terms of educational and philosophical thinking (Englund, Chapter 2, and Kilbourn, Chapter 3). Second is the matter of how the substance of items on the curricular menu appears in text and classroom—that is, how companion meanings materialize. In Chapters 8 and 9, respectively, the curriculum emphases Self as Explainer and Science, Technology, and Decisions are featured in analyses by Munby and Roberts, and by Geddis.

Uncovering the "unintentional" companion meanings that accompany such matters as the concept of race (Willinsky, Chapter 6) or the vision of science as a culture with a "border" to be negotiated (Aikenhead, Chapter 7) leads to a different point about diversity. Such analyses suggest that there should be more, and different, items on the curricular menu, especially if one takes seriously the currently fashionable slogan "science for all."

The second analytical theme, communication, is the focus of two chapters. In Chapter 4, Roger Säljö takes a sociocultural perspective on learning that enables one to see how language and contexts communicate to students. Leif Östman takes up the theme in Chapter 5, discussing in detail the general features of communicating companion meanings in textbook and classroom discourse.

The themes of ideology and power that are part of curriculum determination are discussed in broad terms by Englund and Östman, and are touched on by Orpwood and Bybee. More detailed examination of these matters is found in Fensham's Chapter 13.

CONCLUDING REMARKS

Science in the school curriculum is a great deal more than a collection of the scientific meanings of the laws, principles, and theories of scientific disciplines. To the extent that companion meanings can be recognized and brought under rational control, a more sophisticated debate about the substance of science curriculum can be undertaken. Such debate is much to be hoped for. At the moment it is not very common.

CHAPTER 2

Problematizing School Subject Content

TOMAS ENGLUND

IN A WELL-DEFINED and structured discipline such as the natural sciences, there is a strong temptation to take the subject matter as a starting point for curriculum development. Whenever that happens, it becomes difficult to "problematize" the school subject content; it is much more likely that it will be taken for granted. In such cases, the meaning that students are offered by their school subjects— what I will call the *educational* content of school subjects—is always at risk of being dominated by a narrow view of the socialization function of education.

This situation unquestionably is linked to the fact that the moral and philosophical aspects of education and socialization have been neglected. To explain the neglect, much has been written about the dominance of scientific-technical rationality in educational thinking during the twentieth century and the consequent adjustment of educational research and teaching to the demands of this rationality (cf. Englund, 1986). One of the casualties of educational research so construed is that the content of education usually is not problematized very well.[1]

Problematizing school subject content is a moral and philosophical endeavor that cannot be addressed by scientific-technical rationality. The central questions of philosophical inquiry in education are about the worth of knowledge and meaning offered to students. Scientific-technical questions about efficiency and effectiveness are quite different questions—indeed they are derived from the central questions of education—yet efficiency and effectiveness questions tend to be more prevalent than philosophical inquiry, on the educational research agendas of many countries.

Sweden has been no exception, yet there has been a substantial renaissance in recent years of educational research with a philosophical purpose. Because it occurred in a relatively well-defined time period, this rekindled interest in a moral and philosophical role for educational research can be examined as a case study with rich potential for addressing some perennial problems of interest to educational researchers elsewhere. It began with a resurgence of interest in "didactic" research—that is, a renewed focus on the importance of subject matter—and it has taken two directions that are described later in this chapter. The key factor distinguishing the two has been the extent to which the subject matter has been problematized, and it is toward understanding this factor and its implications that the chapter is devoted.

Some readers may find the term *didactic* to be old-fashioned, or predominantly European. Both perceptions are essentially correct. (See Hopmann & Riquarts, 1995, however.) The term, as an adjective, basically means "instructive," but most significantly it tends to be associated in practice—in teacher education, for example—with traditional school subject areas such as science, social studies, and mathematics. "Science didactics" probably would be expressed approximately as "science education" in North America, Britain, or Australia, and the science education research tradition in those places certainly shares the important feature of having developed in the two directions being explored here with respect to didactic research in Sweden.

The argument in this chapter proceeds in three sections. The first outlines the development of didactic research in Sweden, with particular attention to the two directions it has taken. In the second, I need to provide the reader with some history of Swedish educational research, because the renewed interest in subject matter occurred in a historical and intellectual context. Especially important is the profound influence of changes in the sociology of education on the preoccupations of educational research in Sweden and elsewhere. In the final and longest section, I examine the educational implications and the potential of different approaches to didactic research generally, with special reference to aspects of science education. Both implications and potential are shown to rely heavily on the extent to which school subject content is problematized.

"NARROW" AND "BROAD" DIDACTICS

Didactics has developed within Swedish educational research in two quite separate directions since the early 1980s—one historically related to cognitive psychology, the other to curriculum theory. As a reflection of and evidence of how the content question was emphasized, it may be noted that in 1981 research groups working within these different directions called their respective research "content-related educational research." The term *didactics*, even if it was known, was not used at that time. In a report 2 years later, Marton (1983) relaunched the term *didactics*, saying that it should deal with "scientific studies of questions connected to what content the teacher chooses to teach and how he or she teaches the specific content" (p. 64). In spite of this rather broad definition, the territory of didactics was in the same report narrowed down to questions of how pupils conceptualize and treat the content of their education.

Countering that narrow construction, curriculum theorists argued that the factors determining educational content and the question of *why* a certain content was chosen were also central concerns of didactics (Englund, 1984). The subsequent evolution of Swedish didactics, at least within educational research, was in two clearly distinguished but simultaneously desirable directions, which I called *broad* didactics—based in curriculum theory—and *narrow* didactics—oriented toward instructional methodology and related to phenomenography (Englund, 1990; Marton, 1980, 1986—especially the contributions by Marton and by Englund & Svingby, in the latter).

During the years since the establishment of these two directions in didactic research, it is the narrower, instructional variety that has become the better known, even if both directions have had quite a major impact. The prominence of instructional didactics springs from two factors in particular: its perceived closeness to the concrete instructional problems of different school subjects and, in the Swedish context at least, its gradually evolving link with phenomenographic methodology, which stresses the differences in student learning by showing how a given content is conceptualized differently by students.

The *narrow* model for didactic analysis entails a focus on the relationship between (1) a version of the subject content that is, usually, an epistemic imitation of the underlying discipline, and (2) the students' learning of that version of content. To put it in the terms being used in this volume, narrow didactic analysis in science education is concerned primarily with getting students to learn "scientific meanings." It is historically based in cognitive psychology and its close relationship to the phenomenographic approach has been noted. It is quite obvious that in many ways this model has been and still is very successful when it comes to analyzing qualitative differences in learning. Nevertheless, it will be critically examined below with respect to some of the societal consequences to which it often leads and that it fails to problematize. This aspect also can be compared with other internationally well-known narrow didactic models such as alternative conceptions, prior conceptions, untutored beliefs, and misconceptions. However, I also will note promising attempts within narrow didactics to widen the view of didactic analysis by contextualizing learning situations.

The *broad* approach to didactic analysis, which I would like to underline in this chapter, is closely connected to curriculum theory as it developed in Sweden in the past few decades. The latter will be characterized below as consisting of three different modes, or stages when perceived in chronological terms. What is important to stress is that these three different modes are based on or linked to different sociologies of education, leading to very different educational implications. Whereas the narrow approach is highly specific about a rather narrow view of educational content, the first stage of the broad approach is indifferent to content, and the second views it as a medium of social control (discussed in the following section). However, in the third stage content is problematized in a manner highly suggestive of the attention to "companion meanings" in the present volume.

I return to narrow and broad didactics later in the chapter. From a historical perspective on the development of curriculum research in Sweden, I will exemplify the benefits when curriculum research takes into account the content of education, that is, when curriculum meets didactics. (The "curriculum meets didactics movement" is a most interesting development in educational research. See Westbury's [1995] examination of this phenomenon.)

THE HISTORICAL BACKGROUND FOR BROAD DIDACTICS

Curriculum research in Sweden started with Dahllöf (1989) and the development of "frame factor theory." This theory can be said to form the first of three stages that give Swedish curriculum research its identity. I will try to show how these three stages have been anchored in different sociologies of education with different world views and perceptions of science.[2]

Stage 1: Frame Factor Theory and Traditional Sociology of Education

The phenomenon on which the frame factor theory focused was the learning process and how it seemed to be affected over time by various structural aspects of the school system. A more natural subject for educational research would be hard to find. Dahllöf (1989) points out that the specificity of the theory

> lay in the fact that it empirically analysed the content and the results of teaching over a longer period for a whole [3-year] stage of the school system. (p. 6)

By analyzing the learning process in such terms, frame factor theory acquired an explanatory value in relation to the space for action permitted by the "frames"— for example, the time available and the rules about size of school classes and grouping of pupils. In its preliminary form, the theory also sought to explain how state decisions about the direction and dimensions of schooling constrained and regulated the actual shaping of education. An example of curriculum-historical analysis in the spirit of this perspective is in Dahllöf (1981), in which shifts in the time available for different school subjects are demonstrated.

The conceptual climate and dominant view of science within which the frame factor theory took shape comprised the efficiency and equality aims of the traditional sociology of education. The view of content held within this tradition cannot be characterized as critical or relativized. It regarded education and its content as good in themselves. School knowledge was viewed as shaped by consensus and in accordance with the cumulative development of underlying disciplines.[3] The concern was in principle a *problem of efficiency* (a question of efficient organization of pupils and of sequencing the given content)—later taking its shape within educational technology. The representatives of traditional sociology of education (and of frame factor theory) also believed that it was possible to draw a clear dividing line between the tasks of scientists and of politicians—for example, by allowing the politicians to decide about the question of ability grouping on the basis of empirical investigations.[4]

Stage 2: Curriculum Theory and the New Sociology of Education

The second stage of the frame factor theory entailed, on the one hand, a deepening of the earlier studies of learning processes and, on the other, a development of the theory into a curriculum theory. Here we can observe a preliminary endeavor to study the historical and societal determination of the curriculum and to supplement the earlier analysis of outer structural frames (timetabling, etc.) with an examination of the structure of teaching and classroom behavior.

New programmatic questions were asked. One such question was how the educational content of a curriculum was built up and legitimated. This question necessitated historical analyses both of how different conceptualizations of the goals and content of schooling were shaped, and of how they were maintained. Researchers began to analyze how the teaching and learning processes differentiated among pupils and how the educational content re-created certain social conditions. The functions of schooling and differences in pupil achievement were formulated in terms of *reproduction* and two other key metaphors, namely, *social control* and *legitimacy*. The teaching process and its content were seen as tools, but what this research perspective overlooked was the differing educational aims of different social forces and their implications. Instead, this perspective emphasized how content selection was legitimated, without making the content itself problematic and contingent—that is, open for different choices.[5]

In summary, the Swedish variant of the new sociology of education and its critical curriculum theory did not really approach teaching from a perspective that implied an interest in differences and change. Rather, the emphasis was on the grounds on which the complicated process of content selection was legitimated, and on the stability of the educational system and its inability to undergo real change regarding its content, owing to its reproductive function. Researchers working within this tradition also rejected in principle the idea of making or attempting to develop a basis for curriculum recommendations, focusing their efforts instead on exposing structures.

Meanwhile, in England the new sociology of education was for a long time rather ahistorical (cf. Whitty, 1985). However, it is interesting to see how, in its criticism of the dominating educational philosophy (e.g., Hirst, 1974) that legitimated school subjects as simplifications of the underlying disciplines, it did develop a critical sociological perspective on curriculum history. This criticism, in which Goodson (1987, 1988) is prominent, takes as its starting point, and demonstrates, the fact that school subjects are historical and social constructions and that they change over time. An important result of Goodson's research in curriculum history is his model for the development of school subjects—"invention, promotion, legislation and mythologization" (1988, pp. 193–194). He asserts that the representatives of a school subject, when it is established, develop a rhetoric of *legitimation* that prevents further change. The main interest of this kind of curriculum-historical research is consequently not to examine different moral and political implications of teaching, that is, the production of companion meanings (cf. Englund, 1991b). Instead, it focuses on the processes and especially the social forces shaping the content in a certain way—in England, the ambition of a school subject to be accepted by the universities.

However, it is quite clear that research into curriculum history that proceeds from the school subject is *one* important starting point for a problematization of educational content and hence for didactic research. The risk inherent in taking the school subject as a starting point is that this easily may result in a confirmation of the content already established and that the analytical perspective may not go beyond the school subject. This point is taken up further in a later section of the chapter.

Stage 3: A "Citizenship" Sociology of Education and Curriculum

Moral and philosophical interest in content was put on the agenda of curriculum theory in Sweden in what I call its third stage. An effect of this new interest was that educational content was problematized through recognition of (1) questions about its selection, (2) manifest differences seen as possible differences in interpretation at all levels in the educational system, and (3) historical change in the "shape" of school subjects. Thus, the third stage did not simply entail an application of the earlier stages of curriculum theory. The result of incorporating the focus on content into curriculum research meant a fundamental change concerning the interest in knowledge and a gradual shift in theoretical perspective.

Didactic research within the third stage emphasizes the question of the choice of educational content and the contextualization of teaching, that is, the content chosen in terms of what meaning and what context is offered to students. The fundamental assumption is that these choices, conscious or unconscious, have crucial implications for teaching and learning. Depending on what content is chosen, what context it is given by the textbook and the teacher, the student will be offered different possibilities regarding creating and constructing meanings. In this view, the content of learning can never be confined to unproblematic "facts" or subject content as such, but must be seen as contextualized in a more or less determinate context and thereby given *different social meanings* or *companion meanings*.

Readers may find that this brief overview of three stages in the development of Swedish curriculum research has important parallels with educational research in other countries, as suggested by the developing international attention to the movement alluded to earlier as "curriculum meets didactics." Whether or not the Swedish case study is representative, for purposes of the present chapter it is important that the three stages be identified, in order to prepare for the analysis that follows. That is, unless one recognizes the significance of having an educational research agenda move on to what I have called Stage 3, it is difficult to apprehend the point of the following arguments about the educational implications and the potential of different approaches to didactic research.

THE POTENTIAL OF DIDACTIC RESEARCH

In the following I will examine in greater depth the significance of problematizing school subject content in terms of meaning making, by returning to the potential of the narrow and broad didactic research traditions. As analytical tools to assist in this examination, I first distinguish among ways of conceptualizing educational content.

Three Conceptualizations of Educational Content

By way of introduction, it can be said that school subject content can be approached and conceptualized in ways that vary greatly. At one extreme, it is seen as unproblematized and given in accordance with educational policy aims. There are different essentialistic interpretations, and content can be seen as well in historically and socially changeable and interpretable terms, as noted below. The phrase "educational content" is used to signify that the focus here is on the meaning and educational worth of what is being offered to students.

Epistemic (School Subject) Content. This version is determined essentialistically and scientistically. In the case of science education, its basis is a school subject's relationship to an underlying scientific discipline, for example, central concepts such as gravity, power, chemical bonds, photosynthesis, electricity, and so on.

Knowledge Content. This version is derived by analysis of relations—such as the relationship between individual and society, individual and nature, and so forth—which are dealt with, explicitly or implicitly, as educational content. The aim of such analyses is to trace different conceptualizations of the relation studied, which can be shown to have different didactic implications—for example, different "curriculum emphases," "subject foci," and "nature languages," which are elaborated in this volume. (See also Englund, 1986, for an example of didactic typologies of the social studies subjects.)

Socialization Content. This version of educational content is developed out of knowledge content analyses. Socialization content includes the different meaning-creation contexts or discourses where different conceptualizations of the relation studied (knowledge content) are expressed. In terms of this volume the result from this type of analysis is companion meanings that constitute and characterize an educational discourse, which could be, for example, patriarchal, scientific-rational, or democratic (Englund, 1986, 1996c).

With these differing versions of content in mind, one can proceed to examining the educational implications and potential of different approaches to didactic research. The important point is that the view of content will influence the kinds of questions seen to be significant within the different approaches.

A Sociocultural Perspective on Learning:
The Potential of Instructional Didactics

Already in Marton (1983) and in the "particular"—that is, subject-specific—didactic research (instructional didactics) that has taken shape, the content–student relationship is emphasized. What is problematized is the students' differing conceptualizations and understanding of the educational content. Generally, that content itself has been looked upon as given in an instrumental sense, in a way that does not go beyond a view of school knowledge as limited to one object or rather one central concept at a time, as noted above.

The learning of these concepts (in relation to different learners) consequently has been problematized, but not the educational content that is to be learned, other than in relation to the problematization of learning. The focus on students' conceptualization and understanding of central concepts derived from academic disciplines—what I earlier have called epistemic school subject content—implies that a learning content that for most students is fragmented, coupled with what in a very narrow sense may be seen as the "right" way of understanding it, has been taken as the point of departure.[6]

Educational content often has been "chosen" on strictly essentialistic scientistic grounds. The phenomenographic methodology, although it is scientifically legitimate, has not been problematized for use within didactics. This has meant that the problematic of learning has excluded many questions; the choice of learning content has not been questioned.

The kind of questions that have been excluded are, for example, what sort of socializing effects (companion meanings) arise from the learning of (or attempts to learn) these fragmented concepts, that is, what meaning-creation contexts, if any, the concepts are set in. An epistemic school subject content can be given totally different (companion or social) meanings depending on its contextualization. Here we can see a need to open the door onto an area of research that has been neglected, an area of research that considers the "meta-lessons" that the educational content implies. These express the reasons or purposes for students to learn it—curricular contexts in which they are to understand the subject (Östman, 1995; Roberts, 1988).[7]

Another question that could be addressed in relation to this, is whether school subjects in their traditional form—for example, science subjects such as physics and chemistry, with their pronounced scientific structure—are the most adequate tools for preparing children for citizenship, and whether mere adjustments within these school subjects (development of their central concepts, or more sophisticated methods of teaching them) are sufficient, or even desirable (cf. Englund & Östman, 1992).

There are certainly potential dangers with a one-sided accentuation of learning at the expense of deliberations about content selection. The societal consequences of the kind of didactic research that has been referred to here as "narrow" could be that a science- and mathematics-oriented view of knowledge will predominate and also will characterize other fields of knowledge. This implies that there will be a focus on epistemically delimited areas of knowledge, irrespective of different views in the scientific community and in society at large concerning their adequate contextualization.

This potential danger can be countered by revitalizing the philosophical dimension of education, in order to evaluate and relativize different knowledge contents in relation to their historical and societal contexts, and not just as expressions of different students' conceptualizations. As I see it, for a relativization of educational content to be scientifically interesting—for example, an analysis of different student conceptualizations of educational content—links have to be developed that provide a perspective on this specific educational content: its historical origins, its formation, different ways of perceiving it, and the different possible angles from which the subject matter or, better, the knowledge content can be delimited. In short, there needs to be a shift from a purely instructional didactic discourse to one that incorporates a supplementary historical-societal dimension.

Among representative examples of research that widens the phenomenographic approach to didactics and that problematizes the epistemic content as the school subject content, I would like to mention the work of Säljö and the research group he is leading. Säljö (1992b) has developed what he calls a sociocultural perspective on the learning process (see Chapter 4 in this volume). In contrast with research in which the learning problem is, as a rule, perceived in terms of the learners' commonsense views versus the adequate, scientific way of conceptualizing, Säljö sees the problem as being that scientific concepts—the epistemic content—are seldom confirmed in social environments other than those of the scientific communities (Säljö, 1995; see also Aikenhead, Chapter 7 in this volume). Because of their specific scientific character, these concepts often are seen by pupils as strange and difficult to understand. Simultaneously, due to our conceptualization of learning as learning scientific concepts—the metaphors of institutionalized schooling (Säljö, 1990)—we often see learning problems as psychological and not as communicative. In a sociocultural perspective there is an awareness that we are not living in an unambiguous "reality," but rather that there are always different perspectives ("meaning provinces") for looking at and understanding phenomena.

A Sociopolitical Perspective on Teaching: The Potential of Broad Didactics

In Stage 3 of the development of curriculum research in Sweden, the stage that gave rise to broad didactics, there is a sociopolitical perspective that sees education and its content as the objects of struggling social forces. The ultimate power center for this struggle is the state, but it is also a struggle at all levels over whose interpretatation is to win out. The way in which the educational system manifests how reality is to be conceptualized and school knowledge constructed means that certain power relations are consolidated or transformed. This transmission of ideology is therefore subject to constant shifts, as power relations gradually change. At all levels there are permanent ideological conflicts, while at the same time a cohesive state power and state apparatus have the task of shaping political compromises out of the various political and ideological interests and making it look "rational" (e.g., through national evaluation programs).[8]

Educational policy documents such as national curricula and syllabi consequently are analyzed within a Stage 3 perspective as interpretable political compromises. The scope for interpretation expressed by these documents shifts over time in accordance with the forces mentioned above. Depending on the forces, different preconditions are created for the concrete selection of educational content, which can be studied more closely by means of various types of theoretically based empirical studies.

Instead of taking their starting point in the way a certain selection of content is legitimated (the perspective inherent in Stage 2), analyses of educational content in Stage 3 are set in another theoretical perspective. This means that the choice of educational content analyzed is limited to knowledge content, as defined earlier. These areas of content can be conceptualized in different ways, with different didactic implications. Different interpretations of the knowledge content can be seen as arranged according to a system of different meaning-creation social-ization contexts and dimensions of citizenship.[9]

What it is crucial to stress is that this research direction has didactic implica-tions, in the sense that *different* ways of conceptualizing knowledge content are exposed. Developing a systematic knowledge of these different ways and assimi-lating this knowledge (the common task of researchers, teacher educators, and teachers) are, as I see it, central elements in the step-by-step development of what could be termed didactic competence.[10]

Compared with the earlier stages of curriculum research, it can be said that the normative implication (from Stage 1) is partly revived here, but now as a pos-sible choice for *teachers*, rather than politicians, and is dependent on a didactic competence within the area of the relevant knowledge content. This didactic com-petence implies an educational-philosophical standpoint and a readiness to dis-cuss the aims of education and to have arguments for a given selection of educa-tional content. The central implication of the broad didactics of Stage 3, however, is the possible reestablishment of the philosophical aspect.

CONCLUDING REMARKS: REESTABLISHING THE PHILOSOPHICAL ASPECT OF EDUCATIONAL AND DIDACTIC REASEARCH

A central challenge for future educational and didactic research can be related to the further development of a critical analysis of the dominant educational philosophy's view concerning the epistemic basis of school subjects. The critical analysis that has been made within the new sociology of education (for an over-view, see Steedman, 1988) can, in the third stage, be further developed in line with the Aristotelian starting point "that education is fundamentally not an epis-temological but an *ethical and political enterprise*" (Schilling, 1986, p. 12; cf. Aristotle, 1990).

This perspective means that the content of education cannot be referenced to any definitive scientific-technical rationality. The content aims that are expressed and the tradition within which, say, science education is embedded (including its relationship to various scientific disciplines) have to be understood as historically and socially conditioned and always open to discussion.

With Aristotle and his modern interpreters, I would put forward a communi-cative-practical rationality, stressing space and procedures for a rational discourse of value questions, as an alternative to the presumed adequacy of scientific-technical rationality. Once different conceptualizations of educational content have been acknowledged, a means is needed for discussing and debating their relative merits. This enterprise also can (given the aims set for the educational system today) be related to the question of values (companion meanings) to be communicated. Thus the educational philosophy that has focused on the relationship between democracy and education is placed center stage.

In line with such a view are the endeavors to revitalize the pragmatic tradition, especially as represented by Dewey (1916/1966), into a neopragmatism. Richard Rorty (1982) and Richard Bernstein (1986) are the leading figures at a general level, and Cleo Cherryholmes (1988) is one prominent example within educational research. There is a need to go beyond the analytical scientistic tradition of philosophy that has dominated this century and that, within educational philosophy, has legitimated an unproblematic relationship between underlying disciplines and school subjects—in science education as elsewhere. To do so means to revive the role of a social reconstructionist educational philosophy in analyzing communication and a sense of community (Englund, 1986, 1996c).

The task before us is one of developing an attitude to educational content that accords with the demands of the "knowledge society" and the pluralist society. In this situation, teachers have to create the preconditions for a public dialogue and try to develop reasonable citizens discharging their civic purpose, the formation of new publics (Giarelli, 1983). Translated into concrete teaching, this means that

> becoming a part of the public does not involve learning what the proper response is to an item stimulus. . . . It is finding a way to enter the conversation about the significance of a flow of historical events and about the meanings that are to be attached to them. (Feinberg, 1989, p. 136)

Teachers (or future teachers) and teacher educators turn out to have a key role to play as carriers of different didactic and educational-philosophical conceptions and different approaches to educational content. I believe that we need to focus more systematically on these differences among teachers/teacher educators (cf. the earlier discussion of ways of broadening the phenomenographic approach). Perhaps such a focus also would forcibly bring about a productive confrontation between the two didactic research directions mentioned.

That confrontation also would create a more genuine basis for analyzing educational-philosophical dimensions that go beyond the questions of learning and selection of content as isolated phenomena. Teaching and learning processes always imply interpretations of knowledge content, and in that connection they are links in the meaning-creation contexts of socialization processes.

CHAPTER 3

Root Metaphors and Education

BRENT KILBOURN

IN THIS CHAPTER I want to explore the question of how the metaphors we use and the circumstances in which we use them can affect what we believe, who we are, and the kind of society we live in and are a part of. Metaphors are closely associated with the production of companion meanings, to use the terminology of this volume. As I have argued elsewhere (Kilbourn, 1974, 1994), school science implies or "projects" different metaphors to students through the science texts they read. The role played by metaphor in the construction of knowledge is familiar, of course, but metaphors and their companion meanings normally are not explicit topics of conversation in the science classroom. Because they are not, students are left vulnerable to unexamined and sometimes questionable ways of making sense of their experience. The mechanical metaphors that are so powerful for understanding aspects of human physiology, for instance, lose their power when applied to interpersonal relationships, moral dilemmas, and social policy. More generally, because the relative merits of implicit metaphors and their companion meanings seldom are brought to the surface in the classroom, issues surrounding the worth of viewing the world mechanistically, formistically, organically, or contextually (these terms are explained later) are left unexamined. As I will try to show, this has potentially serious consequences for individuals and for society.

I begin by capturing some of the concerns of men and women as we approach the twenty-first century. I suggest that one ground for understanding these concerns lies in the fundamental metaphors that we use to construct our social reality, and I discuss the work of Stephen Pepper (1942, 1945) as one way of conceptualizing these metaphors. I develop the concept of crude metaphors as a way of expanding Pepper's refined metaphors into the common experience of everyday life. I close with thoughts about the educational merit of classroom conversations about root metaphors.

MAKING SENSE OF EXPERIENCE

Charlie and I talked last night. We manage to talk about once every other month. I'm here in Canada; he's down in the States. We've kept in touch since our undergraduate days. Our talk last night was typically less than systematic. We ranged over a number of topics: the downsizing of corporations, automatic bank tellers, straightening roads, destroying iron bridges, talk shows, the Oklahoma tragedy, my son's acid rain project, the state of education, the influence of the media on society. By the time we hung up, I was mildly depressed.

Later, musing about the possible connections among the disturbing things we had discussed, I found myself searching for some fundamental ground from which to start. How could a society come to the point where it celebrates the miraculous survival of a corporation, while thousands of people are put out of work? How could a society produce an arms industry and arms trade that could be turned on its own soldiers and citizens? How could a society arrive at a state where talk show hosts flame the fires of conspiracy and suspicion, then blandly deny any culpability whatsoever? How could we come to the point where we would demand rigorous scientific proof for the connection between violence in the media and violence in the home and on the streets?

And I wondered about the role of education. I mulled over the thought that the current rhetoric on accountability and traditional content seems to offer so little by way of critical discussion of what it is that we should be teaching our children. I chuckled at the questions running through my mind—at their naivete and simplistic framing.

A more sophisticated beginning for making sense of these troubled times lies in the metaphors we have at our disposal for constructing meaning and interpreting experience. The interest in metaphor outside the confines of literature (e.g., Lakoff & Johnson, 1980; Munby, 1986) supports the notion that a society's metaphors are central for shaping what that society is to become. Metaphors are not the only things that shape a society, of course, but for present purposes I will confine the discussion to these literary and philosophical aspects of the determinants of social life. Furthermore, I will confine the discussion to the work of one individual, Stephen C. Pepper. As I will try to show, Pepper's treatment of metaphor has the breadth needed for encompassing far-ranging questions, and it has the specificity needed if the discussion is to avoid lapsing into vague generality. His work offers the kind of grounding that helps me make sense of the kinds of issues that Charlie and I discussed.

QUALITIES OF PEPPER'S THINKING

World Hypotheses: A Study in Evidence was published in 1942. It was published in the heyday of logical positivism, and that is remarkable because it is a book about metaphysics, a topic that logical positivism and the intellectual fashions of the time had made all but obsolete. Its author, Stephen C. Pepper, had an interesting biography. His father was an artist, a painter. Pepper followed this artistic strand in his work on aesthetics. By the time he came to the end of his long career, he had been chair of the departments of both Art and Philosophy at Berkeley. In his memoir, Robert Armstrong (1980) said:

> What comes to mind as I draw these remembrances to a close is a powerful impression of a man who was full of life. More than anyone like him that I can remember, he seemed to enjoy almost every moment of life both sensuously and reflectively. He really was both an artist and a philosopher. He had mastered what I like to think of as the artist's ability to fully enter into the sensuous depths of immediate experience. But also he seemed to equally enjoy the philosopher's ability to reflect on the meaning of human experience. (p. 217)

Pepper's driving concern about issues of truth and evidence found their expression in *World Hypotheses* (1942). His central argument in that work is that philosophical conceptions of truth and reality vary, but not so much as to suggest that they are thoroughly relative. (James Ford, 1990, has called Pepper a systematic pluralist, a description that he also applies to the thinking of Richard McKeon.) Different conceptions of the nature of reality coalesce or gel around a handful of central ideas or, as Pepper calls them, root metaphors. As he argued in a later review,

> Through the whole history of human thought there have probably been only about seven world hypotheses conceived in this broad sense, and of these seven, reasons were advanced in my book for regarding only four as worthy of serious consideration today. . . .
> These four I called formism, mechanism, contextualism, and organicism. None is completely corroborated by its evidence, so that we cannot accept any of them as an entirely true or adequate description of our world. We might regard them as four different approximations to the nature of the world. They are cornering it, so to speak, from different sides. (1945, p. 9)

According to Pepper, each root metaphor generates an internally consistent set of categories, forming a hypothetical view about the nature of truth, evidence, and reality. The metaphors are simply stated. The root metaphor of *similarity* (and its implied opposite, dissimilarity) gives rise to a view of the world preoccupied by the idea of forms and categories. The metaphor of *machine* views the universe as a gigantic machine made of discrete parts that causally act on one another. It is a view commonly associated with Isaac Newton and with science in general. The root metaphor of *integration* emphasizes the interconnectedness and organic wholeness of things and processes. Whereas formists and mechanists tend to view the world as parts, the organicist approaches reality as complex wholes. The root metaphor of *context* emphasizes the ever-changing quality, immediacy, and intu-ited wholeness of situations, and the extent to which our constructed sense of reality is dependent on context.

Pepper (1942) articulates the root metaphors and central categories of (what he argues are) the four most adequate world views in occidental philosophical history. He shows the world views at their best; his aim is to demonstrate the way in which the central categories of each view are connected and can be seen to emerge from its root metaphor. The connections are of logical entailment rather than contingent association. Consequently, the rigor of Pepper's account and of the world hypotheses themselves comes from the logical relationships among the categories. For instance, our ability to notice different types, forms, categories, genres, and so on, is predicated on the root metaphor of similarity/difference; it can be said that the concept of "type" logically emerges from the root metaphor of similarity.

Before sketching each of the four world hypotheses and their central catego-ries, I want to raise three issues. One concerns a book that Pepper published 3 years after *World Hypotheses*. In 1945 he published *Basis of Criticism in the Arts*, where he continued the work done in *World Hypotheses* by showing that each of the root metaphors generates a framework for aesthetic criticism. This work is a significant contribution for the present discussion because it makes clear a host of issues surrounding questions about what a society values. While it is clear that Pepper is talking about aesthetic values, it is a short (if provocative) step to suggest that much of our daily experience lies along an aesthetic continuum. That is, experience is (or can be construed as) aesthetic in nature, experience as art. Consequently, when I sketch the four world hypotheses, I also will comment on what the categories say about aesthetic criticism.

The second issue returns to the nature of each of the world hypotheses. Pepper was interested in depicting each of the world views in as pure a form as possible. That was necessary in order to show the internal consistency of a view and to show that it arose from a dominant metaphor. Consequently, when reading *World Hypoth-eses* or *Basis of Criticism in the Arts*, one is reading about idealized forms of each of the world views. In an idealized form, all of the categories would be logically con-nected to each other; there would be no loose threads, no contingently associated categories. It is what one would expect from systematic philosophical work.

However, the power of Pepper's notion of root metaphor for thinking about society and education, particularly the diagnostic potential of root metaphor, is enhanced geometrically by considering that each of the views also has a "crude" form. These crude forms contain contingently associated categories. In other words, at one end of the continuum lies the idealized, thorough, logically connected, internally consistent world view arising from the root metaphor as seen in Pepper's articulation; at the other end lies the crude form, also "arising" from the root metaphor but (unlike its rigorous cousin at the other end) shot through with contingently associated categories.

The more refined the world hypothesis, the more logically connected are its categories; the more crude, the more the categories are only contingently associated with the root metaphor and with each other. Pepper himself did not explore the idea of crude forms of the metaphors, but clearly he was aware of it. He noted in *Basis of Criticism in the Arts*, for instance, that the notion of "genres" in literature could be justified within a formist conception of literary craftsmanship, "though they are likely to become rigid and can be a source of abuse"(1945, p. 106). To continue the example from formism, it is clear that the concepts of "similarity," "type," and "genre" are logically related, whereas the idea of psychological rigidity, while highly associated with a crude version of formism, has no logically necessary connection to the root metaphor of similarity. Why this is a useful way of thinking about Pepper's root metaphor theory as it relates to society and education will become apparent shortly.

Finally, before proceeding to the views themselves, let me reiterate that it will be a sketch. As with a painting, each reader will have a slightly different interpretation of the root metaphors, and each successive view introduces fresh meanings and brings further understanding. Some interpretations might emphasize some aspects over others. Consequently, my aim is not to provide a definitive interpretation. Rather, it is to sketch with a broad brush, with the intent of showing the potential of root metaphor for furthering our understanding of education and society.

PEPPER'S FOUR ROOT METAPHORS

Formism

The formist root metaphor is similarity. A thoroughgoing formist intuitively gravitates to the stark realization that there are similarities and differences among things and experiences. A formist conception of the world emphasizes that particular things and ideas exist and have characteristics that make them what they are. Particulars and characteristics always come together. A formist also stresses that things grow and are made according to plans or norms that are responsible for their being similar to each other and their being of one kind or another. Truth to a formist is a matter of the correspondence or similarity of one thing to another, normally interpreted as the correspondence between statements and reality. The upshot of the root metaphor of similarity is the formist preoccupation with noticing categories, kinds, types, and classes of things; these are all *forms*.

Members of a form share common characteristics. The view of aesthetics that emerges from the root metaphor of similarity is one that traces a path through the notion of forms and norms. A formist tends to find beauty in the realization of form. The closer (more similar) a piece of art is to the ideal of its type or genre, the more beautiful it is. Early Greek statuary, for instance, was focused on fulfilling the characteristics of the ideal form of the human body. As Pepper (1942) points out, there is a preoccupation with notions of normalcy, either with respect to the "normalcy" of the art itself, or with respect to the intuitive reaction of a normal person to a work of art. Many questions come to mind with respect to what is regarded as normal, of course, but setting those aside for the moment, suffice it to say that representation (growing out of similarity) is a strong thread in a formist aesthetic, particularly with respect to visual art.

Let me comment on the crude version of formism. The crude version of any one of the root metaphors is difficult to articulate because the characteristics of a crude version are contingently rather than logically connected to the metaphor. Consequently, associations can work their way into almost every facet of experience and it is hard to draw the line as to where the refined version ends and the crude version begins. It is also difficult to tease out the overlappings of the crude versions with each other. Nevertheless, I think some quick strokes will give a general picture; it is easier to begin with observations about a crude formist aesthetic. A crude formist aesthetic reduces to the idea that the only kind of art with merit is that which corresponds to the everyday experiences of an average person. The function of art in this view is to mimic reality—representational art is supreme—and in the crude view, representation is seen as the attempt not to express essences, but to come as close as possible to photographic images. The only good art is that which corresponds to familiar, normal experience.

Crude formism has several associated and interrelated characteristics that highlight its weakness as a way of making sense of experience. Stale habit, form followed for form's sake, and mindless tradition are all variations of the emptiness and unthinking quality of crude formist actions; they depict a shallow understanding of experience and a way of thinking that is unthinking. Ritual that has become detached from the spiritual reasons for the ritual in the first place is a common example. Closely associated with stale habit and mindless tradition is rigidity; the rigid tenacity with which empty form is defended, is often in inverse proportion to the degree of connection that the form has to actual experience. The Achilles' heel of crude formism is the certainty with which the crude formist assumes what is normal and the certainty with which what is perceived as normal is automatically regarded as superior to all that lies outside the boundaries of normalcy. Nothing in the categories of refined formism would suggest that we know with certainty what the bounds of normalcy are or that ideas, things, and persons outside the bounds of "normal" have less value, but these are unproblematic leaps for the crude formist. The root metaphor of similarity and the crude formist's preoccupation with "type" manifest themselves in the obsession with distinguishing between the similar members of one's own group and dissimilar others. The concepts of certainty, rigidity, type, and normalcy in the hands of a crude formist reach a nadir in the varieties of prejudgment of value—prejudice about race, gender, ethnicity, ability, and religion. (See Willinsky's discussion about the topic of race in science education, Chapter 6 in this volume. The language of racism is the language of crude formism.)

Contextualism

If formism was historically one of the earliest root metaphors, brought to flower with early Greek thought, contextualism (pragmatism) is the most recent and, particularly with Dewey's work (*Art as Experience*, 1934), can be seen as an attempt to address the categorical rigidity of formism. The root metaphor of contextualism is the active present or changing situation. The contextualist emphasizes lived experience and the changing qualities of situations as they play themselves out through time. The contextualist does not deny categories and types of things, but argues that they have no immutable reality; rather, they are concepts that are more or less useful for making sense of situations. In other words, the concepts of form, type, normalcy, and so forth, are primary categories for a formist, but they are derivative categories for a contextualist. The primary categories for a contextualist are change, novelty, quality, texture, spread, fusion, strand, and, of course, context. A contextualist focuses on the intuitive understanding of the nature of a situation and revels in the experience of it.

The contextualist notes that events in real life have no "real" boundaries; any experience has strands that reach into the past and anticipate the future. The contextualist also emphasizes the fusion of experience. Our attention to details and parts is secondary to the experiential, fused, holistic quality of a situation. A glass of lemonade is the classic example of fusion. Lemonade is experienced as a fusion of water, lemon, and sugar, and, in fact, we could not say that we taste the individual parts. A contextualist emphasizes the fused wholeness of events. Wholes are primary, parts derivative. Contextualists argue that the search for absolute truth is in vain. Rather, truth in contextualism is regarded as relative to the context in which claims are asserted and situations experienced. Theories and explanations are regarded as provisionally true or intellectually satisfying if they parsimoniously account for the phenomenon in question. New information, discoveries, insights, and ways of thinking and seeing may make these provisional truths obsolete.

A contextualist aesthetic focuses on the vividness of experience. It focuses on how well a work gives us a sense of a situation or state of being, regardless of pleasure, pain, or distaste. This last point is important for understanding contextualist thinking in aesthetics. The contextualist can find aesthetic merit and place a high value on a work of art that commonly would be regarded as ugly, so long as the work gives us a vivid sense of situational experience. A comparative example is helpful here.

A crude formist would view Henry Moore's bronze *Warrior with Shield* (1953–54, Art Gallery of Ontario) as grotesque. The abstract head does not look like a human head. It is oddly flattened in back and it is hard to tell if there is a nose, nor is it clear whether the sightless eyes really are eyes or nostrils that seem to go nowhere. The left leg and arm are missing, as is the right foot. The left hip is caved in and most of the body parts are distorted in ways that seem plainly abnormal. All in all, it is a thoroughly unpleasant sculpture to view and clearly depicts an abnormal human being, according to a formist.

The contextualist, however, would value *Warrior with Shield* as a work of art, not because it is beautiful, but because it so vividly portrays the grotesque and horrible qualities of war. The contextualist would ask that viewers let themselves experience the fused, immediate quality of this horror and then (and only then) look to the strands and qualities that work together to form the immediate experience of intuited horror. The sightless, dehumanized face and missing appendages are symbolic of war's horror; the shield is a strand that reaches into early Greek history, and yet the armored face is a strand reaching into the future, almost as a sci-fi image; the hammered bronze has an impenetrable quality of armor, and yet the missing appendages vividly illustrate vulnerability. As Pepper (1945) points out, contextualism is an aesthetic view that allows us to deal with and appreciate the ugly and the unpleasant.

Crude contextualism reduces to a simpleminded relativism. For instance, a fairly complex and difficult idea that truth lies in a context and that we provisionally regard ideas as true if they can adequately account for the phenomena in question becomes a shadow of itself in the dictum that truth is merely what works—truth as expediency. Consequently, as with most root metaphors, the insights of contextualism are, in its crude versions, also its liabilities. The insight that our empirical understandings, moral judgments, and aesthetic values are relative to the context in which they function can, in the hands of a crude contextualist, be reduced to the intellectually flabby idea that nothing much matters since everything is relative. In other words, crude contextualism runs into trouble because of a difficulty in making even provisional distinctions and boundaries. In the field of art, for instance, it is difficult for the crude contextualist to distinguish good from bad. Further, the specter that grows from crude contextualism and persistently haunts the refined contextualist categories is moral relativism.

Organicism

The root metaphor of organicism is integration. As with contextualism, organicism is a view that is essentially holistic. However, unlike a contextualist, an organicist fundamentally believes in an absolute truth (unattainable, but worth pursuing) and stresses the nature of the integrative links that ultimately form that truth. The primary categories for the organicist are fragments, nexuses, contradictions, organic whole, implication, coherence, transcendence, and economy. The organicist sees all manner of contradictions in everyday life, but is quick to point out that those apparent contradictions (or fragments) are resolved (or integrated) at successively higher levels of analysis and insight. It is a view that emphasizes not the vividness of experience, but the integrative quality of experience. The essential "connectedness" of things and events is a hallmark of organic thinking. The entire field of ecology is based on the root metaphor of integration, for example, as is the metaphoric grounding for most present-day environmental concerns. The idea that there is a "balance of nature" that can be disturbed when the (apparently) most inconsequential organism is destroyed rests on the fundamental intuition of the integration and connectedness of all living things. Truth for the organicist is a matter of coherence, the integrated quality of experiences and ideas that allows us to come to a firm belief about something.

Organicist aesthetics values the integration of feelings. When examining a work of art, the organicist looks at the work as a whole, but with a view to comprehending those aspects that help it become a whole. Pepper (1945) points out:

> To reach the organistic idea, one is not far off if he starts with the vivid situation of the contextualist and instead of stressing the quality and defining the unity of the situation by the quality, stresses the organization and defines the unity of the situation in terms of its organization. (p. 77)

The organicist would look at Moore's warrior holistically, as would the contextualist, but the organicist would pay more attention to those aspects of the work that produce a unity of power and horror. The organicist would stress the integration of the bronze metal medium with the theme of battle, for instance. She or he would be quick to point out that the grotesque stumps, where an arm, leg, and foot used to be, are startling fragments, but they are fragments that find resolution or integration in the more inclusive theme of war. In other words, the work exhibits a high degree of unity because of the nature of the fragments. Once one thinks about what the work means, it becomes clear that the initial perception of fragmentation is resolved at a higher level of abstraction, a level that comes closer to the organic whole.

Pepper (1945) talks about the integrative feelings experienced by an organicist:

If you ask an organicist what these feeling connections are, he will ask you in effect if you have not felt the demand of pleasant things for other pleasant things to complete them or fill them out. Have you never been a bit of a creative artist in planting a garden, arranging flowers, putting a room in order, hanging up tools in the basement, making a speech, or even just carrying on a conversation? Do not gaps appear that ask to be filled in certain ways—ways that practically or logically are not called for, but that just make you feel better when they are followed out? . . . Well, that is a feeling connection. (p. 78)

Crude organicism can exhibit an unreflective mysticism about integrative experience. By that I mean that the intuitions of connection are taken for granted rather than traced in any rigorous fashion. In the context of a trial, for instance, it could lead to a conviction based on flimsy, circumstantial evidence. Weaving flimsy, circumstantial evidence into a knowledge claim or verdict is using a pale shadow of the coherence theory of truth that the refined metaphor demands. The drive for integration at successive levels of abstraction in the hands of a crude organicist also can lead to ignoring important distinctions (fragments of experience), as when, in the interests of consensus at a meeting, critical differences are neglected.

Mechanism

Machine is the mechanistic root metaphor. No other metaphor has had as profound an effect on the present-day world. The strident success of mechanistic ways of viewing the world in modern science and technology is evidence of the power of this metaphor. The increasingly obvious failures of the metaphor are an equal sign of its power. A simple machine is a good way of coming to understand the mechanistic root metaphor. A machine has parts, and the parts are articulated in such a way as to affect one another once the machine is set in motion. Each of the parts is discrete—each part has a reality unto itself and is existentially independent of other parts. It is only when the parts are put together in certain ways that they will affect one another. The discrete reality of *parts* located in time and space is a vital concept in a mechanistic view of the world.

Quantification is also an important notion in mechanism because the ability to count allows the parts to be physically located in time and space. In extreme views (pushing into crude mechanism), things are not real unless they can be quantified. The preoccupation of a mechanist is on how things work, that is, how the parts are arranged such that the machine can do its job. Consequently, explanations for how the machine works (and explanations in general) are, as commonly noted, "reduced to" the parts. This reductionist view can be seen in the following excerpt from Swerdlow's (1995) article on the brain:

Scientists increasingly argue that everything we experience can be reduced to a physical component. These "reductionists" are the ultimate cartographers: Everything, they say, exists at a particular point on the brain map. Some reductionists stake out an extreme position. Francis Crick, who along with two colleagues won the 1962 Nobel Prize in medicine for deciphering the DNA code that defines genes, says that "You, your joys and your sorrows, your memories and your ambitions, your sense of personal identity and free will, are in fact no more than the behavior of a vast assembly of nerve cells." (p. 20)

The theory of truth in mechanism is what Pepper (1942) calls the causal adjustment theory. Rather than a matter of correspondence or coherence, statements are manifestations of physiological responses to stimuli. This stimulus–response account of truth, not surprisingly, focuses on the mechanism by which we regard things as true.

Pepper's (1945) discussion of mechanistic aesthetic criticism has several aspects, but his starting point is the reaction to pleasant and adverse stimuli. In other words, his entry into mechanistic aesthetics is through a stimulus–response theory of truth:

> That pleasure is good and pain is bad is generally taken as fact not to be doubted without ridicule, so evident as to need no further evidence. On this datum the mechanistic theory of criticism is based. (p. 36)

The "pleasure principle," in combination with the idea of individuals as discrete, unconnected entities, leads to a mechanistic aesthetic that is basically hedonistic, according to Pepper (1942). Mechanistic hedonism is more complicated than our commonsense, puritanical image of it, but several points merit attention. One is that it is highly individualistic. Pepper (1945) puts it thus:

> There is no literal community of feeling possible on a mechanistic view. I may feel badly about your toothache. But my sympathetic pain is my own pain in my own body spatially separated from the pain of your toothache which is your own pain in your own body. Feelings on a mechanistic view are radically individualistic. Furthermore, and this cannot be too much stressed, it is the insulation of the bodies spatially separated from each other that guarantees the individuality of the feelings. (p. 38)

A second point relates to the mechanist's focus on pleasure. In more refined versions of mechanism, there is a push to seek pleasure beyond the bounds of our own parochial experience. (One should give oneself a fair chance to like sushi for there are many pleasures to be had from raw fish.) A third point concerns how pleasures are produced and relates to the mechanist's preoccupation with how things work. In the visual arts, for instance, the mechanist focuses on the various techniques that give rise to an overall effect: principles of contrast, gradation, theme-and-variation, pattern, form, line, mass, color, and so on. A mechanist would likely judge Moore's warrior as distasteful but would quickly turn to a discussion of how the effect of power is produced in the work with the techniques of mass, form, and medium.

As in the case of the other root metaphors, the boundaries of crude mechanism are somewhat arbitrary. Several points are worth noting. Crude mechanism exhibits a simplistic, linear conception of causality in which single causes are thought to produce single effects. For example, a crude mechanistic conception of causality lies behind the demand for "scientific proof" that violence in the media has anything to do with violence in society. The penchant for quantification in the hands of a crude mechanist conveniently reduces to valuing all things in monetary terms. Those things that cannot be quantified in dollars and cents have little or no value. The rabid materialist quality of much of Western society emerges from this aspect of the crude mechanistic metaphor. Efficiency for efficiency's sake and, in material production, the implicit principle of *doing* (producing) that which is *possible to do* (produce) are common attributes of crude mechanism. In crude mechanism the hedonist principle reduces to satisfying oneself with little or no consideration for others—in its virulent form, it is a rampant disregard for anything other than personal gratification. The atrophied sense of morality in crude mechanism manifests itself as every-man-for-himself; consequences of one's actions are something for others to worry about. Drug dealers, pornography, and the arms industry are particularly good examples of a mentality based on crude mechanism.

METAPHORS, CURRICULUM, TEACHING, AND RESEARCH

Let me finish the sketch of the root metaphors and of crude mechanism by returning to the phone call with Charlie and to the sophomoric but sincere questions that two middle-aged men wonder about. It is easy to slip into simplistic answers to such questions as how a society could spawn an arms industry that fuels the fires of ethnic hatred throughout the world. It certainly is not a case of simple causality. However, it is not farfetched to suggest that root metaphors are somehow implicated. Root metaphors are, in a way of speaking, metaphors of possibility—they give rise to ways of thinking about the world and ways of being in the world. They, at once, extend and limit our conceptions of what is, what is beautiful, what is possible, and what is right to do. The refined root metaphors of similarity, context, machine, and integration are, indeed, metaphors of possibility—but so are their crude counterparts. It is perhaps not well understood that issues of selfishness, cruelty, waste, greed, immorality, rigidity, and blind tradition (usually discussed in political, sociological, and psychological terms) are related to the philosophical traditions undergirding our sense of reality, related to the crude cousins of refined root metaphors.

The issues I have been discussing are ripe for serious inquiry, particularly as they relate to the nature of the school curriculum and teaching and, more particularly in this volume, science teaching. Before bringing this chapter to a close, I would like to note the modest amount of work that has been done in this area (so far as I am aware), at least as it relates to Pepper's notion of root metaphor. One category of work concerns inquiry into the nature of inquiry in science education. Roberts (1982c) analyzed the quantitative/qualitative research debate in terms of Pepper's root metaphors and showed in considerable detail how the methodological tenets of quantitative research stem from formism and mechanism, while those of qualitative research stem from contextualism and organicism. Roberts's analysis convincingly illustrates how the different root metaphors give rise to equally stringent, but quite different, standards of epistemological rigor. This discussion, of course, needs to be seen in light of the lively debate on the relative merits of quantitative and qualitative research that has been going on for some time.

Another category of work is aimed at classroom practice. In one study (Kilbourn, 1974) I developed a scheme for analyzing textbook material and showed how the scheme could be used to detect world views implied in written work. I developed the concept of "projection" (itself a metaphor) in order to highlight the active quality of metaphors, and took pains to work out in detail the evidential basis for claiming that a textbook passage or statement or phrase projects a world view. In a similar vein, Östman (Chapter 5 in this volume) shows how metaphors contribute to the production of companion meanings in classroom communication. The tone of both of these works is essentially descriptive.

Anderson and Kilbourn's (1983) discussion of the creation/evolution controversy is based on a descriptive approach as well. We used Pepper's framework to argue that the creationist position is grounded in a nonevidential world view of animism, whereas the evolutionist position is based on an eclectic mix of the four evidential world views. We also sketched what teaching might look like if these radically different ways of explaining phenomena were to be treated with dignity in the science classroom.

Geddis (1982) aimed at a slightly more prescriptive tone when he showed how four different conceptions of evidence could lead to different teaching strategies. As with the notion of "crude metaphor" outlined in this chapter, Geddis showed the limitations of each of the four root metaphors when their categories are treated superficially. The works cited above all involve Pepper's conception of root metaphor and his treatment of world hypotheses. In the same general vein is Cobern's (1991) review of "world view" as it relates to science education, although the conception of world view is broader than Pepper's.

CONCLUDING REMARKS ABOUT CLASSROOM CONVERSATIONS

Let me bring this discussion to a close with a few general comments about root metaphors and teaching. We can better understand people's construction of social reality if we think of it as based on bits and pieces of these world views or root metaphors. Some of us might exhibit preferences, but most of us are eclectic. And most of us are not conscious of the eclecticism; we tend not to bring forward to conscious awareness the mixed metaphoric nature of our understanding of experience.

Pepper (1942, 1945) argues that we should aim for eclecticism in practice— that we will reach fuller understanding of a phenomenon if we view it through all of the root metaphors. But the eclecticism he envisions is an informed and refined one. It involves being consciously aware of the way we view a phenomenon and consciously attempting to see it through the lenses of different metaphors. It suggests the kinds of conversations we might aim for in classrooms as learners attempt to make sense of experience and construct meaning. In short, the metaphors we use to make sense of our experience could be the object of discussion and conscious awareness in our classrooms. We could help our students become aware of the power of refined metaphors for shaping the way we see and think. We could help them see that when the crude cousins of these metaphors are used to construct social reality, we encourage the cynical use of language to think and talk about the human condition. The amoral celebration of the triumph of downsizing among the corporate elite is one stunning, if pathetic, example. If "the economy" is construed as a machine, whenever it has too many component parts to function efficiently some parts have to be dropped out. It doesn't matter that the parts are people—the idea is to make the machine function efficiently. Yet, if "the economy" is seen as an expression of a society's integration of its people in meaningful work, both problem and possible solutions appear to be different.

The science classroom would be one good place to start such conversations. At present, the issue is only partly what we do say in the classroom; more significant is what we do not say. We do not talk about the metaphors we use to construct our reality—certainly not in the pervasive, world view senses described above. We do not talk about the character of those metaphors, about the important differences between the refined and crude cousins. We do not talk about where the metaphors are useful and where they are not. And because we do not talk about these matters it is quite possible that we leave our children vulnerable to the crude versions of formism, mechanism, contextualism, and organicism. It is quite possible that we leave them vulnerable to crude interpretations of science, to the cheap ranting of pseudoscience. It would help explain some of the concerns that Charlie and I expressed over the phone; it would help explain our perception that society is increasingly desensitized to crude, artless metaphors and dehumanizing rhetoric and practice.

CHAPTER 4

Learning Inside and Outside Schools: Discursive Practices and Sociocultural Dynamics

ROGER SÄLJÖ

THE ABILITY TO LEARN and to adapt flexibly to many different conditions of life is no doubt a prominent feature of the human species. Helpless at birth, the young child has to acquire a broad range of skills and varied forms of knowledge to function in social situations. As infants we are biologically preprogrammed, as it were, to communicate. We orient ourselves toward people around us, and we respond to physical and verbal attempts to interact from the very moment we are born (and, in fact, even earlier).

What the adult person masters in terms of intellectual, social, and physical skills must be understood in terms of the interaction between what is biologically given to the species, on the one hand, and what has been acquired subsequently by the individual during his or her exposure to particular kinds of social experiences, on the other. In obvious respects, our capacities are constrained by the biological resources available to us. As far as physical performance is concerned, our limitations in strength, endurance, and so on, are apparent. But also when it comes to intellectual performance, it is evident that our abilities are highly restricted; we are not very good at memorizing or remembering, our attention span—that is, the ability to simultaneously register and recall events in the surrounding world—does not exceed what is captured by the famous 7 +/– 2 formula (Miller, 1956), and our ability to handle logical problems is far from impressive (Wason & Johnson-Laird, 1972).

However, at the same time as we make these observations that point to limitations inherent in the human species, it is obvious that in relation to many of the activities we engage in, we are not constrained by these biological shortcomings. To compensate for the meager resources given to us by nature, as it were, humans have developed tools and instruments by means of which they can perform operations that would be impossible to manage without such external aids. When moving a heavy object such as a stone, we are not limited by the strength of the human body. We have invented increasingly sophisticated tools that help us achieve our goals; the technique of using a lever has been known for a long time, and recent technologies offer devices such as excavators, bulldozers, and tractors by means of which we can solve problems of this kind while exerting almost no physical energy. The limitations of our visual system are compensated for by devices such as the microscope, camera, and binoculars, technologies that allow us to see what is not readily visible under natural circumstances. Technological development also implies that intellectual problems are solved through the use of artifacts. To a society that uses the technology of text production, the limitations in memory capacities of individuals are not critical when it comes to retaining information about matters such as ownership of land and other property, debts, kinship, and so forth, or when central texts such as laws, religious stories, and so on, have to be remembered. Instead of committing such texts to memory, we can write them down and retrieve them whenever called for (Ong, 1982). The use of paper and pencil, the abacus, and more recent technologies such as the slide rule, calculating machine, and electronic calculator make it possible to solve complicated multiplication and division problems that would be very difficult, maybe even impossible, to handle without such artifacts.

Theories of learning, however, generally focus on the individual as if he or she were acting in isolation from other people and without the support of artifacts. The processes through which people acquire knowledge are seen as residing within individuals; the dominant metaphorical construction of learning sees it as the "taking in" of information into the mind of the individual. Knowledge is construed as a truthful copy of what is "out there" in the physical world, and it is strictly mental and private in nature. Manual skills either are seen as independent of linguistically mediated knowledge, or, alternatively, they are conceived as the mechanical application of what has been acquired through previous acquisition of rules and information. If we follow the traditional mentalist conception of human thinking and action, learning is disembodied.

But if we are to follow the spirit of the observations commented on above—and those reported elsewhere in this volume—an initial commitment to the conceptual separation of the individual from the collective (society and its cultural practices) is hardly feasible, when it comes to either thinking or acting. People do not learn in isolation, and their knowledge and skills are intimately dependent on those of the more experienced members of their society and culture. Nobody learns how to become a blacksmith (Keller & Keller, 1993) or a tailor (Lave & Wenger, 1991), the skills of downhill skiing (Fuhrer, 1993) or navigation (Hutchins, 1995), how to read (Heath, 1983) and use numerical systems (Cohen, 1982), unless they are exposed to situations in which they become familiar with these human practices. Also, anyone learning such skills today relies on insights and techniques developed over a long time, maybe even thousands of years as in the case of navigation, where there is an historical continuity in certain elements of this practice that goes back at least to Phoenician sailors in the Mediterranean some 3,000 years ago (Hutchins, 1995). Rather than reducing learning to an individual and private phenomenon, it must be understood as a problem of how collectively shared knowledge and practices are made available to, and are appropriated by, individuals inside as well as outside the formal activities of schooling.

HUMAN LEARNING AND SOCIOCULTURAL CHANGE

In a sociocultural perspective on human action (Säljö, 1992a, 1996b; Wertsch, 1985, 1991), the integration of artifacts—manufactured tools—into social practices is seen as a basic starting point for the understanding of any human activity. To learn and to develop is to appropriate and master artifacts within meaningful social activities. The fundamental unit of analysis in such a perspective on human learning and development implies that individuals are conceived as operating in social situations with mental and physical artifacts as resources (Chaiklin & Lave, 1993; Goodwin, 1998; Hutchins, 1995; Hutchins & Palen, 1998). Such a formulation challenges the basic tenet of most modern dualist psychology in that it explicitly counterargues the feasibility of assuming that there is something inside the heads of individuals—cognition—that can be understood as separated from what is "outside"—culture and social life. On the contrary, a central assumption of a sociocultural perspective is that mind and culture co-constitute each other (Cole, 1991) and develop in close interrelationship. The link between cognition and culture is discourse. But before continuing along these lines of arguing for the central role of discourse, let me return to some of the Vygotskian themes on the appropriation of cultural tools that have been alluded to above.

The claim that there is an intimate interplay between culture and cognition—between a world of objects, events, and discourse, on the one hand, and the human mind, on the other—has several important consequences when it comes to understanding human learning and development. One of the most decisive elements of such a position is captured in Vygotsky's (1986) famous dictum that human development must be understood at two levels. First, there is the biological level where the early development of a child can be understood largely in terms of the unfolding of innate resources. Then, there is the cultural level where the "child's intellectual growth is contingent on his mastering the social means of thought, that is, language" (p. 94). This implies that later stages of learning and development—those characterized by the mastery of language and other cultural tools—

are not uniform across cultures and societies, and that the "nature of the development itself changes from biological to *sociohistorical*" (p. 94).

At the cultural level the concrete differences in life-conditions between (and also within) societies result in radically different assumptions regarding how to think and act in social situations. What differs between societies in cultural terms is not just ideas and worldviews, but also the nature of artifacts that are used in daily life and the social organization of knowledge. In some societies, artifacts such as telephones, computers, television sets, and faxes are commonplace, and they play a critical role in production and in the management of everyday life. In other societies, these particular artifacts play a very limited, if any, role. In some contexts, agricultural production is carried out by means of artifacts such as tractors, mechanical ploughs, and complicated reaping machines, while in other places different technologies with draught-animals instead of tractors, and groups of people with scythes and similar tools instead of reaping machines will be used for agricultural production. The knowledge that people need to master these different systems of production will, of course, differ. In the former case, it is absolutely necessary to know about the maintenance of engines and machines, while in the latter case knowledge of how to provide for animals will be essential.

In a sociocultural perspective, learning (and development) implies mastering the particular tools that are prevalent in society. This implies that in order to understand thinking and learning, "it is necessary to go beyond the limits of the organism and to search for the roots of these complex processes in the historically formed environment, in the communication of the child with adults" as well as in the "relations among objects, tools and language which have been laid down in the course of social history" (Luria, 1971, p. 260). At a general level, tools can be described in two major categories: practical (or physical) tools and psychological (or intellectual) tools. The concept of tool is suggestive, and it deliberately puts the use of concepts and linguistically mediated knowledge into the same category as the use of practical tools and instruments; just as we do things with physical tools and instruments, we do things with words.

As I alluded to above, the link between mental and physical tools must be understood as discursive in nature. Thus, even physical tools—such as the compass, the clock, or the minicalculator—are manifestations of human conceptual distinctions that originate in social activities. The system for describing directions by means of degrees and minutes on the compass; the measuring of time with units such as hours, minutes, and seconds; and the use of the zero, the decimal, and algorithms for multiplication and division that we find in the calculator are conceptual conventions that have been implemented into instruments. Thus, artifacts are not dead objects in the sense that they do not communicate artificial distinctions. On the contrary, they speak back to us in categories that have been created by people to provide knowledge, overview, and systematicity.

DISCOURSE AND THE RE-PRESENTATION
OF OBJECTS AND EVENTS IN LANGUAGE

In most accounts of the role of language in human activities, there is an assumption that words and concepts primarily represent the world; that linguistic expressions are somewhat like pictures or abstract images of objects and events in the "real" physical world in which we have our primary commitments and interests (cf. Wittgenstein, 1953/1995, pp. 20ff, for a systematic critique of this assumption and the philosophy of language that goes with it). Following this construction of the nature of language, we often talk about communication and verbal interaction as "just talk" rather than "action." This tendency of opposing the use of language to physical action can be seen as yet another element of what philosophers refer to as a dualist perspective on the human being, separating mind and matter; the "real" world is what is tangible and physically present, and words are mere representations or abstract copies of that reality. This has been, and still is, a very pervasive metaphor for understanding mental phenomena (including linguistically codified knowledge) and their relation to practical activities.

In a sociocultural perspective on thinking and learning, in which human learning is understood in terms of the appropriation and use of intellectual and practical tools, this traditional view of language as a simple and straightforward representational device cannot be taken as a valid point of departure. There are many reasons for this. It is obvious that there are many significant human phenomena and events that cannot be understood in terms of images or pictures in this simplistic manner. Concepts such as loyalty, justice, irony, equality, and democracy, to mention but a few examples, do not correspond to objects and events in the world in the simplistic manner assumed within a picture theory of language. Still, they can be meaningfully applied when talking about and analyzing events in concrete settings, and they play an important role in social life. Even such an elusive phenomenon as time can be understood and communicated about in a meaningful and precise manner by grounding it in human experiences and activities. This is clearly illustrated in the analysis provided by Lakoff and Johnson (1980) of the metaphorical construction in everyday language of the concept of time, presented in their seminal work on "metaphors we live by." When analyzing contemporary English, the authors found that the idea that "time is money"—a very central assumption in Western capitalist societies—is reflected in a broad range of expressions:

> You're wasting my time.
> This gadget will save you hours.
> I don't have the time to give you.
> How do you spend your time these days?

That flat tire cost me an hour.
I've invested a lot of time in her.
I don't have enough time to spare for that.
You're running out of time.
You need to budget your time.
Put aside some time for ping pong.
Is that worth your while?
Do you have much time left?
He's living on borrowed time.
You don't use your time profitably.
I lost a lot of time when I got sick.
Thank you for your time. (Lakoff & Johnson, 1980, pp. 7–8)

The systematicity of these expressions in depicting time as a commodity and a limited resource analogous to money is apparent. It is also quite obvious that these manners of speaking in no way can be considered as mere reflections of an objectively observable reality. On the contrary, and as I have already pointed out, they form part of a particular conception of time that is far from universal. This metaphorical construction of time reproduces a particular social order, and it is material in its consequences; people experience time in accordance with these metaphorical constructions, they act accordingly, and they evaluate how they "spend" their time along these lines. The particular mode in which time is talked about in everyday parlance no doubt reflects culturally significant connotations or "companion meanings" (Östman, 1995; Östman & Roberts, 1994). In fact, several medical and psychological ailments, such as ulcer and stress symptoms, can be related to this manner of conceiving of time. The individual who feels that she is "wasting" her time rather than "using" it "productively" eventually may develop severe psychosomatic symptoms.

The dominant picture theory of language is also incapable of dealing with cultural differences in interpreting the world. The famous examples of the many words that Innuit populations in Greenland and Arctic regions use for snow, or that migrating peoples living in deserts use for sand, alert us to the complex manners in which the surrounding world is made "meaning-full" by means of linguistic resources. While for most people in the world a single concept of snow is sufficient to cover a wide range of situations in which we communicate about this substance ("Be careful when driving; there is snow on the roads," or "I hope we get some snow for Christmas this year"), Innuits find it functional to operate with finer distinctions that communicate more effectively the salient features of snow that are relevant to pay attention to in their social practices. The particular quality of powder-like snow that Innuits refer to as "quanik" (Hoeg, 1995), for instance, is distinctive, since it easily results in avalanches and other kinds of problems.

What is even more important when it comes to the simplistic conception of language implied by the picture theory, however, is that a closer scrutiny of the relationship between language and action in human activities tells us that language is a field of action in itself. As Harré and Gillett (1994) put it, words "can be meant as invitations, warnings, promises, threats, apologies, reprimands, congratulations and so on" and "these are not expressions, but ways to do things" (p. 32). In fact, the very activities of teaching and learning are predominantly ways of doing things with words. Such conversational projects aim at introducing people to terms, concepts, rules, methods, and so forth, that allow them to understand and simultaneously do things in other settings. But in many other areas of life as well, language, or rather discourse, is a means of social action—the lawyer defending his client in a court procedure; the police officer, social worker, therapist, or physician giving advice to people in need of help; the salesperson trying to communicate the advantages of a commodity to a potential client are all examples that illustrate that many pragmatic actions are achieved by means of language as the dominant tool.

HUMAN KNOWLEDGE AND MEDIATION

A central assumption in what has been said so far is that language mediates— refracts rather than reflects (Voloshinov, 1930/1973)—the world for us (Vygotsky, 1986). Objects and events thus are never perceived per se but always mediated in language in line with situational and communicative expectations. This feature of language is easily recognized in the context of media in modern societies. Soldiers in a war may be referred to in sharply conflicting manners. Some may refer to them as "persons doing their duty for their people," "brave freedom fighters," or "courageous defenders of the free world," while others may describe them as "merciless killers," "undisciplined bandits," or "invaders." The truthfulness of any of these statements cannot be established by just looking at what is happening, but is clearly relative to the different discourses of which they form a part. Another famous example in the history of human debates on ethical dilemmas is, of course, whether a pregnant woman is to be referred to as carrying a fetus or an unborn child. The two expressions have different connotations and they are relevant accounts in different discourses.

Human knowledge thus is largely codified in language. Even in physical activities, linguistically mediated knowledge will, on closer scrutiny, be found to be an essential ingredient. The blacksmith deciding when to start working with the hot iron has at his or her disposal a series of linguistic distinctions in terms of which, for instance, the quality of the melting iron and its appropriateness for being worked with can be analyzed (Keller & Keller, 1993). These distinctions mediate the relevant qualities of the physical objects in situationally functional manners, and they can be used for communication within the community of practitioners familiar with the practice and its terminology. The meaning of terms and linguistic expressions therefore should be sought not only in their reference to an outside reality, but rather in their insertion into systematic discourses in which terms and concepts acquire their meaning in relationship to other terms and to human practices. The "sense" of an expression, to use Vygotskian language, therefore is always relative to a situated practice, and the task for the user/learner is to identify the relevant contextual specification of a term. In a complex society (Hannerz, 1992), that is, a society with a high division of labor, advanced technologies, and differentiated social systems, the objects, events, and relationships are contextualized very differently across social practices. Terms such as energy, atom, and force (see below) are used as parts of different discourses, and their meaning will differ as we move between the everyday conversation among neighbors and the scientific colloqium in the famous university laboratory.

Terms and conceptual conventions thus are grounded in discursive practices, and the relevant referents of an expression often will differ across social practices. This point was clearly illustrated in a study by Säljö and Wyndhamn (1988) in which children's awareness of the relevant referential meaning of the term *week* was tested in some empirical studies. The term *week*, like other terms for quantifying time, such as hour and month, varies in its meaning in different human practices. A week can refer to a period of 5 days (such as in the context of work or school in most, although far from all, countries) or 7 days (which is the formal definition), and there are other alternatives as well. In an empirical study among fifth and sixth graders (aged 12–13), pupils were given one of two types of tasks. "A cow produces about 18 liters of milk per day. How much does the cow produce during one week?" and "Kalle goes to school and on the average he has seven lessons a day. How many lessons does he have per week?" The first task, in which the relevant referent of week is 7 days, was correctly solved by more than 90% of the participants in our study, and none of the participants made a mistake with respect to the number of days that was relevant. With respect to the second type of task, however, about 30% of the children used 7 days in their calculations, and among those that the teacher characterized as poor achievers in mathematics 40% did so. Thus, even though the second type of problem referred to the children's own everyday circumstances, the relevant referent of the term *week* was more difficult to find. The interesting point here is that none of the children were unaware of the fact that they went to school 5 days a week only. However, when operating in a world on paper in the classroom, determining which type of specification is relevant becomes a problem; I return to this problem later.

COGNITION AND LEARNING: EVERYDAY EXPERIENCE AND INSTITUTIONAL ACCOUNTING PRACTICES

The principle of conceiving language as a tool for mediating the world so that it can be talked about meaningfully in human practices applies to our everyday language. In this sense, knowledge relevant for daily activities is built into our language, although this normally escapes our attention. In everyday practices we treat language as transparent, and we seldom, if ever, reflect on the nature of knowledge represented by our natural language unless it becomes obvious to us that there is something problematic about our use of it in a particular setting. For instance, today most people avoid expressions that once were associated with colonial attitudes toward indigenous populations. Thus, terms such as "Native Americans," "African Americans," "Innuits," "Sami people," and so on, are used instead of earlier expressions that often reflected alien perspectives on these groups.

In a complex society, however, powerful mediating tools are developed within institutional activities such as science and research, art, schooling, production, bureaucracies, health care, and other similar activity systems. This process of institutionalization of knowledge and mediational means results in the creation of abstract, but at the same time powerful, intellectual and practical instruments that are no longer rooted in everyday understandings and perspectives on the world. Rather, the knowledge now represents a more specialized and narrow interest in furthering a particular activity. In science and research, which is one of the activity systems that has profoundly influenced modern schooling, a prominent interest is the systematic understanding and explaining of natural and social phenomena. In everyday life, on the other hand, our interests tend to be more pragmatic. We are generally happy to use whatever knowledge or principle works, and we do not necessarily bother about understanding why and how it works.

This growth of partially autonomous, institutionalized discourses is characteristic of a complex society, and it has modified the conditions of human learning dramatically. Much of the learning that people have to engage in is no longer part of ongoing, everyday activities. Learning has been decontextualized from other such daily projects, and it has emerged as the leading activity of a particular institution largely separated from production and other activity systems in society. In this process of decontextualization, a distancing between everyday, pragmatic knowledge and insight, on the one hand, and institutionally sanctioned forms of knowledge and understanding, on the other, inevitably takes place. Learning becomes subordinated to the discursive traditions and principles of communication characteristic of school subjects, which, in turn, generally have been modeled on academic disciplines.

In a sociocultural perspective this implies that schooling forms another, and slightly different, context for action and understanding than everyday life, with different priorities as to what counts as knowledge and adequate solutions to a problem. In a complex society schooling in itself has become a semiautonomous activity system with specific criteria for what counts as valid forms of communication and appropriate definitions of knowledge. There are two consequences of this decontextualization of learning, and its subsequent recontextualization into the particular context of school, that I would like to comment on, since they illustrate how new and complex discursive practices emerge as a consequence of the institutionalization of human activities.

The institutionalization of learning implies that the dominant forms of mediating the world change. In contrast to how knowledge reproduction was organized in the learning of crafts such as tailoring in an apprenticeship system (Lave & Wenger, 1991), where there was a close proximity between producing clothes and learning how to do this, schooling increases the distance between the original activity—production—and training to master the skill. In previous systems, people learned, but very few, outside small elites, studied. A very important consequence of this development is the more indirect and complex relationship between everyday experiences that people have and the knowledge they encounter in institutional settings. When learning is subordinated to the conceptual frameworks and knowledge interests of school subjects, the discourse that students meet no longer corresponds to what we see and hear, in the manner that characterized, for instance, apprenticeship situations. The dominant discursive constructions now derive from the principles of organizing knowledge that characterize school subjects and academic discursive traditions. This conceptual loyalty to fairly abstract conceptual systems is immediately apparent when looking at textbooks in school. Consider, for instance, the following passage from an introductory textbook in chemistry, analyzed by Östman (1995), in which students are offered an explanation of what water is:

> If you let a hydrogen flame burn under the opening of a cool and dry beaker, you get mist—drops of water—on the inside of the beaker. The water has been formed through a chemical reaction between hydrogen, and oxygen from the air. Water, thus, is the oxide of hydrogen. The simplest possible formula for water (hydrogen oxide) could be written HO. This implies that there would be one hydrogen atom for every oxygen atom. Through experiments, however, it is possible to show that there are two hydrogen atoms to every oxygen atom in water. The chemical designation will then be dihydrogen oxide and, consequently, the formula will be H_2O. (p. 84, my translation)

When analyzing this short piece of introductory science text from a discursive point of view, we see a transition from an explanation of something that can be observed and felt (or at least we can imagine doing so), the formation of water, to an account in which the formation is explained by means of abstract concepts and principles that have no direct relationship to our senses. We cannot perceive atoms and their behavior, and we may not be able to delimit what a chemical reaction is or describe its essential features. The descriptions and explanations are grounded in accounting practices (Shotter, 1992) characteristic of scientific forms of reasoning that describe objects and events in accordance with abstract principles rather than on the basis of the experiential qualities that we register with our senses. In this very important sense, learning is no longer necessarily supported by observations we make in everyday situations. On the contrary, learning often presupposes that we disregard what are "obvious" constituents of a phenomenon, an event or an object in the world as we encounter it in everyday practices.

This latter point has been illustrated in interesting ways in much of the recent research on students' understanding of scientific principles and explanations. For instance, the research on students' understanding of the physical concept of force (Johansson, Marton, & Svensson, 1985; cf. Säljö, 1996a) illustrates the difficulties students have in adopting a scientific mode of reasoning when explaining movement. Instead of considering (uniform) movement as the natural state of objects (which is the Newtonian point of departure), and using the concept of force to explain differences in velocity (acceleration and deceleration), students (often well into their university studies in physics/mechanics) seem to prefer an accounting practice more familiar to everyday experience (and everyday language) in which rest is seen as the "natural" state that does not have to be accounted for. The idea that rest is the natural state of objects no doubt is supported by everyday experience, where we are used to assuming that "force" is something that sets objects in motion and that is somehow transferred to an object while it moves. Loss of speed consequently is interpreted as the loss of the "force." Thus, to learn to use the discursive practices of physical reasoning, is to learn to disregard features of relationships that might appear obvious and that are sustained by commonsense assumptions and observations.

A second aspect of the sociocultural development of forms of learning is that the institutionalization of learning processes results in an increased reliance on texts as mediational means. In formal schooling, texts were adopted as the most important form of mediation, and reading (and writing) became dominant activities in the teaching and learning process. Indeed, learning to read and write came to be seen as the core idea of the educational enterprise. In a sociocultural perspective this focus on written texts can be understood as a decontextualization of mediational means (Wertsch, 1991), that is, the practice and mastery of forms of communication emerge as a significant activity per se within the institution. Thus, reading not only serves concrete purposes of communicating events, but it also becomes the dominant form of communication. This reliance on texts has had profound effects on learning and on our interpretation of what constitutes knowledge. The prototypical conception of knowledge has become the explicitly formulated statement—a fact or a proposition—and learning has been identified with memorizing such pieces of information.

However, from a sociocultural perspective, the use of texts as the prime vehicle for communicating knowledge can be seen as a further step in the adoption of experience-distant accounting practices for understanding the world. Texts have been used as prominent socializing devices, and they promote the use of literate conceptual frameworks that are defined explicitly and delimited according to a set of abstract principles. As Olson (1994) has analyzed in great detail, reading (and writing) highlights the problem of interpretation of messages. Successful communication via text presupposes familiarity with hermeneutic principles that allow the reader to go from what is written to what is meant. Readers have to learn how to take meaning from a text, to use Olson's expression. For instance, the meaning of such "biblical statements as 'The kingdom of heaven is within you' or 'This is my body'" (Olson, 1994, p. 29) is not self-evident, nor is it located entirely within the text.

A very interesting study that illustrates the powers and potentials of textual (and institutional) practices to get people accustomed to certain hermeneutic principles—ways of fixing and taking meaning—was carried out by Luria (1976) in the late 1920s and early 1930s in the remote parts of what were then the southern regions of the Soviet Union. The purpose of Luria's empirical research was to document the consequences of the introduction of literacy, schooling, and a new social order with "new forms of social activity: the collective evaluation of work plans, the recognition and correction of shortcomings, and the allocation of economic functions" (p. 13) in these remote areas with a "backward economy" (p. 13), as the author put it. The new type of discourse encountered in books and in schooling was more abstract and "theoretical" in the sense that it reflected a more analytical and textual orientation toward objects and events. The attitude to the world promoted by education and literacy was very much in line with the quotation from the chemistry textbook above: Phenomena such as water were held at arm's length, as it were, and described and talked about as autonomous entities for the sake of being able to define them according to some abstract analytical principle. Phenomena were no longer discussed primarily in the immediate context of practical human concerns, such as drinking or irrigating fields, in the case of water. Rather, the attitude toward knowledge now implies that there is a decontextualization of phenomena from their appearances in daily practices, and a subsequent recontextualization into the discourse of school subjects, science or some similar institutional framework.

In a sociocultural perspective this is a dramatic shift in our relationship to objects and events in the world around us. The new types of discourse, grounded in institutional traditions and interests, entail accounting practices that give priority to text-based versions of the world. Exact and unequivocal definitions as well as general relationships between phenomena within the context of some general, and often idealized, theoretical framework—such as an academic discipline—form the resources and contexts for communicating. In such text-based discursive practices, it becomes relevant and interesting, even necessary, to approach the world by formal definitions and careful delimitations of the conceptual tools by means of which we interpret phenomena. But this discursive practice represents an attitude to the world that will appear strange to many, children as well as adults. In Luria's study there are many interesting illustrations of how questions generated from such a discursive position appeared alien to the unschooled—what Luria refers to as "illiterate"—people who were interviewed. In the following case, a peasant responds with a certain suspicion when he is asked a typical school-type question analogous to "What is water?":

> Subject: Illi-Khodzh., age twenty-two, peasant from remote village, illiterate.
>
> Try to explain to me what a tree is.
>
> "Why should I? Everyone knows what a tree is, they don't need me telling them."
>
> Rejects need for explanation
>
> Still, try and explain it.
>
> "There are trees everywhere; you won't find a place that doesn't have trees. So what's the point of my explaining?"
>
> But some people have never seen trees, so you might have to explain.
>
> "Okay. You say there are no trees where these people come from. So I'll tell them how we plant beetroots by using seeds, how the root goes into the earth and the leaves come out on top. That's the way we plant a tree, the roots go down." (Luria, 1976, p. 86)

As can be seen, the interviewee refuses to accept the question, since he obviously cannot see the point in asking, when "everyone knows what a tree is." The question "What is . . . ?" in relation to a familiar object such as a tree seems strange, and the respondent—unlike the student in the classroom—cannot spontaneously find a context in which it makes sense. When the interviewer makes a discursive move and positions the respondent differently in relation to the question by claiming that the point of the explanation is to inform someone who has never seen a tree, the question makes more sense (even though the peasant still appears somewhat hesitant). However, the straightforward question about definitions of objects in this manner is typical of the language game of formal schooling, which focuses on text-based realities in which objects and events are defined and attended to as discursive entities rather than acted upon.

Similar observations also were made by Luria when unschooled interviewees were asked to solve problems of deduction and inference. In the following excerpt, a peasant is presented with a so-called syllogism that gives two premises and the task for the respondent is to establish whether the conclusion is true or not:

> Subject: Abdurakhm., age thirty-seven, from remote Kashgar village, illiterate.
>
> Cotton can grow only where it is hot and dry. In England it is cold and damp. Can cotton grow there?

"I don't know."

Think about it.

"I've only been in the Kashgar country; I don't know beyond that."

Refusal; reference to lack of personal experience.

But on the basis of what I said to you, can cotton grow there?

"If the land is good, cotton will grow there, but if it is damp and poor, it won't grow. If it's like the Kashgar country, it will grow there too. If the soil is loose, it can grow there too, of course." . . .

But what do my words suggest?

"Well, we Moslems, we Kashgars, we're ignorant people; we've never been anywhere, so we don't know if it's hot or cold there." (p. 108)

This example very clearly illustrates the problems that the interviewee has in identifying the logic of this particular conversation. He does not operate according to the assumption that the truth of the conclusion should be evaluated with reference to what is said in the premises, which is the logic of this typically literate language game. Instead his reasoning is grounded in considerations about an empirical reality in which certain climatic conditions have to be at hand if cotton is to grow. He also refuses to make statements about whether cotton grows in England, since he has never been outside his own region. This would be, of course, a very relevant argument, if the discussion had concerned where and how cotton could grow. But this was not the point of the discussion (at least not from the interviewer's perspective). It took place fully within a text-based reality, and the question can be correctly answered if one pays attention to the words uttered and to the relationships between them. The interviewee takes meaning from the utterances as if they were about the world, while what is needed is attention to the meaning of words in relationship to each other. What is possible or reasonable in the real world—in which the interviewee is operating when trying to answer—is temporarily of no interest when relating premises to conclusions.

CONCLUDING REMARKS

Human knowledge—whether mediated by language in the form of concepts and rules or implemented into artifacts—is discursive in nature. Sociocultural development implies that increasingly sophisticated accounting practices and conceptual realities are created, by means of which events and objects in the world can be brought under conceptual control. In a complex society these discourses are reproduced by individuals acting in social institutions that have the power and resources to cultivate and sustain them over time. The knowledge produced within these discourses does not remain inside the heads of individuals, nor can it be reduced to mental structures residing in the biological substrate of the brain unaffected by cultural assumptions and values. Rather, knowledge emerges as properties of tools and socially organized practices in which individuals participate, and which by necessity are ideological in nature—without values there can be no knowledge. The acquisition of knowledge cannot be conceived as the absorption of value-neutral and objective images of the world, as the dominant metaphor has it. On the contrary, learning is the appropriation and mastery of artificial tools that have developed on the basis of human interests inside or outside social institutions. Knowledge is therefore fundamentally argumentative in nature; it moves the world rather than reflects it.

CHAPTER 5

How Companion Meanings Are Expressed by Science Education Discourse

LEIF ÖSTMAN

MY AIM IN THIS CHAPTER is to focus closely on communication from the point of view that in science education, as elsewhere, we create and take part in systematic discourses. The chapter, and indeed this entire volume, brings together two elements: the creation of meaning in communication, and the potential socializing consequences of such meaning in the formation of consciousness and identity in the younger generation.

It is tempting to focus on surface features of communication in science education, despite Lemke's (1990) detailed use of semiotics to demonstrate the complexity of establishing what is referred to in the present volume as scientific meaning. Further, a great deal more than scientific meaning is communicated in science education discourse. Companion meanings are communicated simultaneously, and these can contribute significantly to the socialization of students—what Dewey (1916/1966) meant when he called education "the process of forming fundamental dispositions, intellectual and emotional, toward nature and fellow men" (p. 328).

To view socialization in this manner is to actively reject the sense in which the term sometimes is used—to refer to attitudes and feelings about matters separated in time and space from the learning of school subjects. (For example, socialization refers sometimes to students' deportment and social interaction.) The "fundamental dispositions" to which Dewey referred have a substantial intellectual component that is learned, usually implicitly, *while science is being learned.* A view of science itself is learned in the science classroom, and so is a view of nature. Also learned is a view of one's fellow human beings—for example, in terms of their race and gender, in terms of who possesses truth and who should listen to whom in matters scientific, and in terms of who has the capability to understand science and therefore can be empowered in a certain way. The learning of all such matters is seen as socializing students toward particular attitudes and viewpoints.

The chapter is presented in four sections followed by a conclusion. Some orienting ideas are presented first, then three sections are devoted to how science education discourse communicates, respectively, (1) a view of science, (2) a view of nature, and (3) a view of the relationship between human beings and nature. The approach used is to analyze teaching vignettes and textbook excerpts. In order to visualize and conceptualize the different meanings produced in science education discourse, three categories are used: curriculum emphasis, nature language, and subject focus. Each corresponds to one of the types of meaning mentioned above: curriculum emphasis to view of science, nature language to view of nature, and subject focus to view of the relationship between human beings and nature. The concluding section extends the discussion to other aspects of science education considered in the third part of this volume.

DISCOURSE AND MEANING

Companion meanings are located in ongoing discourses (cf. Säljö, Chapter 4 in this volume). A discourse can be viewed as a systematic process of inclusion and exclusion, regarding what to say and what *not* to say, how it should be said and how it should *not*. Thus, to understand or clarify the production of companion meanings, it is necessary to switch constantly between what is included and what is excluded. By paying such close attention to language use, it is possible to get a grip on the discourse and thereby clarify the meanings created. Citing Wittgenstein (1953/1995), Cherryholmes (1988) describes the close connection between language use and discourse rules as follows:

> Discourses are not composed by randomly choosing words and statements. Instead, rules constitute and regulate language use. . . . Such rules help shape a discursive practice that produces a specific discourse. (p. 3, citation omitted)

I will illustrate how meanings are produced in science education by systematically discussing what *is* said in relation to what *could have been* said, how it *is* said in relation to how it *could have been* said. The comparison exposes choices made about the meaning to be communicated. Such a comparison is grounded in poststructural theory, and it depends on having available some alternative possibilities (about what could have been said and how). Some alternatives are drawn from the array of curriculum emphases that have appeared in science education history (Roberts, Chapter 1 in this volume). Others will be presented in the course of the analysis.

The next three sections concentrate on analyzing how three types of ever-present companion meanings are produced in science education—views of science, views of nature, and views of the relationship between human beings and nature. Production of such meanings has been discussed for views of science (curriculum emphases, in Chapter 1). Two complementary conceptualizations will be used; I call them nature language and subject focus. I will argue that any teaching concerning nature automatically will also produce these three types of companion meaning. The examples I use are vignettes drawn from my own early experience as a teacher in the 1980s in chemistry classes at the lower secondary level in Sweden. These are complemented with analyses of excerpts from science textbooks.

HOW DISCOURSE COMMUNICATES A VIEW OF SCIENCE

Vignette 1: What Is (Really) in the Black Box?

One day, looking through a newly released textbook, I found a description of a technique referred to as "the black box," which probably will be familiar to many readers. I asked the craft teacher to make six identical wooden boxes and to put five or six small objects in each of them, the same in each box. I told him to make sure the boxes were very difficult to open and not to tell me what items he had put in them. I divided the class into six groups and directed them to find out, without damaging the box, what was inside it. Some students asked for a magnet, others for a stethoscope. Each group was very secretive, anxious not to reveal which tools they were using.

Each group found six objects, four of which were described in similar terms: a wooden object, a metal screw, a piece of cotton wool, and a needle. I asked how they could tell, and they described their evidence in terms of such categories as magnetism and sound. As for the remaining objects, the groups differed in their descriptions and all were uncertain. I summarized the results by saying that the box probably contained the four objects all groups had found, but we did not know about the rest.

Some of the students asked who had won and what was the right answer. I replied that the purpose of the exercise was to illustrate that scientists often cannot see directly the objects they are studying, so they have to use indirect techniques. Nobody has direct access to such objects; hence there is no absolutely right answer—the scientists have to argue in favor of their findings and arrive at an agreed conception. It is exactly the same thing with our research into the black box, I continued. Some students grasped the point immediately and drew a comparison with atoms. Others got quite upset and complained—so scientists do not really know the truth? I was amazed at the upset the exercise caused for some of the students.

The Influence of Everyday Discourse Rules

What I did not recognize was that my normal teaching—the way I presented science, in both my way of using language and my way of teaching—was communicating another view of science, one that ran counter to my aim in using the black box. In particular, I was not careful about how I used the word *is* in statements. Consider the usage of that word in the following textbook excerpt:

TEXT 1: MOLECULAR COMPOUNDS

Water is a compound of hydrogen and oxygen. Two hydrogen atoms are bound to one oxygen atom. Together they form a group of atoms with the formula H_2O. Water is a molecular compound. Other simple compounds that form molecules are carbon oxides. One molecule of carbon dioxide consists of one carbon atom and two oxygen atoms. The carbon monoxide molecule contains one carbon atom and one oxygen atom. (Borén, Moll, & Lillieborg, 1988, p. 24, my translation)

The excerpt contains a series of assertions. It states in a straightforward manner that water *is* a molecular compound. It does not tell the reader how scientists know this, nor does it provide any evidence for the statements or give any clue that a specialized set of discourse rules applies to understanding the use of the word *is* in this context. (Notice how one would read it differently if it were preceded by the words, "In the light of atomic theory, . . .")

In everyday language, there is a set of discourse rules for the word *is*. We use the word often to confirm, to express that something has the status of truth, as in the statement, "The chair is made of wood." (Similar everyday discourse rules apply to such words in the textbook excerpt as *consists of* and *contains*.) The statement can be checked easily by anyone who doubts its accuracy. The word *is* signals that we can get agreement by using our senses—by looking at or touching the chair. Our everyday experience of using such words as "is" and "consists of" and "contains," and interpreting other people's use of them, is connected with giving statements a specific epistemological value, namely, that they are true and readily confirmed by using the senses: looking, touching, and so forth.

Taking this experience and their everyday discourse rules with them into the science classroom, my students probably would have gotten the message from my day-to-day teaching, which was consistent with the textbook excerpt, that science is absolutely true. The products of science are something everyone will agree upon, if they just use their senses—to smell, taste, listen to, and look at nature. Therefore, through this way of using language in the classroom, my students were offered a naive realist view of science, which was certainly contrary to my intention when setting the black box task. No wonder some of the students were upset.

It is by comparing a specific way of talking about science with other possible ways that we can clarify what epistemological value science statements are being given. (As discussed later, science statements can be given other types of value as well: technical-practical and moral.) By paying attention to aspects of communication that give science statements a value, explicitly or implicitly, we can detect the way a curriculum emphasis is expressed (see Roberts, Chapter 1 in this volume). In the case under discussion, the emphasis is Correct Explanations. Its most significant discourse rules have to do with what is *not* said. This emphasis is characterized by a series of assertions made without reference to evidence, methods, everyday matters, or moral issues (all of which are possible and, to varying extents, present in other curriculum emphases). Statements with theoretical content are therefore vulnerable to interpretation according to the discourse rules of ordinary language.

Some Potential Consequences

Students have no means of judging statements put forward without evidence and reasoning. They are being socialized to see that science is "true knowledge," but they are forced to take the teacher's word for it. If students accept the epistemological value of this view of science, there could be consequences for how they will perceive themselves in relation to society and its decision-making processes. The people who possess a great deal of this true knowledge will be accorded the status of experts on nature. Students who do not become scientists might see themselves as nonexperts on nature and therefore not capable of reaching decisions on controversial issues concerning it.

COMMUNICATING SCIENTIFIC MEANING AND A VIEW OF NATURE

Whereas the previous section concentrated on epistemological features of discourse rules in science education, this section discusses some broader considerations. The discourse rules discussed in this section pertain to the way language is used to portray nature itself. Specifically, I will examine how scientific discourse about nature is governed by conventions.

Vignette 2: Talking in the Wrong Language

The main idea that I took as my starting point in planning a course of grade 7 lessons on acid rain was the experience that most traditional teaching is overloaded with scientific concepts and so-called facts. I eliminated a lot of material from my old planning on the topic "Acids, Bases, and Salts." The concepts that became central were acid, base, neutralization, and pH—concepts important for understanding the phenomenon of acidification in the natural environment. I introduced the key concepts through a lot of experiments based on everyday experience, using household chemicals and other items familiar to the students.

On the final test, many students answered *sweet*, *salt*, or *bitter* to the question, "What is the opposite of *sur*?" (the Swedish word *sur* can mean acidic, sour-tasting, or surly). Despite my teaching them for a couple of weeks and assigning sections of their chemistry books to be read at home, the students still failed to understand the concept "acidic." Or so I thought. Were the students weak or lazy, or could it be something else?

The Influence of Language and Context

The view of learning that steered my teaching at that time was totally cognitive and heavily focused on concepts. I saw concepts as entities, in which the word and its definition were inseparable. Learning these entities meant that students installed them, so to speak, in their brains, like filling their rucksacks with different objects, always replacing inappropriate concepts with appropriate ones.

My view of learning missed an important point: A word is not linked automatically to a single idea or definition (Culler, 1992; Eagleton, 1989) as a railway carriage is linked to a locomotive.[1] *Sur* has at least three definitions (like the English word *sour*). Even if students looked up *sur* in their chemistry books, the definition would help them only partway. The explanation for the word *sur* can be given only by using other words (pH, for example), and some of them certainly will have to be looked up. The explanation for these new, unknown words and terms contains other new, unknown words and terms (hydrogen ions, for example), which, in turn, have to be looked up. In principle this process is everlasting and it is in this sense that one can say the meaning of a word or utterance always will be some way ahead, located in the future.

This phenomenon is, of course, a genuine problem for us as teachers—how can we get our students to associate a word with a scientific definition if it is not possible to nail down meaning? It has to be possible to do this; otherwise we would not be able to communicate with each other. The way it works is that learning scientific meanings—the scientific definitions of words or utterances—requires learning a specific way of using language (Lemke, 1990, is helpful in this regard). It is by using a language in accordance with specific, agreed-upon conventions that one can understand and communicate scientific meaning; to understand the meaning of a word, one has to understand both the words that make up the definition and how these words are supposed to be used in relation to each other and in context. Thus, what distinguished my students' everyday meaning of the word *sur* (sour-tasting) from the scientific meaning I wanted them to express (acidic) is the fact that everyday language use is steered by conventions other than those that apply in the language of chemistry. Thus the alternative explanation for their examination results is that they did not have enough opportunities to practice the language use to which the concept *sur* belongs. It is mainly through practicing scientific language in relevant situations that students can get a grip on the scientific meaning of a specific word (scientific concept). Retrospectively it also can be questioned whether the test results really showed that the students had not acquired an understanding of the scientific meaning of *sur*. It could be that they did not recognize the contextual demands for scientific rather than everyday conventions. (This could have been influenced by my heavy use of everyday household examples in their experiments and classroom work.)

Discourse Rules for Talking About Nature: The Concept of a "Nature Language"

Scientific language is language for talking about nature according to certain demands that make it intelligible in a special, scientific way. That is, the use of scientific language is governed by specific conventions regarding how to explain and investigate nature. According to von Wright (1991), the scientific revolution that began in the seventeenth century was governed by three new requirements for explanation and investigation: an objectified approach (nature is an object distinct from human beings), an atomistic approach (the actions of larger entities are understandable in terms of their smaller components), and a mechanistic approach (some discrete mechanism is responsible for events). I have referred to such a coherent account of language usage in science, constituted and governed by intelligibility demands of the sort exemplified by von Wright, as a *nature language* (Östman, 1994, 1995). I have identified several types of nature language, as discussed later; what I see as a nature language that follows von Wright's conventions I have called *Classical*. The example of my students' use of the word *sur* provides an opportunity to explore the three intelligibility demands expressed by a Classical nature language.

The main convention that has to be followed to use *sur* in a scientific way is that *nature has to be dealt with in isolation from the human being*, that is, nature is to be perceived as a thing, an object distinct from humans (subjects) and their values and feelings. In everyday usage, though, the word *sur* is connected with feelings—with likes and dislikes based on how things taste.

Another convention that has to be applied in the scientific use of language is *an atomistic way of comprehending nature*, which means that first the whole has to be dissected into its basic components (analysis). On the basis of the properties and modes of action of these components, the whole then can be explained (synthesis). To talk scientifically about *sur* (acidic) means that, sooner or later, it will be explained in relation to atoms and ions: The whole is explained with reference to its component parts.

The third convention to be applied is that *sur has to be explained in a mechanistic sense*: The mechanism responsible for acidity is the movement of bodies (ions). Its atomistic and mechanistic conventions especially make the Classical nature language quite different from everyday language, in which *sur* means sour-tasting and the attribution is more holistic.

In his description of the root metaphors we use to conceptualize reality, Kilbourn (Chapter 3 in this volume) discusses the taste of lemonade in a way that sets the Classical nature language in even starker contrast to everyday language. One of the key terms associated with the root metaphor of contextualism is *fusion*; the sour taste of lemonade is offered as an example of experiencing the fusion of water, lemon, and sugar. What tastes sour is not the individual ingredients in lemonade, the contextualist would argue, but the mixture as a whole. This link is not mechanistic, it is contextualist. That is, the lemonade tastes less sour if one has just eaten a slice of lemon, more sour if one has eaten something sweet.

A Very Different Nature Language and View of Nature

As noted earlier, I have identified several nature languages; this was done by analyzing biology and chemistry textbooks in use in Sweden during the 1980s. To continue using Kilbourn's terms, one could say that a nature language is governed by a root metaphor or a blend of different root metaphors. Clearly in the case of Classical nature language, it is mechanism. A root metaphor gives rise to a specific way of talking about nature, and this way of talking/using language gives certain words and utterances a scientific meaning and at the same time expresses a world hypothesis. These different world hypotheses make up different views of nature.

Classical nature language predominates in the first textbook excerpt identified (Text 1). That is, water is talked about as a thing, an object; it is explained in relation to its basic components (atomistic approach); and the form of explanation used is mechanistic. In biology textbooks, I have found a way of talking about nature that is governed by conventions quite different from those of the Classical nature language, one that I call an *Organicist* nature language (closely related to the organicist root metaphor Kilbourn discusses). It is exemplified in the following textbook excerpt:

TEXT 2: THE INTERDEPENDENCE OF ORGANISMS

The distribution of living creatures in nature has not come about by chance. All plants and animals have definite living requirements which have to be met. Every natural area provides its particular inhabitants with shelter, food and opportunities to develop. If the environment changes, the potential for life will also be affected. . . . The plants in an ecosystem are dependent on moisture, light, soil type etc. The ecosystem's plants are the main source of food for its herbivorous animals. Herbivores in turn provide food for carnivores. Everything within an ecosystem interacts and is tied together by invisible threads. The organisms form food chains, with each of them constituting a link in one chain or another. . . . Let us say that a sparrowhawk has a weight of 1 hg. To build up the cells of the hawk, it will have taken 10 times that weight of flesh from small birds, i.e. 1 kg of small birds. The weight of a willow warbler is about 10 g. Thus, approximately 100 willow warblers have presumably been consumed. We can go further back in the food chain and for each link find out the total weight and number of the organisms involved. . . . Herbivores obtain their nutrition from green plants and thereby use some of the solar energy stored in them. Different predators utilize this nutrition at the third, fourth and fifth levels. A hawk thus obtains energy that has been radiated by the sun, built into the leaves of plants and passed through three different animals. The path taken by this energy constitutes the food chain, in which top predators constitute the last link. (Andréasson, Bondeson, Forsberg, Gedda, Luksepp, & Zachrisson, 1986, pp. 96, 98, 100, 101, my translation)

Kilbourn points out that the world hypothesis called organicism is characterized by a holistic view. Similarly, for the Organicist nature language the first intelligibility demand is *the view that phenomena and events in nature are to be explained in relation to a larger whole.* This whole is the life existing within a specific system, a limited area in time and space. It may be the biosphere, an aquarium, or, as in Text 2, an ecosystem.

Part of the idea that life is a uniform phenomenon within a system is the perception that the system is in balance. This is the second convention of Organicist nature language: *Nature is to be understood and explained as a life system in equilibrium.* Text 2 points out that a disturbance in the environment will change the preconditions for life: The system is in balance and even the smallest change could wreck this balance.

The last convention concerns what Kilbourn describes as the hallmark of organicist thinking, namely, the "essential 'connectedness' of things and events." Formulated somewhat differently, this convention says that *phenomena in nature are to be explained in relation to other phenomena.* Generally, as in Text 2, the requirement of connectedness is reduced to a question of material exchange (Worster, 1985).

Together, these three requirements mean that natural phenomena are to be investigated and explained in relation to life as a unity, by showing that one organism is dependent on another for its survival and that the life of one organism is affected by other organisms, phenomena, or events. This, in condensed form, is a statement of the conventions or demands that have to be complied with in the use of Organicist nature language if specific words—for example, relations, ecosystem, food chain, balance—are to be given a *scientific meaning.* At the same time, these conventions convey a *companion meaning—*a specific *view of nature* itself as a system of life-giving relations that is in a state of equilibrium. Students are socialized by it to perceive nature as an organism, a life-giving entity, in which the parts are subordinated to and intelligible in relation to the whole—almost the reverse of the view perpetrated by Classical nature language.

Other Nature Languages

The Classical and Organicist nature languages represent two polar extremes. In my investigations I found two others, both of which are blends of the two extremes. An *Ecomechanistic* nature language blends the Classical and Organicist by portraying nature as a self-regulating whole that can be explained by atomistic and mechanistic reasoning; the Organicist language is dominant in this blend. In a *Biomechanistic* nature language, which is also a blend, the Classical language predominates. (An example might be the prominence of biochemical pathways.)

COMMUNICATING A VIEW OF THE RELATIONSHIP BETWEEN HUMAN BEINGS AND NATURE

In this section the scope is broader still than in the previous one. There it was shown that scientific discourse presents a view of nature itself. Using the same post-structuralist methodology (paying attention to what *is* said compared with what *could be* said), this section explores what is communicated about the relationship between human beings and nature—the essence of environmental ethics.

Vignette 3: Ethics in the Science Classroom

My colleagues and I were trying to decide what it means in teaching terms to get students to become environmentally conscious. We came up with two solutions.

First, some of my colleagues argued that it is not suitable to bring an ethical dimension into science education and that the best solution is therefore just to give students the scientific background of environmental issues. The following textbook excerpt describes, I think, what my colleagues had in mind:

TEXT 3: WHAT HAPPENS TO THE SEA

An area of water such as the Baltic Sea can be said to constitute an ecosystem. A disturbance of the balance in one part of the system causes changes in other parts of it. . . . Many watercourses and outfalls discharge plant nutrients, for example from agricultural fertilizers. In the Baltic Sea, which was originally poor in nutrients, this has resulted in a sharp increase in the quantity of algae, and consequently in the numbers of animals which feed on algae and bacteria. Consumption of oxygen in the water is thus increasing. Should it increase too much, the ecosystem will be unable to cope with the stress, and the result will be an environment deficient in oxygen, which will affect organic life. (Mårtensson & Sandin, 1988, p. 199, my translation)

This textbook excerpt (which incidentally is a good example of Ecomechanistic nature language) says that the interaction of human beings with nature is threatening organic life, and explains how this is happening. However, it says nothing about how to view this threat or what to do about it. This omission constitutes an implicit message that the threat does not lead to any moral deliberations or decisions, that it has no implications for our subsequent thinking and actions. Thus human beings have no moral obligation to change the ways in which they interact with nature. This meaning is ascertained in light of the comparison between what is said and what could be said but is not. So, being silent about the ethical dimension in a science classroom is not really being silent at all.

Second, some of us (myself included) came up with a two-phase approach. Students would first learn appropriate scientific concepts (Phase I) and then apply them to an environmental-ethical issue (Phase II). For my grade 7 students, Phase I involved learning concepts of acid, base, pH, and so on (Vignette 2), followed by application of the concepts, in Phase II, to issues associated with acidification of the natural environment. This sequencing was based on an idea that the first phase was to be free from any communication about how we should relate to and treat nature. The latter was to take place only during the second phase, in which teaching would explicitly address the general question of how we should treat nature, with the help of a concrete example—acidification. Attention to Texts 1 and 2 will show that this assumption was not very well considered.

Saying Nothing Is Actually "Saying" Something

At first glance it appears absurd to claim that "Phase I teaching" and textbook language such as that of Texts 1 and 2 can express a view of the relationship between human beings and nature. After all, no explicit reference to human beings is made.

This suspicion springs from a specific view of language, namely, as something apart from action—language is just a means of expressing our thinking. Säljö (Chapter 4 in this volume) offers some illustrative examples from everyday situations showing that language use also can be viewed as a social act. When we talk, we also do something (see also Cherryholmes, 1988). Let us then look at Texts 1 and 2 from the viewpoint of social action.

The section in which Text 1 appears is headed "Air and Water," yet the main purpose is to teach students the concepts of atom, molecule, and molecular compound, and the relationships among them. Water and air are not the main focus of the text, but merely illustrations. In Text 2 the point is the same. The sparrowhawk and willow warbler are used to exemplify the food chain concept. The main lesson to be learned is not the relationship between these two birds, but the concepts of ecology.

Using examples from nature as a pedagogical device to make abstract concepts more understandable is quite common in science teaching. Of course, when planning a series of lessons, one tries to choose natural events or phenomena that are not only illustrative of the concepts, but also important for the students to understand scientifically. It is not a big step from using water or birds to communicate the scientific meaning of concepts in atomic theory and ecology to the way we sometimes use animals in teaching to communicate general scientific knowledge about classification, morphology, and physiology. It is unlikely, at least in a Scandinavian context, that a teacher would have students dissect an animal without discussing its ethical dimension. This would likely be done to avoid having students surmise that nature is only an instrument to serve our purposes and that we do not have any moral obligations regarding the way we use it.

Of course, it is more obvious in the case of dissection (or vivisection), but in principle there is no difference between using water or birds as a means of communicating scientific meaning to students and using a living animal in an experiment. Both acts give rise to the same view of the relationship between human beings and nature: Nature is an instrument that humans can use for their purposes, in this case, to teach students scientific concepts. Since nothing is said about the responsibility of human beings when they use nature, one can add that humans have no moral obligations in this action.

Thus, in an action-based view of language it makes no sense to think, as I did when determining the sequencing of my lessons on acidification, that some science teaching (Phase I type) does not express a view of the relationship between human beings and nature. In other words, students do not wait until Phase II to hear about this relationship—they get the point during Phase I. In certain respects, then, my sequencing of the lessons was undercutting the goal of making students environmentally conscious.

With respect to Phase II, my teaching was consistent with the following textbook excerpt. The moral question of how to view our dealings with nature is addressed explicitly, and the question is elaborated with the help of science:

TEXT 4: LOOKING AFTER THE WATER WE BORROW

The eternal cycle of water in nature, between oceans, atmosphere and continents, was discovered about 1600. Now that we know about this cycle, and also know that water is involved in processes vital to human life, we must also realize that what we release into the atmosphere and water travels far and wide, even through plants and animals. We must never lose control of how we utilize water. We must be careful with water when we "borrow" it from the eternal cycle! In order that water can suffice for all our needs, we have to "borrow" it many times over from the same water system. Because of the great need for water in our technological society, water pollution by waste matter released from households and industry has quickly become an enormous problem. In order to tackle this problem, increasing numbers of treatment plants have been constructed close to urban areas, and more are being built. (Sonidsson & Hörnqvist, 1984, pp. 74–75, my translation)

The text has a direct moral message: We must never lose control of how humans utilize water; we must be careful—otherwise human survival will be in danger. Our moral responsibility for our interaction with nature thus is motivated by our responsibility for each other, for the survival of *Homo sapiens*. Another way to motivate moral responsibility for our dealings with nature is to argue that nature has an intrinsic value, which human beings do not have the right to violate. In both cases nature is assigned a value that humans are to respect. The first way of reasoning is called human-centered or anthropocentric, and the second biocentric. They constitute two different systems of environmental ethics.[2]

Discourse Rules About Relating to Nature: The "Subject Focus" Concept

To conceptualize the ever-present communication of a view of the relationship between people and nature in science education, I have invented the concept of *subject focus* (Östman, 1994, 1995). One conceptualizes a subject focus by paying attention to those aspects of language usage that, explicitly or implicitly, attribute a value to nature. Through this aspect of discourse, a companion meaning is communicated about the moral responsibility of human beings to nature. There are two very broad categories of subject focus: *Induction into Science* and *Learning from Science*. This distinction was used by Fensham (1988).

Texts 1 and 2 express the subject focus *Induction into Science*, in which nature is nothing more than an educational device to make scientific meaning easier for students to understand. As discussed earlier, the view expressed about the relationship of human beings to nature is that nature is merely an instrument for our purposes, implying that we have no moral obligations regarding the way we use it.

The subject focus of Text 3, which I call *Human Being as a Threat*, is one of the four I found in my investigations that make up the major category *Learning from Science*. All four share a common feature that distinguishes them from *Induction into Science*, namely, that science is used as a device for describing and explaining what our relationship to nature looks like or ought to look like. With the *Human Being as a Threat* focus, the aim is for students to learn that human beings are threatening themselves and other living organisms and the ways in which they are doing so. The language used is characterized by not assigning nature any value at all and by describing humans as a threat to life. This language thus communicates that human beings are a threat to life, but have no moral obligations in their dealings with nature.

The subject focus illustrated in Text 4 I call *Survival of Homo sapiens*. It finds expression when the aim is for students to learn a responsible attitude toward the way we deal with nature. Here, language usage is characterized by explicit moral statements or utterances, and nature is ascribed a value by referring to the responsibility of human beings for each other. The view of the human–nature relationship expressed is that we ought to interact responsibly with nature insofar as the survival or well-being of other human beings could be at stake.[3]

Subject Foci, Curriculum Emphases, and Broad Educational Goals

My analysis of subject foci was the result of my interest in science education goals that foster environmental consciousness, which is an important part of science education in Sweden. Such goals were not prominent in Roberts's analysis of curriculum emphases (Chapter 1 in this volume), simply because environmental education goals did not appear frequently in the historical time period he examined for North America. The subject focus concept functions in a way analogous to the curriculum emphasis concept, namely, by forming a conceptual bridge between generally stated goals and actual communication in science education. Where they differ is that a subject focus conceptualizes aspects of language use that attribute a value to *nature*—and thereby expresses a view of human beings' relation to nature—whereas a curriculum emphasis attributes a value to *science*. As noted earlier, three types of values can be discerned: epistemological, practical-technical, and moral.

Science is attributed an *epistemological value* through the kind of language usage illustrated by Text 1 (and any science teaching consistent with it)—particularly the use of the word *is*. It has been pointed out that the Correct Explanations curriculum emphasis is expressed there. Text 2 is another example: The statements imply that "this is simply the way things are." A common alternative to Correct Explanations is the curriculum emphasis Roberts called Structure of Science. It finds expression when teaching or text seeks to convey to students knowledge about the intellectual character of science, such as how the relationship between evidence and theory is to be perceived, the historical growth of science, and other explicit talk about the epistemological value of science. Often a positivistic view of science is produced, but it is possible to express other views, for example, relativistic or neopragmatic ones. Unlike Correct Explanations, this emphasis gives students a chance to judge knowledge claims and therefore to exercise some autonomy in relation to their teacher (cf. Munby & Roberts, Chapter 8 in this volume). Nevertheless, if a positivistic view is expressed, Structure of Science will have the same potential consequences as Correct Explanations when it comes to the students' future position as citizens.[4]

In Text 3 science is attributed a *practical-technical value*, expressing what Roberts calls an Everyday Coping curriculum emphasis. Here scientific knowledge is used to explain how an ecosystem works and how our dealings with it can cause serious problems. The companion meaning communicated is that science is directly useful in understanding and controlling our interaction with nature. In other words, science is assigned the value of being directly applicable to practical, everyday situations. The potential consequence regarding the students' future role as citizens is that they could become passive, for the same reason as when science is put forward as absolutely true in the Correct Explanations emphasis.

Science teaching consistent with Text 4 attributes a *moral value* to scientific knowledge (descriptions of nature), communicating that science has a role in deciding moral issues. In Roberts's terminology, this form of teaching expresses a Science, Technology, and Decisions emphasis. In the particular case of Text 4, scientific knowledge appears to lead directly to a moral stance, directly to norms governing the way in which human beings should treat nature. The text first puts forward statements about nature—the eternal cycle, that water is crucial to human life, and that water passes through plants and animals—and finally sets out a moral stance regarding how we should treat water: We must never lose control; we must be careful. Nothing is said to indicate that the statements about nature can be seen as *arguments for* the moral stance. Instead, the relationship between the scientific descriptions of nature and the moral prescription is put forward as direct and logical, without any complication or doubt. Science thus constitutes a basis for making correct moral judgments regarding our way of interacting with nature, and scientists must be seen as experts when it comes to deciding about environmental issues. Those who do not have access to this moral foundational knowledge are mere laypeople and therefore not suitable for deciding such issues. It should be noted that it is possible, within this curriculum emphasis, to give science a value other than that of a foundation for moral judgments—for example, the value of being one *consideration* among many.

Companion Meanings, Ideology, and Power

The concepts of subject focus, curriculum emphasis, and nature language share an important feature, namely, all can be used to foresee and discuss potential socialization consequences of science education discourse. Taken together, the nature language and subject focus concepts capture central aspects of an environmental ideology/morality: a view of how nature is to be understood and a view of how human beings are to value and treat nature. Depending on the particular combination of nature language and subject focus, different environmental ideologies will be produced in science education discourse. Different potential socializing consequences for students can readily be seen to follow.

It is also readily seen that there are connotations about power relationships in the views of science expressed by different curriculum emphases: it is Absolute Truth (or not), it is accessible to only a few (or to many), it leads directly to moral stances (or not), and so on. The power relationship is between human beings. These views also have different potential socializing consequences for students. To use a currently fashionable term, students can be empowered or not, with respect to science, depending on the qualities of the discourse they experience in science education. In both Chapter 8 of this volume (Munby & Roberts) and Chapter 9 (Geddis), this phenomenon is examined in some detail through analyses of the way power is distributed inside the science classroom.

Outside the science classroom, ideology and power relationships are also at work to influence a student's science education. The character of discourse—what *is* said compared with what *could be* said, *how* it is said compared with how it *could be* said—represents the outcome of choices, and these in turn are governed by power, values, and interests. The companion meanings about view of nature, view of science, and view of the relationship between human beings and nature are thus an effect of power and ideology, and constitute "socialization content" (see Englund, Chapter 2 in this volume). It is not by accident that socialization content is present, or by some foreordained, automatic chain of reasoning. Some of the complexity of the choices that have to be made is shown in Solomon's discussion of European science curricula, and the effects of influence are seen in Fensham's analysis of power relationships associated with science curriculum in Australia (Chapters 12 and 13, respectively, in this volume).

CONCLUDING REMARKS

The characteristics of science education discourse are an outcome of power and ideology. What counts as science education is a battle among different stakeholders, different social groups. Generally speaking, it can be said that different social groups promote the knowledge and the world views they think most suitable for the next generation to acquire. Mannheim (1968) expressed this social basis for schooling very neatly when he observed that

> every historical, ideological, sociological piece of knowledge (even should it prove to be Absolute Truth itself), is clearly rooted in and carried by the desire for power and recognition of particular social groups who want to make their interpretation of the world the universal one. (pp. 196–197)

Science education thus can be viewed in the light of an ongoing struggle over what knowledge and world view students are to be offered. Behind it lies an aspiration within different social groups to achieve power and thereby a position from which to design future society in accordance with their own interests and values (Englund, 1986).

The effect of this struggle is that certain knowledge is chosen, while other alternatives are excluded. Choices cannot be made without involving values, criteria, and interests. The metaphors, world hypotheses, interests, and so forth, that form the basis for different choices will, to use Cherryholmes's (1988) term, be "sedimented" in the constitutive rules (conventions, demands) of any given educational practice—such as language usage. Thus, the values and interests forming the basis for the choices sometimes will be formulated as goals for education but, more important, will be sedimented in the rules that constitute and regulate the language used to talk about the things that have been chosen. This language use will help to create or re-create a discourse—a regular exchange of ideas—in which the meaning of words and statements will be located (see Cherryholmes, 1988).

The personal experience I have shared in this chapter can be seen in this light. Behind my different choices of what to teach and how to teach it one can discern certain values concerning how to view nature, our relationship to nature, science, science teaching, and also certain interests. These values and interests were partly hidden from me. However, they manifested themselves in my use of language, with the result that certain companion meanings were communicated. Some of these I have illustrated.

The companion meanings I created can be seen as those that the students would be socialized into if they fully participated in the discourse. As I have discussed in detail elsewhere (Östman, 1994, 1995, 1996a, 1996b), this socialization has some important potential consequences for the way in which the students will look upon and treat other human beings and nature. The companion meanings produced in science education can, indeed, have an impact on the formation of an identity in the younger generation. For anyone wanting to consider the companion meanings investigated here in their planning and teaching, the categories of subject focus, curriculum emphasis, and nature language may be helpful tools.

PART II _____

Into the Classroom

THE AUTHORS of the four chapters in Part II all focus on issues surrounding companion meanings by examining science textbooks and classrooms. In each case one of the concerns raised is the need for *more* and *more explicit* communication about the companion meanings, which, of course, is a direct outgrowth of their largely implicit nature.

John Willinsky's Chapter 6 is one of the best examples we have seen of the power of critical methodology for the study of science education. While many critical analyses focus on general features of science itself (most sociology of knowledge critiques and feminist critiques do, for instance), Willinsky has grounded this work in a recognizable problem of science education practice: teaching the concept of race. He argues convincingly that the epistemological features of the concept and its relationship to societal issues are badly in need of attention, largely because students live with race every day as a sorting device for social relations. (The everyday concept of race is a good example of the crude version of the formist root metaphor described by Kilbourn in Chapter 3.) Dealing with the two discourses—everyday and scientific—regarding this very specific concept is a nice extension also of Säljö's work in Chapter 4.

Glen Aikenhead in Chapter 7 uses the concept of "border crossing" as a basis to explain why students have differential success at entering the school science subculture. He allows one to "see" from the student's point of view the companion meanings that "tell" students what that subculture is like, and what they have to do in order to cross into it. He further shows how the companion meanings that go into building science programs can be planned and changed for students who have different kinds of difficulties crossing the border. This chapter also extends and applies the analysis by Säljö in Chapter 4.

In Chapter 8 Hugh Munby and Douglas Roberts present a way to analyze the distribution of power in the science classroom, to explore the potential link between science teaching and the development of an attitude of questioning, wanting evidence, and making judgments for oneself, which are attributes of responsible citizenship in democratic societies. (The latter attitude is what is meant by Munby's original concept of intellectual independence.) Arthur Geddis picks up the theme in Chapter 9 by looking at power and control issues associ-ated with high-quality classroom discourse about controversial issues in a science-technology-society curricular setting. The companion meanings in both of these cases constitute subtexts that are profoundly moral in their import and substance.

Readers who are particularly interested in Part II will want to examine a recent work edited by Judith Green and Gregory Kelly, a special issue of the *Journal of Classroom Interaction*, *32* (Summer 1997). Analysis of science classroom dis-course is a special feature of that work.

O CHAPTER 6

The Obscured and Present Meaning of Race in Science Education

JOHN WILLINSKY

THE CONCEPT OF RACE is at once obscured and present in today's science classroom. On the one hand, it is *obscured* when curriculum fails to clarify the historical and contested status of race, and when it is silent about science's contribution to defining the significance of racial difference over the course of the past 2 centuries. On the other hand, race as an everyday lived idea is still *present* and felt in the experiences of students and teachers. It is one of the primary categories in the meeting of human biology and identity.

The textbook analysis presented later in this chapter suggests strongly that the recent tendency in science education has been to wash its hands of race as a topic. I ask, instead, that we consider the potential consequences of providing students with an understanding of how the scientific conception of race developed, how the truth and values of that element of scientific work were tested, and how this knowledge might assist the young, if only in a limited way, in comprehending and debating the scientific dimensions of this social issue. I will argue that we owe students an account of the relationship between race and race science because each of us has come to bear, in different ways, the weight of that area of scientific inquiry. The potential consequences of studying the race concept in an epistemological, historical, and social context have to do with understanding one's own racialized identity as still working in the world, despite the protestations of color-blind curricula and classrooms.

STUDENTS, RACE, AND RACE SCIENCE

The Interests of European Imperialism

This chapter is drawn from a larger study I conducted into the educational legacy of European imperialism as an intellectual enterprise that still has a hand in how students learn about the world.[1] Science's contribution to the era of European expansion included the provision of navigational aids, engineering principles, and other technological innovations, many borrowed from around the world. It encompassed the immense taxonomic ordering of flora and fauna, with breakthrough understandings of structure and function. Valuable developments in astronomy, meteorology, and medicine were greatly assisted by field stations and observatories dispersed throughout the colonial world.

Science's give-and-take with the imperial order also entailed the anthropological and biological inquiry into human differences, which was every bit as instrumental and foundational for a European ordering of the globe as the spate of technological devices that were incorporated so readily. We should not be surprised that some of the best scientific minds to be found in Europe and America were devoted to measuring and postulating the nature of differences among humankind. Empires have always operated with the harshest of regard for the barbarians beyond the gates, but then empires tend to collapse eventually, leaving behind ruins and memories. The scar tissue left on those touched by the modern science of race has survived the end of European empires. This legacy of deeply set racial distinctions needs to be examined as a function of its academic construction, it seems to me, if we are ever to move beyond what this legacy has made of the world.[2]

The Making of a Racial World

Even after the considerable efforts of the anthropologist Franz Boas (1908/1974) and others against the misuses of race earlier in the twentieth century, even after the years of UNESCO committees that sought to distinguish the myth from the fact of race (Montagu, 1972), and even after such brilliant exposés on the fallacies of race science works as Stephen Jay Gould's *Mismeasure of Man* (1981), science's contribution to the meaning of race has not yet come to an end. In the closing decade of the twentieth century, pernicious aspects of this concept still find support from the work of a very small, but hardly insignificant, segment of the profession through a number of scientific journals (Ziegler, Weizmann, Wiener, & Wiesenthal, 1989). That support has found its revival in the popular press also, most recently in the bestseller *The Bell Curve: Intelligence and Class Structure in American Life* (Herrnstein & Murray, 1994).

Nancy Stepan (1982) neatly captures the pervasiveness and commitment that have marked the science of racial differences, as she charts the (never quite complete) "disappearance" of the race paradigm in science after the Second World War:

> For more than a hundred years the division of human species into biological races had seemed of cardinal significance to scientists. Race explained individual character and temperament, the structure of social communities and the fate of human societies. In fact commitment to typological races often appeared to have been deeper, because psychologically more necessary or satisfying, than the commitment to revolutionary change in science itself. (p. 170)

It may be that the new biology of behavioral genetics has moved beyond such a deep commitment to racial differences. However, the search goes on for gene structures that "determine" intelligence, homosexuality, and certain diseases, as well as tendencies toward crime, alcoholism, and poverty. The links between science and the social order continue to be forged, suggesting that a great deal of interest remains in continuing to divide the world along racial orders.

THE SCHOOLING OF RACE SCIENCE

College/University Potential Influences on Teachers

Whatever else science teachers learn about race science, they are surely influenced by what biology and/or anthropology professors teach them, and what their college or university textbooks have to say. In an extensive survey of American professors and textbooks in these two fields, the team of Lieberman, Hampton, Littlefield, and Hallead (1992) found a striking difference between the two disciplines. In the 1983–84 academic year, 73% of the biology professors surveyed (105 of 144) accepted the race concept as valid, compared with only 50% of professors of physical anthropology (73 of 147). Only 12% (17) of the biologists rejected the concept, whereas 42% (63) of the physical anthropologists did so. For the remainder of both groups the information was indeterminate. This provides its own interesting perspective on how scientists, thought to hold common standards of objectivity, can come to differ on what might seem to be a fundamental and long-standing matter of basic classification.

Textbooks published during the period 1975–1984, still in use in the 1983–84 academic year, showed the following: A slight majority of the biology books examined (52%, 11 of 21) accepted the concept, 10% (2 books) rejected it, and for the remainder the information was indeterminate. Of the physical anthropology texts, only 21% (7 of 33) accepted race as a valid concept, while 39% rejected it, leaving the remainder indeterminate.[3]

In another survey, the Lieberman team examined eight college/university textbooks used in the period 1987–1989, and found that one trend was simply to expunge any reference to the race concept. Thus, consider how Joseph Birdsell claims in the first edition of *Human Evolution: An Introduction to the New Physical Anthropology* that "today new races are in the process of being formed" (1972, p. 598), only to announce blithely in the next edition that the "use of the term race has been discontinued because it is scientifically undefinable and carries social implications that are harmful and disruptive" (1975, p. 505).[4]

It is not clear how such comments are helpful to students in biology or anthropology. Do they not simply obscure how the race concept lives on in so many scientific and nonscientific forms? Nevertheless, the Lieberman team (1992) viewed the reduced exposure "as preferable to presenting race as if it were an accepted concept but not as informative as presenting both the new information and the issues that have been debated" (p. 310). Not only do I side with this more informative approach, but I also want to see it introduced at the high school level rather than reserving it, as the Lieberman team seemed to suggest, for the limited number who take biology in college or university.

What influence might all of this confusion have on prospective science teachers? This is hard to trace, for an individual. However, imagine a curricular setting in which different teachers have learned different versions of the status of the race concept in their university courses. (We will see that this happens.) Is there a democratic process for arriving at a definition of race's scientific status, for the sake of the science curriculum? Does the meaning of race require a majority decision? Does race work well for one discipline and not another? At the very least, such questions add to the sense that such categories, per se, not only are constructs of the mind, but also are badly in need of epistemological clarification.

What, then, of race science and the high school? To get some sense of the situation, we interviewed prospective and experienced high school teachers about their understanding of the scientific status of race, and examined what a number of textbooks from the past few years have made of the idea.

Race Science and the School: Teachers

The five experienced and five prospective high school biology teachers we interviewed are all from the Vancouver area in Canada. They are evenly divided by gender, and each had taken university courses in biology.[5] They spoke about their own biology instruction, their ideas about race, and where, if at all, they envisioned race fitting into the school's science program. No claims are made about the representativeness of the sample, but the range of articulations this small group offered on the concept and how it figures in the classroom are most informative for surfacing issues.

As the Leiberman team found for professors, these teachers were divided on the scientific idea of race. They were divided as well on whether the concept has a place in the high school biology classroom. We found the following polar opposites, and some positions in between:

MEANING OF RACE

Different races classify nothing significant; all people belong to the same species and to the human race.

versus

Different races are [very close to being] different species, or at least subspecies, of *Homo sapiens*.

RACE IN CURRICULUM

Race is an important issue and must be discussed in high school biology classes.

versus

The issue is not appropriate for a biology classroom—"too emotionally charged," "not science," and so forth.

There is much here for a science department to deliberate about, if this variety of talk about race represents in any way the variety of positions science teachers hold. How are impressionable adolescent students supposed to deal with such mixed, vague, and implied messages? Here are selected excerpts from the interviews, to provide more substance about the teachers' positions.

The Meaning of Race. The importance of a teacher's education in biology as a source of understanding—and sometimes the recollection of an individual professor—came through in the comments, as this prospective teacher conveys:

I think one of the most important things that I can recall about my education at [university] is a professor who . . . asked us the question, "Is there such a thing as race?" And that was a really important question and we debated it for a long time and resolved that really we are all part of the human race.

Compare that recollection, which casts doubt on the viability of race as a way to divide the human species, with the report of another prospective biology teacher as she described how her university education taught her the very opposite:

> My professor was telling us that there is a scientific basis for differentia-
> tion of race based on genetic stuff, that actually the different races are
> different subspecies of the human species, but that you can't say that
> because it's not politically correct or proper. . . . He mentioned that
> interracial couples, like black and white . . . when they have children, they
> have major orthodontic problems because the jaw is structured differently
> or the size is different.

Aside from the quaint sense of scientific innocence or objectivity associated with
this focus on orthodontics, consider how *difference* was made to loom large in
that account. For this person a course in evolution similarly had taught her that

> Yes, there is a scientific foundation and we are different, we can't dispute
> that, there are differences.

These are fair scientific points, of course. The race concept is meant to make
sense of differences. What is worrisome here is that the emphasis on difference
for the sake of difference in this prospective teacher's education seems meant to
keep peoples apart. "Difference" provides the excuse that helps us set aside the
terrible mess we have made out of being different, not to mention the deliberate
abuse and exploitation of the idea. We need not deny difference either. In schools
we can inquire about the particular history and significance of what appears to
divide us. But is there anything in this person's preparation for a career as a science teacher that enables her to reflect on her own education and help her students ask these sorts of questions about race and other categories of consequence
to people's lives? This in essence is the issue Kilbourn raises in Chapter 3 about
the difference between crude and refined versions of the formist root metaphor.

Another prospective teacher also came close to linking race and species, in
conceding her own confusion:

> I don't know if you can . . . I don't know if I would equate race and
> species together; I don't know if they're the same thing or different.

This confusion—about whether "separate races" refers to species other than *Homo
sapiens*, hence nonhumans—is a malicious thread of race science that Darwin and
others attacked,[6] although it can be traced well into this century. One can imagine
from this prospective teacher's remarks how her future students might come to
confuse the two concepts in ways that only heighten the difference and distance
thought to stand between people.

Appropriateness of Race in the Curriculum. Some of the prospective teachers
were less confident about the place of race in the school biology course than were

the experienced teachers. In the case of one of the latter, with 20 years experience, the teaching of race in his biology class has a rather traditional ring to it and expresses a slightly different take on the matter of separating race from species. His approach includes naming the number of races (four) and identifying both the physical and genetic basis of those races:

> We talk about different features, such as shape of nose, thick lips, hair texture, and that basically there are four races; some people put it at five. I also talk about the idea of classification as a sort of a human thing; we look for basic characteristics, and basically there may only be, say, five or six genetic differences between races. We're basically the same species but there are significant differences in races and these probably originated as adaptations to different environments.

Consider the ambiguity in this teacher's account: First he limits the reach of race—by allowing that classification is "a sort of human thing" and suggesting "there may only be, say, five or six genetic differences." But then he goes on to extend it with his talk about "significant differences in races." I hope that I am not being unfair in thinking that his identification of human beings as "basically the same species" could be said to suggest an almost reluctant sense of inclusion of all races.

We have to remember that such scientific perspectives are taken up by students bombarded by what can only be characterized as a wide range of attitudes toward racial difference. Science teachers need to consider whether what they say about race can be taken as leaning either way, toward a strengthening or weakening of the hold of race on our thinking.

One of the prospective teachers, who gives a fairly confident and accurate reading of evolutionary forces, still is a bit unclear about distinguishing race from species:

> And if the environments are different enough and the separation has been long enough, then . . . you'll get two different species or two different races.

If this does not equate race and species, it certainly suggests that they are closely related categories. This young man related to us his own untroubled experiences growing up as an African Canadian, alongside his puzzled observation that others (native Canadians) were not so untouched by race:

> There was a *big* difference between the First Nations population and the town population and I always felt that was rather strange—how I fit in and someone of First Nations [ancestry] didn't in that town.

However, his bewilderment did not extend to a professional commitment to sort out the issues of race and species in his biology class; in fact, he allowed that such issues as race did not belong in a biology class at all:

> I just think that they're too emotionally charged, too full of opinions to really do anyone any good.

A second-year biology teacher expressed his aversion to teaching about race in his class because he felt the topic to be

> social studies or something, that is, more like personal development. It's not my job to get into that kind of thing. . . . I'm a scientist and I try to see things objectively, in a scientific way, and I just think that you can get into all kinds of things here that don't belong in science.

A teacher with 5 years experience made it clear that he was not so hesitant to have race issues discussed in his science class. He noted that students in his classes feel free to ask about the concept as a matter of managing difference and identity:

> Kids want to know what is the advantage of living in a more uniform environment. They want to know why Asian eyes are different, and what are the advantages and disadvantages to vision of these differences. About advantages and disadvantages of interracial marriages where there are children, are we moving towards a more universal person with all of these? I throw it back to them, ask what they think. They note that children who have one Chinese parent often look more Chinese than anything else.

Part of what these students are wrestling with is surely the identity themes of race, nation, and culture—as we see in the comment about looking "more Chinese than anything else." We might well ask what good it does them to have a discussion of the issues and yet have the teacher just "throw it back to them." When asked about whether his own ideas about race had changed over the years, he responded that they were "definitely more fuzzy." So here we have an example of allowing the discussion of race in the classroom but apparently teaching nothing helpful about it.

Another teacher with about the same amount of experience (in his fifth year) was adamant about the importance of discussing race in science class, but stressed a bit more about the teacher's role. He told us he has come to believe that race "has nothing to do with biology," but has to do instead with the culture in which one is raised. He also was one of two teachers we interviewed who cited the media attention paid to Philippe Rushton's questionable work on race:

> I got all kinds of questions about him. A lot of our kids are Asian, and there were a lot of questions. "Are kids from Asia smarter?" "Do they have bigger brains?"[7]

His final words in the interview located the issue within his own life and need for understanding:

> For me it's a big issue. I've seen a lot of racism in my time and it really bothers me. . . . I remember when I was young my grandmother coming to the house and the neighbors burning a tire in front of our yard and telling the squaw that she should go back to the reserve. And when you're 6 years old this makes a big impression on you. I couldn't understand, this was my grandmother, why were these people mad at her?

It would be discouraging to think that it might take this level of personal suffering for a teacher to feel that race warrants inclusion as part of a science course. Nevertheless, it reminds us of the magnitude of the issue in everyday life, and the corresponding need to develop an approach in science classrooms that contributes to the meaning and presence of race in what students make of their lives.

Race Science and the School: Textbooks

In reviewing fifteen biology textbooks published for American and Canadian high schools over the past 2 decades, I found two stances toward the scientific status of race. Either the books treat race as a given category, without clarifying the scientific status and relevance of the concept, or they do not treat it at all.[8] In the more recent (1980s) group of eleven books, all of them American, eight had no index entry at all on race. (Avoidance has long been the school's response to controversy.) Two of the remaining three are approved for school use by the Ministry of Education in the Canadian province of British Columbia, and I want to draw on those two for the following analysis.

In grade 11, students typically use the Macmillan *Biology,* which, in its chapter "Life in the Past," points out "that the concept of race has become increasingly blurred in the last few thousands of years" (Creager, Jantzen, & Mariner, 1986, p. 282). Here, I thought, is a good point for jumping in to explore with students the fine distinctions that need to be made in the conceptualization of difference. But there is a paradox. Shipman (1994) points out that although the distinctions among once-isolated peoples have indeed diminished, the *concept* of race actually has gained *precision* through scientific usage beginning a little over 2 centuries ago. The text recapitulates this paradox in a rather interesting way, if seemingly unintentional.

On the one hand, the book offers a sense of racial blurring and an explicit undermining of any specific classification of humans into a fixed number of races:

"We see that such systems fail to hold any real meaning" (Creager et al., 1986, p. 282). On the other hand, it nullifies that message by providing a set of four photographs, each depicting a family of what clearly is meant to represent different races. The caption reads, "Selection, drift, and isolation were important factors that produced differences between *early* human populations" (p. 282, emphasis added), yet the visual reinforcement in the photographs is of distinctly *modern* racial differences. The contradiction leaves one wondering how students would approach the chapter question that asks why the "biological definition of 'race' is based on allele frequency, not on appearance" (p. 283), since appearance has figured so prominently.

So this text supports the idea that science continues to have something to say about race and difference, even if it would be difficult to say precisely what. The opportunity is there to clarify issues about the way the race concept functions as a classification category, but nothing happens. Geddis (Chapter 9 in this volume) speaks of this kind of missed opportunity as "epistemologically flat" text or teaching.

For grade 12 students in British Columbia, the prescribed biology text at this time (Mader, 1988) evidences no desire to blur the concept of race. It points out that "all human races of today are classified as *Homo sapiens* . . . because it is possible for *all types of humans* to interbreed and bear fertile offspring" (p. 638, emphasis added). The set of race-type photographs positions what appears to be a professional fashion portrait of a young "Caucasian" woman with the more typical anthropological shots labeled Australoid, Negroid, American Indian, and Mongoloid (referred to as Oriental in the text). The caption for the photographs reiterates that "all human beings belong to one species, but there are several races" (p. 639), without specifying whether the five depicted are exhaustive or merely suggestive.

The chapter ends with another excellent instance of trying to clear up a concern in a manner that raises as many questions as it answers:

> While it has always seemed to some that physical differences might warrant assigning human races to different species, this contention is not borne out by the biochemical data mentioned previously. (p. 639)

What is one to think? That wanting to assign those who differ to another species is a natural inclination, while the biochemical data are a sort of buffer against that? What is the point of the contrasting photographs, if not to suggest that attention be paid to difference and distance?

In both of these substantial biology textbooks, the matter of race takes up a very small section. However, as can be seen, the concept possesses a particular relevance to the lives of students and the future of the globe. It therefore seems worth dwelling more on the scientific status of race, in that it is the brevity of the treatment itself that makes for the confusing messages in these books. My concern is that as part of what students study in science class, and in the face of the lessons on race that they bring to those classes, they need a better understanding of science's role in the making of this conceptual divide between peoples.

BECOMING MORE SOPHISTICATED ABOUT RACE SCIENCE

An Antiracist Program of Science Instruction

Fortunately, there are indicators within science education that some professionals refuse to avoid and obfuscate the issue of race. During the 1980s, a group of London teachers tapped into a segment of the scientific community that was actively working for social change. They developed an antiracist science program that effectively addresses the links between such topics as nutrition and management of world hunger, biology and the construction of race, and ecology and African game preserves. As well, the group took on issues of ability labeling and other evaluation practices that can have a racial impact on science teaching. These educators assumed responsibility not just for teaching the subject, but for teaching about its place within the prevailing economic and ideological system as well. The companion meanings of concern to them are expressed this way:

> Science teaching [usually] masks the real political and economic priorities of science; hides its appropriation of non-Western scientific traditions; often attributes people's subordination or suffering to nature—be it biological or geographic factors—rather than to the way science and nature itself have been subordinated to political priorities. (Gill & Levidow, 1987, p. 3)

With an interesting twist on the scientific theme of discovery, sometimes led with a heavy hand, they turn students' attention to the political causes and consequences of scientific concepts such as race. The program provides a different way of reading the interests of the most objective of disciplines.[9]

A Remarkable Textbook

This critical approach to race and science has managed in recent years to find its way into at least one traditional textbook as well. An excellent instance of an introduction to the topic is to be had in the general science textbook *Science Probe 10*, which is used in many schools in British Columbia (Bullard et al., 1992). The book includes in its chapter on recent advances in genetics an extended warning note under the label, "The Potential for Misuse of Genetic Ideas" (pp. 428–429). The section presents a brief history of the eugenics movement, including its origins in Francis Galton's work and the sterilization and antimiscegenation laws passed during the 1920s and 1930s in North America and Europe, before arriving at Nazi Germany and the master race.

The book's explicit stand is that there are no pure races, yet it also goes so far as to cast doubts on the scientific determination of any sort of reliable racial boundaries. It also has the courage to identify the continuing support that eugenics receives from "a certain number of scientists and others" (Bullard et al., 1992, p. 429). The book stands apart in asking students to remain vigilant against abuses of new developments in genetics. It creates an imperative for understanding genetics. Otherwise, it states, it will be easy "once again for a few people to mislead others with their biased and narrow-minded ideas" (p. 429).

The image of informed citizenship and historical awareness that this book encourages is remarkable. I feel that holding "a few people" responsible for eugenics is a debatable point, given America's "Fitter Families" contests, Race Betterment Conferences, and International Congresses on Eugenics (Rydell, 1993). Nor am I comfortable with the suggestion that the problem with eugenics is one of mistaken applications of, and ill-founded assumptions about, genetics by scientists. These are minor points, though, compared with the importance of having a textbook raise these issues and pursue these important companion meanings in science classrooms.

More Talk, Not Less

In the 1950s, UNESCO called for a moratorium on the use of the term *race* (Montagu, 1972). This has, in effect, happened among the majority of high school biology texts of the 1980s that I surveyed. I remain convinced, however, that silence is as much a disservice to today's students as the often confused and prejudicial treatment of race was to a previous generation.

Students need to learn more about race, not less. They need to understand race through understanding the nature of classification itself. All that is named and classified represents a tireless effort to render difference sensible, to work with an unsettled and shapeless world that can be brought to order through the civilizing force of language. Where precisely the sense of subspecies can be said to reside—in the eyes of the beholder or the creatures themselves—must be made problematic. Such questioning of the nature of knowledge and the knowledge of nature can spill over into other ways of dividing up the world and experience.

The social implications of race classification need attention also. The "racialization" of the West has meant, in Michael Banton's (1977) compact formulation, that "race, like class and nation, was a concept first developed to help interpret new social relations" (p. 13). In that regard, consider that gender has been treated by scientists as directly analogous to the developmental scale of race, equally aimed at interpreting new social relations. Stepan (1993) describes not only the ascriptions of character (primitive, child-like) but also the elaborate anatomical measurements (brain weight, jaw protrusion) that were devoted to "linking lower races and women" (p. 363) in the anthropological, biological, and medical literature of the 1860s and 1870s.

Into the Curriculum

At this point in our history, science's assistance in the racial and gendered ordering of social relations needs to be promoted as a candidate for the science curriculum and the preparation of science teachers. I think there is room for it within the initiatives to increase scientific literacy. It seems to bring a new dimension to constructivist approaches to science; it certainly lends itself to the initiatives in the curriculum now called science-technology-society. Our understanding of both *race* and *science* can be enriched in the most academic sense; and students as well as teachers can be assisted around more personal issues of identity.

We all need to appreciate the scientific history of this concept, which includes an ongoing questioning of race as a viable biological category (Barzun, 1937; Gould, 1977; Livingstone, 1964). But then I also advocate that we not hide from the young the elements of an unsavory history, or try to protect them from the ethical controversy associated with this concept as well as the scientific controversy. Students do find themselves living within racial designations, after all.

Science teachers can share this history with their students by having them examine various editions of biology textbooks, to reveal science's changing regard for race. Students can pursue the continuing controversies surrounding race and science that crop up in the popular media, most recently around the issue of IQ (Fraser, 1995). They can gather and compare selections from the scientific debates over race that have occupied the nineteenth and twentieth centuries (Harding, 1993). They may well find, as I have found, that the scientific constitution of race in the West brought greater force and precision to the significance of difference, to the naming of the other.

I do not assume that studying race science can or should put an end to racial identification. My aim is to give students an account of how science has worked in consort with other social forces in bringing us to this point in the complex and polysemous meaning of race. My feeling, after having immersed myself in this history over the past few years, is that a science curriculum that obscures science's contributions to the meaning of race is incomplete and irresponsible given the continuing significance of this legacy for all of us. The obscured and present element of race science in science education, if it were to be made part of the curriculum, has the potential of serving both those students who understand race as a part of who they are and must be, as well as those who have learned to think of race as the *other*.[10]

CHAPTER 7

Border Crossing: Culture, School Science, and Assimilation of Students

GLEN S. AIKENHEAD

THE TERM "COMPANION MEANING," as used in this volume, identifies and distinguishes among different messages that are communicated about a school subject such as science, when students are learning it. This chapter advances a perspective that views learning as culture acquisition. The companion meanings offered to students are components and aspects of the "culture," in this view.

A cultural perspective treats the science curriculum (including its companion meanings) as a cultural artifact and characterizes the typical science classroom as the scene of many cross-cultural events. A cultural perspective affords an intuitive, holistic, and rich account of students' lived experiences in a science classroom by considering those experiences in terms of students crossing cultural borders from subcultures such as peers, family, media, and the school, into the subcultures of science and school science (Costa, 1995; Hawkins & Pea, 1987; Phelan, Davidson, & Cao, 1991). "Learning science in the classroom involves children entering a new community of discourse, a new culture" (Driver, Asoko, Leach, Mortimer, & Scott, 1994, p. 11).

A cultural perspective recognizes conventional science teaching as an attempt at transmitting a scientific subculture to students. According to Baker and Taylor (1995) and Battiste (1986), cultural transmission can be either supportive or disruptive. If the subculture of science generally harmonizes with a student life-world culture, science instruction will tend to support the student's view of the world (enculturation). On the other hand, if the subculture of science is generally at odds with a student's life-world culture, science instruction will tend to disrupt the student's view of the world by trying to replace it or marginalize it (assimilation).

Two scenarios will illustrate some features of border crossings between cultures or subcultures:

- Three Aboriginal children in Heather Kaminski's fourth-grade science class again had not followed her directions. Her frustration peaked as she explained to them what they had done wrong. "Look me in the eye when I am speaking to you!" she demanded. The three children had crossed physical borders by coming to science class, but Heather had not crossed cultural borders and therefore had failed to realize the deep respect the three children thought they had shown her by not making eye contact when she spoke.
- University science student Stirton McDougall disobeyed his faculty advisor by avoiding geology courses throughout his career. Stirton did not want to spoil his aesthetic understanding of nature's beauty by polluting his mind with mechanistic explanations of the earth's landscapes. He understood science all too well and chose not to cross one of its borders. His advisor thought he was soft-headed and not worthy of a science scholarship.

These scenarios portray cultural clashes in which intentional actions were misunderstood because some actors had not crossed cultural borders. They suggest implications for curriculum developers and teachers more far-reaching than the traditional call by C. P. Snow (1964) to close the gap between society's "Two Cultures," scientific and nonscientific. Snow's analysis, however, lends credence to the metaphor of cultural border crossing.

This chapter argues that in any school jurisdiction dedicated to the goal of "science for all" (Fensham, 1992), the onus falls on educators to recognize the cultural borders that students must cross before the taught science curriculum becomes accessible to them. Once the borders are recognized, border crossing needs to be taken into account when science educators develop and teach a curriculum. The argument proceeds in several stages: (1) a description of culture and subcultures, (2) a synopsis of research into the borders that students cross to learn science, and (3) a recognition of critical issues to be resolved.

CULTURES AND SUBCULTURES

Students' understanding of the world can be viewed as a cultural phenomenon, and learning as culture acquisition (Wolcott, 1991), where culture means "an ordered system of meaning and symbols, in terms of which social interaction takes place" (Geertz, 1973, p. 5). This anthropological definition is given more specificity by Phelan and colleagues (1991), who conceptualize culture as the norms, values, beliefs, expectations, and conventional actions of a group. We speak about, for example, a Western culture, an Asian culture, or an African culture. An interesting cluster of subcultures was used by Phelan and colleagues (1991): "families, peer groups, classrooms, and schools" (p. 224). This cluster will provide the generic framework for the chapter's analysis of border crossings by students in science classrooms.

The Subculture of Science

We need to recognize that science itself is a subculture of Western or Euro-American culture (Baker & Taylor, 1995; Jegede, 1994a; Ogawa, 1986; Pomeroy, 1994), and so Western science can be thought of as "subculture science." Scientists share a well-defined system of meaning and symbols with which they interact socially. This system was institutionalized in Western Europe in the seventeenth century, and it became predominantly a white, male, middle-class, Western system of meaning and symbols (Mendelsohn, 1976; Simonelli, 1994).

Science has norms, values, beliefs, expectations, and conventional actions that generally are shared in various ways by communities of scientists, although these norms, and so on, vary with individual scientists and situations (Aikenhead, 1985; Gauld, 1982). (Canonical scientific knowledge is included within the category "beliefs.") The following terms dominate the literature that describes the subculture of Western science (although some items turn out to be merely public facades): mechanistic, materialistic, masculine, reductionistic, mathematically idealized, pragmatic, empirical, exploitive, elitist, ideological, inquisitive, objective, impersonal, rational, universal, decontextualized, communal, violent, value-free, and embracing disinterestedness, suspension of belief, and parsimony (Cobern, 1991; Gauld, 1982; Kelly, Carlsen, & Cunningham, 1993; Simonelli, 1994). To summarize the terminology, *subculture science* (Western science) possesses cultural features that define the subculture of science (the culture of Western science).

The Subculture of School Science

Closely aligned with subculture science is *school science*, in which a student is expected (to varying degrees) to acquire science's norms, values, beliefs, expectations, and conventional actions (the subculture of science) into his or her personal world (American Association for the Advancement of Science, 1989; Cobern, 1991; Gauld, 1982; Layton, Jenkins, Macgill, & Davey, 1993; Pomeroy, 1994). School science, however, has been observed by educational research as attempting, but often failing, to transmit an accurate view of science (Cobern, 1991, Ch. 5; Duschl, 1988; Gaskell, 1992; Ryan & Aikenhead, 1992). Unfortunately, the taught science curriculum, more often than not, provides students with companion meanings that science is, for example, socially sterile, authoritarian, nonhumanistic, positivistic, and preoccupied with absolute truth—meanings associated with a stereotypic view of scientific culture. These companion meanings tend to have a negative effect on the career choices made by some bright, imaginative science enthusiasts who quickly get out of science upon graduation from high school (Oxford University Department of Educational Studies, 1989). Therefore, one can well imagine the impact that these same companion meanings might have on students who are less sympathetic to the subculture of science. This issue is taken up later in the chapter.

Science education's goal of cultural transmission runs into ethical problems in a non-Western culture where Western thought (science) is forced on students who do not share its system of meaning and symbols (Baker & Taylor, 1995). The result is assimilation or "cultural imperialism"—forcing people to abandon a traditional way of knowing and reconstruct in its place a new (scientific) way of knowing (Battiste, 1986; Jegede, 1994a). Cultural imperialism can oppress and disempower whole groups of people (Hodson, 1993). School science traditionally attempts to enculturate or assimilate students into the subculture of science. Of interest to this chapter will be the vantage point achieved by taking a crosscultural perspective on the daily experiences of many North American students in science classrooms.

School science has other social functions that characterize its cultural makeup, functions familiar to science educators as educational goals. Fensham (1992) pragmatically summarizes these goals in terms of societal interest groups competing for privilege and power over the curriculum and its companion meanings. For example, school science (most often physics) can be used to screen out students belonging to socially marginalized groups, thereby providing high status and social power to the more privileged students who make it through the science "pipeline" and enter science-related professions (Anyon, 1980; Posner, 1992)—those who can "cut the mustard," to use the rhetoric of the scientific community. School science is a potent cultural force in any society, a force that impinges on most students daily.

Other Subcultures

In our everyday world, we all exhibit changes in our own behavior as we move between different groups of people, for instance, from professional colleagues at a conference to our family at a wedding. As we move from the one subculture to the other, we intuitively and subconsciously alter certain beliefs, expectations, and conventions; in other words, we effortlessly negotiate the cultural border between a conference and a family wedding.

Similarly, students must deal with, and participate in, an array of important subcultures in their lives, including: (1) school science, (2) science, (3) the institution of school itself (society's instrument of cultural transmission), (4) peer groups, (5) the family, and (6) the mass media. Participation in different subcultures creates the need to cross borders between these subcultures. Researchers Phelan and colleagues (1991) have investigated this phenomenon and describe their findings this way:

> On any given school day, adolescents in this society [the United States] move from one social context to another. Families, peer groups, classrooms, and schools are primary arenas in which young people negotiate and construct their realities. For the most part, students' movement and adaptations from one setting to another are taken for granted. Although such transitions frequently require students' efforts and skills, especially when contexts are governed by different values and norms, there has been relatively little study of this process. From data gathered during the first phase of the Students' Multiple Worlds Study, it appears that, in our culture, many adolescents are left to navigate transitions without direct assistance from persons in any of their contexts, most notably the school. Further, young people's success in managing these transitions varies widely. Yet students' competence in moving between settings has tremendous implications for the quality of their lives and their chances of using the education system as a stepping stone to further education, productive work experiences, and a meaningful adult life. (p. 224)

When students cross cultural borders between their science class, school, peers, and family, these borders can seem invisible to educators, for example, to Heather Kaminski in the earlier scenario. Borders can even seem invisible to the "unfortunate" students who find science a foreign experience. Cross-cultural studies in science education in non-Western countries can help clarify the border crossing problems for the conventional North American student. In Japan, Ogawa (1995) contemplated why certain groups of non-Western students living with "traditional" beliefs about the physical world achieved academic superiority over certain groups of Western students on "Western modern science" examinations. He concluded that the culture of Western science is equally foreign to both groups of students, for similar reasons. Non-Western students have acquired a traditional culture of their community, which interferes with learning Western science. Similarly, Western students, with their everyday commonsense understanding of their physical world (that is, their "traditional" science that makes sense within their subcultures of peers, family, and public media), have difficulty acquiring the culture of Western science. However, I would quickly add, so do nonmasculine students, humanities-oriented, non-Cartesian thinking students, and students who are not clones of university science professors (Haste, 1994; Seymour, 1992; Tobias, 1990).

Western students' difficulty learning science concepts has been the object of research in science education. Over the past 2 decades the research program "personal constructivism" has revealed not only that students harbor alternative frameworks (Driver & Easley, 1978), commonsense conceptions (Mayer, 1984), untutored beliefs (Hills, 1989), or preconceptions (Driver et al., 1994), but also that these personal conceptual constructions inhibit science achievement, that is, they inhibit rational conceptual change (West & Pines, 1985). Most students are not about to risk altering a useful commonsense conception in favor of a counterintuitive abstraction advanced by a teacher or textbook. Students may be uneducated, but they are not stupid.

The constructivist research program has expanded to take into account nonrational aspects of conceptual change: the context-dependent nature of concept development (Solomon, 1984) and students' personal orientation toward their sociocultural environment (Shapiro, 1992). This "social constructivist" research program investigates how students' social worlds influence the way they make sense out of their natural world. Solomon (1987) and Driver and colleagues (1994), for instance, show how science concepts have a socially negotiated meaning shared within a group such as a science class or peer group.

This chapter proposes an even more expanded perspective on learning science: a cultural orientation toward concept development. From a cultural perspective, familiar problems with conceptual change are seen in a new light. Within Western culture, and therefore within every North American science class, the subculture of science has borders that many Western students may find difficult to negotiate. We now turn to some empirical evidence that documents this viewpoint.

BORDERS AND STUDENTS

Transitions Between Multiple Worlds

The model of students' multiple worlds proposed by Phelan and colleagues (1991) explores how students move from one world to another. From their data, they suggested four types of transitions: Congruent worlds support *smooth* transitions, different worlds require transitions to be *managed*, diverse worlds can lead to *hazardous* transitions, and highly discordant worlds cause students to resist transitions, which therefore become virtually *impossible*.

The Border Crossers—Costa's Categories

Guided by this model, Costa (1995) gathered qualitative data (the words and actions of students) on 43 high school students enrolled in chemistry or earth science in two California schools with diverse student populations. She concluded: "Although there was great variety in students' descriptions of their worlds and the world of science, there were also distinctive patterns among the relationships between students' worlds of family and friends and their success in school and in science classrooms" (p. 316). Costa described these patterns according to five categories, which are summarized here in terms of a cultural perspective on learning science.

Potential Scientists. For Potential Scientists, the worlds of family and friends are congruent with the worlds of both school and science. These students hold professional career aspirations for which their science classes play a significant role, and, therefore, they work diligently. A family member or friend usually serves as a role model or, if not, at least provides strong encouragement. Generally, Potential Scientists view themselves as having the potential to participate in society's power structures and to generate knowledge. They appear comfortable with a traditional positivist view of modern science, described earlier as a stereotypic view of subculture science. They enjoy the challenges of academic subject matter, not needing (even shunning) efforts to make science socially relevant to their everyday lives. Even bad experiences with science teachers are overlooked in order to sustain the centrality of science for their career plans. Not surprisingly, Costa found a disproportionately high number of Euro-American males in this group.

Potential Scientists may or may not actually become scientists and engineers, but in any case school science for them is a type of "rite of passage." Border crossing into school science for Potential Scientists is so *smooth* and natural that borders appear invisible. For these students, events in the science classroom are not really cross-cultural events because of the congruence between family/peers and school/science. The curriculum's companion meanings will likely be recognized and accepted by Potential Scientists.

Other Smart Kids. For Other Smart Kids, the worlds of family and friends are consistent with the world of school but inconsistent with the world of science. These students do well at school—even in science, although science is neither personally meaningful nor useful to their everyday lives. Science is, however, necessary for their postsecondary plans. Like Potential Scientists, Other Smart Kids do not question the stereotypic public norms, values, beliefs, expectations, and conventional actions of the scientific community. They prefer, however, to engage in creative activities that require self-expression and human interactions, making themselves candidates for C. P. Snow's (1964) nonscientific culture.

Other Smart Kids *choose* not to take up science once they graduate (cf. Tobias, 1990) because they find the subculture of science to be personally unimportant and inconsistent with the subcultures of school, peers, and family. But border crossing into school science is *managed* so well that few students express any sense of being in a foreign culture. Nevertheless, Other Smart Kids *are* in a foreign culture, and events in the science classroom *do* represent cross-cultural events that require border crossing. If teachers are unaware that learning science is a cross-cultural phenomenon, they will be unable to provide border-crossing assistance. Students are then left to manage on their own and to interpret the curriculum's companion meanings as best they can.

"I Don't Know" Students. Costa's "I Don't Know" Students were labeled for their ubiquitous ("I don't know") response to a host of questions about science and about school, and for their noncommittal overall attitude toward school science. Their worlds of family and friends are inconsistent with the worlds of both science and school. Generally, for them, science classes are no different from other classes. The subcultures of school and science are equally inconsistent with their subcultures of peers and family. Although "I Don't Know" Students take only a minimal number of science courses and tend to occupy lower-track classes, they usually achieve reasonably well. School grades have personal meaning—"I don't want to look like a dummy!" The students have learned to play the school game of memorizing content and conforming to teachers' expectations, almost as successfully as Other Smart Kids have. Consequently, they pose few problems for their science teachers, as long as the teachers do not expect them to construct their own knowledge and engage in inquiry other than going through the motions of getting the right answer.

"I Don't Know" Students do not know much about the subculture of science and when probed they fall back on "I don't know" or simply submit to the wisdom of the media and treat scientists as experts. Border crossing into school science poses real *hazards*, but these students generally navigate successfully around those hazards. In a classroom where no border-crossing assistance is furnished by teacher, by text, or by the curriculum's companion meanings, students—like refugees in a foreign culture—learn to cope and survive. But their perception of the curriculum's companion meanings will likely be worlds apart from the intended meanings.

Outsiders. For Outsiders, the worlds of family and friends are discordant with the worlds of both school and science. These students experience great difficulties in the subculture of school, difficulties that lead to failure and alienation for themselves and problems for their teachers. For Outsiders, all schoolwork is busywork and emphasizes compliance to directions from authorities. Outsiders do not know anything about the subculture of science, but even more important, they do not care. School and science are perceived as very foreign cultures—"I feel like chemistry is another world."

Some Outsiders are savvy enough to figure out the system and manipulate it enough to pass their science course. But for most of them, border crossing into school science is simply *impossible*. Border-crossing assistance from teachers would likely be rejected because the culture of science, or even the value of doing well in school, has little significance for these students. The companion meanings related to subculture school science are all but irrelevant.

Inside Outsiders. Costa discovered a group of bright students interested in science but inhibited from crossing the border into school science because of (1) their school's abject discrimination and discouragement, and (2) lack of support from peers and family. These students, called "Inside Outsiders," happened to be female African Americans in Costa's study. Their worlds of family and friends are irreconcilable with the world of school, but are potentially compatible with the world of science. They possess an intense curiosity about the physical world but have developed a mistrust for the school's gatekeepers. Their unconventional lives caused almost *impossible* border crossings into the subculture of school, which in turn prevented them from participating fully in the subculture of school science.

Students, Borders, and Companion Meanings

Costa's five categories of border crossing, as reviewed here, were derived empirically from the lived experiences of high school students enrolled in science classes. Conceptually, it is helpful to view their different responses to science teaching as a function of their responses to companion meanings about the features of subculture school science as normally portrayed in science curricula. Can these features be changed? Surely curriculum materials can be altered to make the companion meanings they convey more compatible with students' different border-crossing "styles." I turn to such considerations in the next section.

ISSUES FOR CURRICULUM DEVELOPERS AND TEACHERS

Costa's (1995) empirical results encourage curriculum developers and teachers to give particular attention to the impact that a science curriculum has on five groups of students. Is there a need to develop a separate curriculum for each of Costa's five categories of border crossings? I do not think so, nor does Costa suggest it. Students who might be categorized as "Inside Outsiders" and "Outsiders" provide educators with challenges that go beyond the scope of this chapter. For instance, given the negative, schoolwide, hidden curriculum that creates "Inside Outsiders," there is nothing a curriculum specialist can do (Apple, 1979; Posner, 1992). Help must come from vigilant teachers who will risk confronting local norms and taboos.

Given the almost impenetrable border crossing experienced by Costa's "Outsiders," what can be done other than creating revolutionary alternative education programs, as some larger school jurisdictions have done? Within such programs, a science curriculum would be integrated with other subject areas and with a student's street or working life—a topic for a much different chapter.

This leaves us with three groups of students to consider: "I Don't Know" Students, Other Smart Kids, and Potential Scientists. What science curricula and companion meanings seem most appropriate for each of them?

Addressing "I Don't Know" Students

This group of students needs assistance negotiating hazardous border crossings into the subculture of science. Against a rich background of research on constructivism—which concludes that students' creativity and intransigence abound in ways to circumvent the construction of meaning within the subculture of science—I will sketch the case of one "I Don't Know" student who illustrates the nonlearning that science teachers will recognize only too painfully.

Melanie, a reasonably conscientious grade 10 student, was enrolled in a science-technology-society (STS) science course. Her teacher and I were collaborating on research into ways to enhance personal constructivism (the teacher's research agenda). Melanie was one of 15 students involved over a 3-year period (five students per year) in a school with a diverse composition of students. During a unit on heat taught each year, I observed the teacher's classes, studied the targeted students' work, observed their social interactions within the class, discussed my observations with the teacher, and interviewed the students before, during, and after the unit of instruction. Melanie clearly fit into Costa's category of the "I Don't Know" Student. Her transcripts are riddled with, "I don't know." One event exemplifies the difficulty Melanie experienced when her teacher and I tried for 5 weeks to have her participate in the subculture of science by experimenting and constructing a concept of heat. During a preinstruction interview, Melanie stated the following (the words are hers but the argument has been collapsed to achieve cogency):

> Heat is the warmth of particles. Temperature is the measurement of heat and coolness. All objects contain both heat and coolness; for example, an object whose temperature is 60 degrees has 30 degrees of heat plus 30 degrees of coolness. (Melanie, April 1992, lines 180–202)

After 5 weeks of student-oriented group inquiry, contextualized in historical and everyday events, and after successfully calculating specific heats of materials and deciding what materials are best for different everyday situations, Melanie's conception of heat became slightly more sophisticated, but not in any intended way. Her degrees of heat and coolness simply became percentages (May 1992, lines 29–35): An object whose temperature is 60 degrees has 80% heat plus 20% coolness. For Melanie, STS content made her science class more interesting, and provided alternative content on which she was evaluated to her advantage, but did not make traditional science content any more accessible. Lijnse (1990) came to the same conclusion based on extensive research and development with STS materials in the Netherlands.

A clue to Melanie's resistance to assimilation into the subculture of science surfaced as she reflected on the nature of heat:

> If I don't know what it is, then I can just leave as it is, and I'll never wonder. Like I'll just say it's that way 'cause it is that way. Same as a person is a way that person is, 'cause of the ways that they're made because; like you may have the eyes of your dad and the chin of your mom and it's just how they are. So you just have to live with it. (Melanie, April 1992, lines 300–304)

Melanie compliantly accepts whatever happens in the natural world, including her own ability to make sense out of that world. According to Melanie, she makes sense out of the natural world by correcting her wrong thinking and memorizing the correct ideas (lines 19–27).

Her teacher and I did not appreciate the hazards she coped with when asked to participate in the subculture of science (with its precise but idealized beliefs about heat—cf. Säljö's discussion of "institutional accounting practices" in Chapter 4 in this volume). We had focused exclusively on her participation, giving no attention to assisting her to cross the cultural border between her everyday world and the subculture of science. Her commonsense culture (with its vague though useful beliefs about heat) could have been legitimately acknowledged, and the transition into the subculture of science could have been openly recognized as a cross-cultural event. In retrospect, we did not appreciate the risk to her self-confidence if she changed her way of making sense out of the natural world—to correct wrong thinking and memorize the correct idea.

Whose interests are served by expecting Melanie and other "I Don't Know" Students to construct new but, for them, irrelevant knowledge about such a topic as heat? Should students be *forced* to participate in the subculture of science? In other words, should the school assimilate these students, thereby attempting "scientific imperialism"? Rather than respond to this ethical issue with an ethical argument, I want to claim *on empirical grounds* that attempts at assimilation most often fail and therefore ought not to be attempted for highly pragmatic reasons.

Researchers Songer and Linn (1991) claim that it takes 12 weeks of instruction to teach the concepts of heat and temperature meaningfully, a time allotment that hardly seems justifiable. Layton and colleagues (1993) discovered that a scientific understanding about heat energy had no consequence to laypeople managing domestic energy problems. The researchers seriously questioned science education's objective to teach what is rarely usable in the everyday world. In the words of Wynne (1991, p. 120): "ordinary social life, which often takes contingency and uncertainty as normal and adaptation to uncontrolled factors as a routine necessity, is in fundamental tension with the basic culture of science which is premised on assumptions of manipulability and control."

For Melanie, and other "I Don't Know" Students, what features of a science curriculum might ease their hazardous border crossing into the subculture of science? A concrete example will suggest a direction to take. The topic of mixtures, for instance, can make sense to students in various ways (in different cultures associated with the home, industry, or science). When salad dressing is made, egg whites and mustard powder can be introduced as ingredients that prevent the dressing from layering. Other substances are introduced to prevent layering in such diverse items as milk, photographic film, and gold jewelry. In addition, the example of milk can clearly illustrate a characteristic of language in the subculture of science: Meanings of scientific terms are tied to scientific classification schemes and may contradict commonsense meanings—for instance, homogenized milk is not a homogeneous mixture. To cross the border from everyday subcultures to subculture science is to change completely one's personal orientation to language (Lemke, 1990). Students will need some way of signifying to themselves and others which subculture they are talking in, at a given time. Border crossing must be explicit, and students will need a "guided tour" of the subculture of science. They are tourists in a foreign culture.

Addressing Other Smart Kids

Similar to the "I Don't Know" Students, Other Smart Kids find the world of science to be neither personally meaningful nor useful to their everyday lives. Thus, knowledge worth learning for both groups normally will *not* include the artifacts of subculture science, and so learning science becomes a cross-cultural event. On the other hand, the differences between the two student groups lie principally in their feelings toward other school subjects (interested and highly successful for Other Smart Kids) and the ease with which they cross the cultural border into the subculture of science (managed rather than hazardous). Thus, for Other Smart Kids, knowledge worth learning in school science will likely be knowledge organized around everyday issues, derived from critical analysis, and involving reflection, self-expression, and humanistic rigor. For these students, bridges to the subculture of science can be constructed out of technological and social issues, and out of the history, epistemology, and sociology of science (all STS content). These bridges should acknowledge the cultural conflicts between the student's world and the world of science, and should help students negotiate that border.

Some students may travel across these bridges and discover a personal attraction to science. For them, school science may become enculturation. However, no student should be coerced into enculturation (that is, no student should be assimilated), if meaningful learning is the objective. (If game playing is the objective, then coercion might be appropriate.) Students should be expected to think critically *about* science and "to think science," but not necessarily believe science (Cobern, 1994). For instance, cultural features of science (its norms, values, beliefs, expectations, and conventional actions) could be made accessible to students through events that inform and shape the students' personal lives, events such as STS content (Solomon & Aikenhead, 1994). The subculture of science would therefore be seen as "a repository to be raided for what it can contribute to the achievement of practical ends" (Layton et al., 1993, p. 135). To understand cultural features of science, Other Smart Kids will not necessarily relinquish features of their life-world subcultures, although they will be expected to examine them critically. As with "I Don't Know" Students described in the previous section, Other Smart Kids will be invited to add to or modify their life-world knowledge, based on their understandings from the subculture of science.

Academic bridges for Other Smart Kids would be somewhat different from the supportive guidance ("guided tours") that "I Don't Know" Students require to negotiate their hazardous border crossings into subculture science. The difference can be characterized in terms of the conceptual construction expected and the degree of academic abstraction and analysis required. A "guided tour" aims at a reasoned and critical appreciation of science (for instance, the salad dressing example above), not unlike a music appreciation course that guides students through the world of music without requiring that they compose music or exhibit virtuosity with an instrument. On the other hand, academic bridges would assist Other Smart Kids to manage the border crossing and to engage in the subculture of science, which would be seen as interacting with the other subcultures that form a fairly coherent unity in students' lives. For example, students could draw diagrams that conceptualize legal and moral reasoning, and concretely sketch in the possible contribution of science and technology to those legal and moral decisions (Aikenhead, 1991). The bridges between the subculture of science and the life-worlds of students would be made concrete. Such science instruction constitutes the essence of most STS education. Lijnse (1990) reports on a promising three-tiered, concept-development model that builds bridges back and forth between students' cultural experiences with energy and scientific concepts of energy.

Addressing Potential Scientists

Potential Scientists enthusiastically engage in a socialization process described by Costa (1993) as a rite of passage into science. These students (as with "Inside Outsiders") derive pleasure from playing with abstract decontextualized concepts and solving idealized mathematical problems. Potential Scientists tend to search for a body of knowledge and apprentice-like activities with which to assimilate the norms, beliefs, values, expectations, and conventional actions of their role models.

Consequently, a number of Potential Scientists would see little value in solving life-world, concrete, and consensual problems typically found in STS courses. To explore subjectivity, epistemology, or cultural values inherent in the subculture of science would approach heresy. Potential Scientists value preprofessional training in the tradition of "advanced placement" courses in the United States. Such courses serve these students' short-term interests very well, although it is interesting to note that "much of the recent research on student learning in the sciences has shown that students exhibit substantial conceptual misunderstandings even after passing university examinations on the topic" (Prosser, Trigwell, & Taylor, 1994, p. 230). Our preoccupation with scientific conceptual fidelity for all high school students is a critical issue that needs our examination and reflection.

Diversity in the ranks of Potential Scientists becomes evident by the number who switch out of science into other fields such as political science, business studies, and law, once they reach postsecondary education. Their disenchantment with science was systematically investigated by Bondi (1985), Oxford University Department of Educational Studies (1989), and Seymour (1992) whose research suggests that a wide range of companion meanings (epistemological, sociological, and cultural), experienced by Potential Scientists in the subcultures of school and university science courses, do not harmonize with their life-world subcultures. As a result, enrollment in university sciences steadily decreases. Contributing to this problem is the lack of clarity in the school's rite of passage designed exclusively for Potential Scientists (Costa, 1993). These students require a more carefully crafted socialization or apprenticeship into an authentic subculture of science (Gaskell, 1992; Hawkins & Pea, 1987; Layton et al., 1993). In terms of the "pipeline" into careers in science and engineering, the traditional school science curriculum has not been very successful. This conclusion forms one cornerstone to the rationale for STS education (Solomon & Aikenhead, 1994). Within the STS movement, people have argued that Potential Scientists should have a foundation for the social, political, and ethical responsibilities that they will certainly face as professionals in the twenty-first century (Aikenhead, 1980; Cross & Price, 1992; Solomon, 1994a). This goal speaks to the long-term interests of Potential Scientists and society.

Interestingly, a humanistic STS science curriculum presents to many Potential Scientists a challenge not unlike (but opposite to) the challenge faced in a traditional science curriculum by Other Smart Kids—who are primarily humanists. A major difference, however, lies in the fact that schools normally provide Potential Scientists with a privileged position (Gaskell, 1992; Hodson, 1993; Posner, 1992) from which they can demean STS curricula as "soft" or for students who "can't cut the mustard."

As Fensham (1992) warned, the science curriculum is a social instrument that serves the interests of those who have a stake in its content and companion meanings. Some influential stakeholders simply want school science to act as a screening device to maintain an intellectual, socially elite status quo for society (Anyon, 1980; Apple, 1979). A second group of stakeholders (many high school science teachers among them) has an interest in maintaining a stereotypic view of science as authoritarian, nonhumanistic, objective, purely rational and empirical, universal, impersonal, socially sterile, and value-free (Duschl, 1988; Gallagher, 1991; Gaskell, 1992). Given the powerful and privileged position that both of these groups of stakeholders enjoy in society, one cannot expect much change to the traditional preprofessional training curriculum with its positivistic companion meanings.

CONCLUDING REMARKS

A cultural perspective on science education lends itself to a new appreciation of science classrooms and what students face when learning science. Old problems become situated in new contexts. For instance, science itself is perceived as a subculture with cultural borders to cross, not only for non-Western students but for many Western students as well.

Conventional science teaching is seen as enculturation for students whose life-world harmonizes with the subculture of science, and assimilation for those whose life-world does not. Many students in the latter group seem to avoid this cultural assimilation entirely by playing clever "school games" (one aspect of the subculture of schools) in which the winners receive socialization-into-science certificates without a genuine understanding of science content. The unintended companion meaning here speaks to "beating the system."

From a cultural perspective, students' experiences with school science are seen as border-crossing events that can be smooth, managed, hazardous, or impossible. When border crossings into the subculture of science are not smooth, students find themselves in a cross-cultural classroom. The learned science curriculum results from the organic interaction among: (1) the personal orientation of a student, (2) the subcultures of science and school science, and (3) the subcultures of a student's family, peers, school, and media.

Seen in this new light, it becomes apparent that the intended and taught curricula need to be redesigned, for a large majority of students, with border crossings anticipated and explicitly facilitated. Border crossings will resemble academic bridges for Costa's (1995) Other Smart Kids, and guided tours for "I Don't Know" Students. Border crossings may be facilitated by examining the subcultures of students' life-worlds and by contrasting them with a critical analysis of the subculture of science, *consciously* moving back and forth from the life-world into the science-world, switching language conventions, switching conceptualizations, switching values, switching epistemologies, and so on, but never requiring students to adopt a scientific way of knowing as their personal world view. However, the "no assimilation" rule does not preclude capturing students' interest and curiosity in science and then doing a good job at a rite of passage into the subculture of science.

A cross-cultural science curriculum could entail STS content with more technology content than is conventional today. The curriculum's scientific and companion meanings would be transformed accordingly. New companion meanings would illuminate subcultures and border crossings. Whose interests are served by compelling a student to construct a scientific concept irrelevant to, or interfering with, his or her life-world? These interests need to be rethought, redefined, and communicated to students as companion meanings.

CHAPTER 8

Intellectual Independence: A Potential Link Between Science Teaching and Responsible Citizenship

HUGH MUNBY AND DOUGLAS A. ROBERTS

THIS CHAPTER STARTS FROM a vantage point developed by Komisar (1969) that teaching is an inherently intrusive social encounter. Consider the prerogatives of the participants in classroom discourse, compared with other types of social discourse. All verbal interactions are characterized by the intrusion of the speakers upon each other's perceptions; yet, in most situations, the participants are at liberty to prevent further intrusion by requesting that the interaction cease. Also, no participants are empowered to coerce the others into taking physical or intellectual action. It is not so in the classroom, where students can pay a heavy penalty if they do not listen to the teacher and take the physical or intellectual action required of them, where they cannot request that the intrusion cease (except by "tuning out"). That appears to be a characteristic of all teaching, and, of course, an unequal power distribution thus is required if teaching is to proceed at all.

As a result, considerable attention has been paid over the years to the moral and ethical demands on a concept of teaching that would allow this social contract with students to be filled honorably. Philosophical analysis of teaching shows a central concern for providing reasons and evidence, for engaging the students' judgment, and generally for conducting teaching in a way that respects the students' integrity, autonomy, and evolving personhood. Teaching that proceeds according to these criteria can be seen to counteract the intrusion and one-sidedness inherent in the process.

In democratic societies there is a further reason for insisting on such features in teaching. Education is expected, generally speaking, to inculcate in students habits of exercising judgment, of thinking actively and critically, of regularly expecting to consider evidence and reasons. This characteristic of teaching purports to contribute to responsible citizenship in all subject areas.

This chapter will argue that these are matters of *the distribution of power* in the classroom: whether the teacher holds on to the power, or teaches students how they can use it responsibly. This is being said in a very special sense. It is power distribution with respect to the *intellectual* aspects of the classroom (providing reasons, and so on)—what might be called the "intellectual climate." Other aspects might be important, but these are not included; for instance, such matters of "managerial climate" as whether students choose their own lab partners.

To set off this special sense, some years ago the terms "intellectual independence" and its inverse, "intellectual dependence," were proposed (Munby, 1973) to capture a distinction between two overall orientations to which students can be socialized. The most significant companion meanings communicated to students being socialized toward intellectual independence are those within the curriculum emphasis Roberts has called Self as Explainer (Chapter 1 in this volume). The consistent, implicit message to the student can be summed up, overall, as this: "You can learn to assess the truth and reasonableness of knowledge claims and explanations; you do not have to remain intellectually dependent on a teacher for such assessments."

The chapter is laid out in three major sections, of which the first is devoted to exploring theoretical considerations about goals and aims in education, and to linking power distribution in the classroom to conceptual roots for the concepts of "teaching" and "indoctrination." The second identifies features of teaching that would be consistent with socializing students toward intellectual independence in the sense described above. The third section demonstrates how these ideas can be applied to understanding the development of intellectual independence in the science classroom, through analysis of two contrasting segments of teaching. Discussion at the end of the chapter returns to the broad theme of potential consequences of these power features of discourse for the student's future role as a responsible citizen.

CONCEPTUALIZING INTELLECTUAL INDEPENDENCE

School science classrooms can be surprisingly authoritarian places—the very antithesis of science education rhetoric. Paradoxically, authoritarianism is communicated by what is *absent*. Schwab (1962) identified a style of science teaching that he called a "rhetoric of conclusions" to capture this point—a style that persuades the listener "to accept the tentative as certain, the doubtful as the undoubted, by making no mention of reasons or evidence" for what is asserted, as if to say, "*This*, everyone of importance knows to be true" (p. 24). Such a style of teaching communicates a powerful companion meaning. Roberts has called this curriculum emphasis Correct Explanations (Chapter 1 in this volume).

Aims and Goals in Science Education

As an unintended outcome of science teaching, authoritarianism could well be a function of the ways we think about educational objectives and how that thinking transfers to classroom practice. A recent review of research on aims and goals of science education (Bybee & DeBoer, 1994) shows that they are usually cast, as ever, in the familiar quartet (stated separately) of knowledge, processes, applications, and attitudes. Knowledge is read as the facts, concepts, laws, principles, and theories of the discipline—what is termed "scientific meaning" in this volume. An untempered emphasis on scientific meaning, which is a possible outcome of the initiative by the National Science Teachers Association in the United States to identify an agreed science "content core," has considerable potential for reinforcing within schools the view that other features of science education are insignificant. That is, to give science content priority in curriculum development is to invite school boards and science teachers to do the familiar—to set up all of the specific objectives concerned with scientific meaning and hope that somehow they will add up to something more. As discussed below, that does not work. Quite clearly, a science curriculum that emphasizes only scientific meaning runs the risk of actually masking the human character of science, by ignoring the reasoned discourse that gives science its life. The obvious consequence for students is that the science curriculum carries a distinctive companion meaning about science that is miseducative because it is authoritarian. So, while authoritarianism might not be found in the objectives of a science curriculum, it can be there quite by accident.

When presented with the challenge of describing the features of a core science curriculum, Munby and Russell (1983) argued against the conventional view of describing a core in terms of content and instead proposed that it be conceived in terms of *manner*. Specifically, the argument urged that of fundamental significance to the education of all students was to have them experience the reasoned nature of science—such matters as the importance of evidence, the consideration of alternative views, and the basis on which ideas are judged to be acceptable or not acceptable. If the curriculum were organized in this manner, the argument went, students would not be left dependent on their teachers' authority for assessing the truth of knowledge claims and the reasonableness of explanations. There would be a deliberately planned antidote to authoritarianism.

The "Manner" of Teaching

If authoritarianism is conveyed when reasons, evidence, and argument are absent, then surely its antidote requires that they be present. A manner of teaching that socializes students toward intellectual independence develops in them the resources necessary for judging the truth of knowledge claims for themselves, independently of other people. We can express this broad educational goal in terms of an ideal. Thus, an individual judging the truth of a claim on the basis of all assumptions, evidence, and arguments necessary for the judgment is exercising intellectual independence.

This expression is an ideal in two senses. First, it is likely that very few people function consistently in an intellectually independent way. For that matter, it is likely that very few people function consistently in the principled manner suggested by Kohlberg's (1966) "Stage 6" of moral development. Second, any professional scientist who does reach a consistent state of intellectual independence probably does so in a very highly specialized and narrow field of study. Neither of these points detracts from the appropriateness of expressing a broad educational goal in an idealized way. The expression does not identify either a perfect, failsafe capability of persons or a definable knowledge base. Rather, it describes a more or less habitual stance toward knowledge claims and explanations, perhaps exemplified in such thoughts and reactions among students as "there is a good reason behind that statement," and "there is a way to assess the truth of that claim," and "there isn't enough evidence for him/her to say that." Contrast these reactions with the typical student reaction when intellectual dependence has been fostered—"It must be true, 'cos the teacher says so!"—and the broad distinction between the two concepts is clear. So the concept of intellectual independence directs attention to the *fashion* or *manner* of science teaching and to the overall goals of education at the same time.[1]

The Logic of Aims and Goals

Intellectual independence shares a frustrating characteristic with all broad educational goals: By their nature they tend to be distant from the immediacies of classrooms. Broad educational goals are not included easily in lesson plans, and it is likely that much more specific objectives are reflected in actual teaching. For example, consider this statement from a Board of Education about its aims for a student's grade 9 education: "The educated student will be able to solve problems and make decisions based on relevant information, will be able to think, act, and learn independently, and will be characterized by flexibility of thought and openness to new ideas." There is a danger that broad objectives of this sort will be "hoped for," even assumed to happen automatically. A teacher's attention, however, is more likely to be fastened on the specific, lesson-by-lesson objectives of a course in grade 9 English, or science, or social studies, and there is no obvious conceptual bridge between the specific objectives and the broader goal—no guarantee, either, that all of the specific objectives will "add up" to the broader goal.

The logic of "adding up" is the wrong logic to use. Specific objectives and broad educational goals are qualitatively different, just because the former typically refer to the *substance* of learning, while the latter refer to the *purpose*. Large numbers of the former do not necessarily add up to the latter in a specific-to-general kind of relationship in which one can grasp completely the meaning of the general objective by identifying all of the specific ones. The conceptual bridge that is missing is found in the *manner* or *fashion* in which the teaching is conducted and, therefore, in the companion meanings that are communicated. In the case of intellectual independence, students need to experience, repeatedly and consistently, such messages as that evidence is needed to support claims, that reasons and arguments are associated with claiming to know in science, that there are publicly acknowledged means for assessing the truth of claims, and—especially—that *students can learn how to use this reasoning power.* That is, the teacher needs to distribute the power inherent in these messages, to "let students in on the secrets" of how science works, rather than cloaking them.

The logic is quite simple to state: If these matters are to be learned by students in the science classroom, *provision has to be made* for that to happen. Such matters must be present in lessons, even if they typically are not included in lesson-by-lesson objectives about the scientific meaning of, say, Newton's laws.

FEATURES OF INTELLECTUAL INDEPENDENCE

This section develops features of intellectual independence as they might appear in science classroom discourse. The intent is to unpack the meaning of the term into components that can be arranged into a conceptual framework for examining instances of teaching.

Some Conceptual Roots

The concepts of intellectual independence and intellectual dependence owe much to the tradition of philosophical analysis of educational concepts, especially "teaching" and "indoctrination." The distinctions are explored in the work of three prominent authors, in order to reveal this ancestry, to give more depth to the phrase "manner of teaching," and to link the two concepts to issues of power distribution in the classroom.

The most common differentiation of teaching from indoctrination is captured in this statement by Scheffler (1965b). It is based on the point that teaching is "practiced in such a manner as to respect the student's intellectual integrity and capacity for independent judgement" (p. 131). By contrast, indoctrinating and similar activities such as propagandizing and conditioning "are aimed at modifying the person but strive at all costs to avoid a genuine engagement of his judgment on underlying issues" (p. 131). If students' capability for independent judgment is to be respected, reason, argument, and evidence must be given. Students are thereby offered the power to judge what is being taught, and are taught how to use it. These features clearly would qualify as providing for the socialization of students toward intellectual independence.

Komisar (1968) makes the distinction between teaching and indoctrination by focusing attention on a special sense of the word *teaching*, which he terms "teaching at the act level" (p. 71). He refers to such intellectual acts as proving, demonstrating, explaining, and the like, all of which make provision, in the following way, for students to move toward intellectual independence. If a teacher is proving something, say, and if the term *proving* is used appropriately, all pieces of the proof may be presumed present. The student's access to these provides for intellectual independence. If a teacher attempted a proof and omitted a part of it, then it would be quite wrong to honor the attempt with the name of the act. The result would be to leave the student intellectually dependent on the teacher; part of the grounds for the proof would be hidden. The power inherent in "knowing how to prove" would be reserved to the teacher, not distributed to the students. The same points can be made about the other intellectual acts noted above.

Green (1968) makes teaching distinct from indoctrination on the grounds that teaching involves matters of truth and falsity, whereas indoctrinating "aims simply at establishing certain beliefs so that they will be held quite apart from their truth, their explanation, or their foundation in evidence" (p. 34). Patently, the potential outcomes of indoctrination and of teaching that provides for intellectual dependence are the same. Both leave the recipient of the act dependent on the perpetrator for assessing the truth and reasonableness of statements made.

These brief ventures into philosophical analysis of the concepts of teaching and indoctrination show an obvious relationship to the distinction between a manner of teaching that socializes students toward intellectual independence and one that socializes toward intellectual dependence, respectively. From such considerations, the following two features of science teaching seem to characterize socialization toward intellectual independence:

- Evidence is provided in support of claims.
- The argument in support of a claim is present.

Often, conflicting evidence arises in the science classroom, suggesting a further feature:

- Discrepancies among observations or evidence are resolved on reasoned grounds.

In light of the considerable extent to which diagrams and models are used in science teaching, a related feature is added:

- Correspondence of a diagram or model to phenomena is demonstrated by evidence and by argument.

These are clearly matters of distributing power to students, based on the point that students are put into a position to make judgments about the intellectual quality of what is taught. If such features are absent, the teaching is seen as socializing students toward intellectual dependence.

Philosophical analysis of educational concepts also has included attention to the concept of knowing. This area is full of controversy, and trying to sort it out is far beyond the scope of this chapter. Nevertheless, any treatment of the concept of knowing requires attention to matters of truth, as well as evidence and arguments on which individuals build their beliefs (Scheffler, 1965a). In science, truth depends for its meaning on quite different views about the nature of science. As a consequence, it would be difficult to comment on the truth of what is asserted in a science lesson (except insofar as it matches with what has been called "valid science"). This is especially so for explanations and theories, concerning which there are very different views of what constitutes truth. This is certainly not an absolute matter for philosophers of science, and different science curricula show some variation in this regard.

So, in the spirit of the present inquiry, it becomes more significant to examine science teaching for the presence or absence of explicit statements about *means for assessing truth*. Thus, rather than analyze teaching for the truth of what is asserted, one can see whether means for assessing truth are made evident to students so that they can learn to judge the truth of statements for themselves. Of course, when teaching contains this information, it moves decidedly toward providing for intellectual independence. Here is the statement of that feature:

- The means are indicated for assessing the truth of statements.

Because models, theories, and explanations do not lend themselves to judgments about "truth" in the same way as many other, more directly empirical statements in science teaching, another feature is noted:

- Students have the opportunity to make judgments about the viability of models, theories, and explanations, including recourse to inspection of phenomena.

The Significance of Alternatives

Socialization toward intellectual independence concentrates on the capacity for making judgments. Thus it is important that students realize that they are choosing among alternatives when they encounter models, theories, and explanations. This happens in one sense every time a student meets an explanation in science class that clashes with his or her own "alternative conception" or "prior conception." Science teaching that presents models, theories, and explanations as *self-evident* essentially violates the student's capacity for judgment. Teaching that provides for intellectual independence would be characterized by acknowledging that alternatives are possible and that judgment among them is based on public criteria that the student can learn. But if alternatives are scorned, or disregarded, then judgments of this sort by students are preempted. This feature of intellectual independence would appear as follows:

- Alternative models, theories, and explanations are respected, and students are taught the grounds for making judgments among them.

Prerogatives in the Classroom

Any discussion of power distribution in the classroom requires that one distinguish prerogatives of students from those of the teacher. Based on what has been said about respecting students' autonomy and integrity, it should be clear that one important prerogative of students is the right (and ultimately the responsibility) to choose how they make sense of their own experience. When we speak of the intrusiveness of teaching, we refer in the first instance to the teacher's prerogative to intrude on the students' attention. Given the unequal power distribution inherent in teaching, more sinister things can happen. For example, the teacher can insist that students pretend to "know" something they don't know, or don't believe—in the sense of requiring that they reproduce the words on a test or in classroom discussion. Nevertheless, teaching cannot proceed if the teacher does not have the prerogative to intrude, and for this final feature of intellectual independence we need to look at how teaching that fosters it, can empower students to counteract the intrusion. We begin with an examination of two contrasting situations.

Imagine that Ken and Joe are chatting at a social gathering. Joe tells Ken that a mutual acquaintance was held in jail overnight for reckless driving. It would be most unexpected, even bizarre, if Joe then started a discussion to the effect that the usual procedure for verifying such a knowledge claim is to refer to empirical evidence—such as the records of the local police station. There is an equal power distribution in these kinds of conversations; Joe is under no obligation to invite Ken to examine the grounds for his assertion.

Now imagine a science classroom in which Ms. Brown declares that three factors will increase the speed with which the granules of a powdered substance dissolve in a liquid: the size of the granules, the temperature of the liquid, and the vigor and duration of agitating the mixture with a stirring rod. Given the unequal power distribution of the classroom, it is Ms. Brown's prerogative to assume that students get the idea that she intends for them to learn, or at least give serious consideration to what she has just said.

It would be neither unexpected nor bizarre if Ms. Brown began a discussion with her students about how these factors might be investigated to determine the validity of the claim about their effects. Indeed, it would be entirely appropriate if she and her students planned to undertake such an investigation to get the evidence they need. The manner in which student contributions to such a discussion are regarded and dealt with is critical. It can be spoken of as the respect shown for students' prerogatives. For instance, when a student offers a response to a question, it is that student's prerogative to have the response honored and treated with due regard to reason. A response rejected out of hand clearly violates this prerogative, for the teaching can be seen as failing to comply with other features of teaching that provide for intellectual independence, such as the provision of evidence or argument. If a student's contribution is unacceptable, it is similarly the student's prerogative to know why. The following two features of classroom discourse that socializes students toward intellectual independence express the foregoing points and bring this section to a close:

- Suggestions, questions, and objections of students are honored and are treated with regard to reason.
- Adequate reasons are given if a student's statement or response is unacceptable.

DEVELOPING INTELLECTUAL INDEPENDENCE IN THE CLASSROOM

The features of teaching identified in the previous section can be used as clues with which to characterize instances of teaching. All of them are associated with companion meanings that provide for students to be socialized generally in the direction of intellectual independence.

In this section two excerpts of science teaching are examined. They are brief, and the intention is to instantiate the features by demonstrating how ordinary classroom discourse can reveal them. Both teachers were interviewed; no pertinent information about supporting claims and similar matters had been provided to students in a lesson beforehand. Presentation of the excerpts is interrupted from time to time for analysis and commentary.

Teacher A

This first sample of teaching is taken from the first 5 minutes of a grade 10 science lesson that is an introduction to static electricity. The students apparently are expected to grasp, or at least reaffirm, the relationship between a condition of low humidity in a room and the occurrence of static electricity discharges as manifest in little sparks and shocks. Also, they are to explain why the discharges occur more in dry air than moist, in terms of an analogy with the speed of light through a less dense, compared with a more dense, medium—which they studied previously. The rich potential of the sample more than compensates for the errors in scientific meaning.

> TEACHER: At what time of the year will static electricity occur more often?
> AMIR: (Quietly) Summer.
> TEACHER: Diane? (No response) Pardon?
> DIANE: I don't know. Spring?
> LEELA: No.
> TEACHER: Mike?
> MIKE: In the wintertime.
> TEACHER: Okay. Jim?
> JIM: In the wintertime.

Canadian youngsters of this age (about 16) have a lot of first-hand experience with static electricity shocks and sparks. They have walked across the carpet in a heated room whose air is relatively dry and been "bitten" by a spark when the hand is just millimeters from a metal doorknob. Yet, in this interchange these students seem to be guessing. Possibly that is because they have not been asked about their experience, which is their personal *evidence*, but have been asked instead to address the question at the level of a conclusion, or knowledge claim, that is either *true* or *false*. That they are dependent on the teacher for this assessment is clear, so the teacher is reserving a great deal of power to himself. *No reasons* are forthcoming for the rejection of Diane's response or the acceptance of Mike's. However, the teacher calls for reasons after Jim offered the same answer as Mike.

> TEACHER: Do you know why?
> JIM: Because the air inside's drier.
> TEACHER: And what's that do—why does dry air help?
> JIM: Er, does it conduct more?
> TEACHER: Okay . . .

The teacher provides the judgment of *truth* about what Jim has said, but the *reasons* that would satisfy the requirements of the knowledge claim have to do with establishing a correlation of air conditions with static electricity manifestations. Once again, the students could have been asked about their *evidence* in that regard. The *explanation* by Jim about conduction, while it pertains to current electricity, has nothing to do with static electricity, but the students are not about to find that out.

> TEACHER: Okay. You have the same . . . the day we were talking about light, what is the medium for light to pass through? (Pause) Or what are some mediums that light can pass through? Wendy?

WENDY: Air, water, and glass.

TEACHER: Okay. Take any one of them—air, water, or glass—and that's a medium and light can pass through it. Electricity has to be able to pass through something too, and they can be *different* mediums. Now static electricity is just like light in air, and that's why in dry air it will pass through better than in, er . . . if the air is moist. All right. (No further discussion of conductivity in the lesson)

The teacher *provides an argument* in the form of an analogy ("static electricity is just like light in air"), but no provision is made for students to *judge its viability* in the case of static electricity (nothing further is said about it). Unfortunately, it is not valid scientific meaning (i.e., neither light nor electricity needs a medium, and the analogy confuses current and static electricity). The teacher withholds the *means for assessing its truth.*

In this short sample of teaching, these students are being socialized in the direction of intellectual dependence. The power distributed to the students is minimal: They are bidden to speak on occasion, but the *kinds of offerings* for which they are asked are trivial. Admittedly this is only a short few minutes in one lesson, but it illustrates clearly how the features of teaching with which we are concerned can be instantiated.

Teacher B

The second sample is also an introductory lesson on the topic of static electricity for a grade 10 science class. The teacher has just completed some standard demonstrations in which the effects of static electricity on pith balls, cork, string, and bits of paper have been observed by the students after a particular kind of rod has been rubbed with some cloth materials.

TEACHER: We've simply taken some (knocking the rod on a desk) . . . some type of ebonite material—it's got an organic base—and we rubbed it vigorously with things like wool and silk, and we noticed it has this effect on small, light objects. (Pause) Those are our observations—that it attracts them and then repels them. (Pause) Now there are our observations, we've organized them, what conclusions can we come to? Can we come to any definite conclusions? How will you explain it? What, what theory can we advance to explain what we see here? Scotty?

The teacher here summarizes the *evidence* that is before the students. The only point for which they do *not* have evidence is that the rod "has an organic base." The *power has been distributed to the students*, to conclude and explain.

SCOTTY: (Indistinct response)

TEACHER: It's somewhat mystifying, isn't it?

SCOTTY: Yeah. (Laughter)

TEACHER: Certainly, we've probably never observed any behavior like this before. (Pause) Richard, have you got any theories to explain this?

RICHARD: Well, maybe, um, just when you rubbed that rod with the cloth . . .

TEACHER: Uh huh . . .

RICHARD: . . . it attracts and then repels the thing. Um, it's . . .

TEACHER: Well that's our, that's our observation, yeah.

RICHARD: Oh.

The teacher has reminded Richard (and the class) that whatever explanation is advanced, it is to be consistent with these observations. Since the *evidence* is available to the students, they are in a position to make a *judgment about the viability of any explanation*. They are *being taught to use their power responsibly*.

TEACHER: That's what we've observed. But what theory can we advance to explain it? Is it because the thing is clean?

The student's *suggestion is honored* and is *treated with regard to reason*. That is, the teacher reaffirms that Richard is still talking about observations, and nudges him in the direction of shifting to an explanation. The teacher does not, however, *take the power away from the student*.

RICHARD: No.

TEACHER: Is it because it's now highly polished? These are the only two things we can observe from this experiment. John?

JOHN: Er, the friction makes it into a temporary magnet.

TEACHER: The friction makes it into a . . . ?

JOHN: Temporary magnet.

TEACHER: A magnet? Then it should attract metals, should it not? Do you think if we tried that with metals . . . ? I haven't got any small strips of metal. Here, let's see if I can get a scalpel blade or something. (Pause) Here's a razor blade. (Suspending the blade on a piece of thread) Just hang it there. Let's see if we attract this when we rub the rod.

In suggesting that John's explanation can be put to a test, the teacher is *making provision for students to judge the viability of the explanation* and is also teaching them *to use their power responsibly* by checking out the explanation. It would have accentuated John's use of his own power *if the teacher had asked John to make his own prediction*.

Teacher: Do you think we'll notice any difference here, because we know that the rod—whatever properties this rod has once it's been cleaned and polished with the wool particularly—it attracts the string . . . (the razor blade and string move) as it's doing there. (Repeats the demonstration) It would also seem to be attracting the metal as well. If we could isolate it a little more carefully you'd see the difference. Perhaps it is a temporary magnet. If that's our theory, how do we explain that it attracts things like pith balls which are made from the, the pith—the center of a woody stem—or bits of cork which are organic tissue from a woody stem, or little bits of paper which once again are light bits of organic material? (Lesson continues on the same manner)

Students observe that the razor blade and string can be seen to move. The teacher accepts John's explanation tentatively ("If that's our theory . . . "), which *leaves the power with the student*, but reminds the class *to use the power responsibly* by raising the issue as to how the theory can explain the attraction of organic materials, which are not affected by magnets. Provision is made for *students to make a judgment* about John's explanation.

These students are being socialized in the direction of intellectual independence. Their responses are honored; they are afforded power and opportunities to learn how to use it responsibly to judge the truth of knowledge claims and to retain control over their own explanations while grounding them in reasons and evidence. This sample of teaching stands in stark contrast to the previous one.

CONCLUDING REMARKS

In this chapter the distribution of power in science classrooms has been examined in a very specific way, namely, in terms of the provision teachers can make to teach students how to use their reasoning power in the service of assessing the truth and reasonableness of what they are being taught. The concept of intellectual independence has served in this venture as both an idealized, broad educational aim and a way to characterize the here-and-now intellectual climate of a science classroom. Features of teaching have been examined in terms of their general contribution to a climate that fosters intellectual independence or its inverse, intellectual dependence. The primary source for doing so is philosophical analysis of educational concepts.

The analysis of two brief segments of science teaching suggests two points to be made in closing. One has to do with the way science lesson planning is conceptualized; the second, with the "bridging" character of the concept of intellectual independence.

One of the least useful features of most lesson planning formats (not restricted to science lessons, of course) is the separation of objectives into separate categories such as cognitive (knowledge), affective (attitudes), and skill (process). This is perhaps a helpful device in teacher preparation programs, but there is a very real sense in which teachers are encouraged to think about these matters separately. Even in research on aims and objectives, as mentioned earlier, the habit persists. In such a separation, a cognitive objective might be (using the example of the mythical Ms. Brown) to have students learn that three factors affect rate of dissolving a powdered substance. The skill objective that coexists beside it might be that students are expected to practice controlled experimentation. The attitude objective might be that students are to grasp the importance of evidence in establishing the claims about the three factors.

What makes the separation unhelpful is that all three of those items need to go together in an organic whole, if the manner of the teaching is to provide for students to develop intellectual independence. That is, it is not the case that one "part" of the lesson is cognitive, one "part" is skill, and so forth. The cognitive part can be accomplished in the absence of the skill part only at the risk of sacrificing the very essence of intellectual independence: namely, the manner in which the reasonableness of the cognitive part is to be assessed. When the objectives are separated, they seem to be in competition. It becomes easy, as every teacher knows, to stress the "coverage" of the cognitive objective at the expense of the attitudes and skills. The side effect is the creeping shadow of authoritarianism.

That brings the chapter full circle to its title, which suggests that intellectual independence is a "potential link," or bridge, between science teaching and responsible citizenship. This is certainly not the first time this point has been made, but perhaps it can be made more clearly with the help of the analysis undertaken in this chapter. Anyone who spends very much time in science classrooms knows that Teacher A's lesson segment is much more likely to be seen than is Teacher B's, at least in secondary schools. Students spend many hours in classrooms like that of Teacher A, where they experience companion meanings that tell them, over and over, that their reasoning power is not adequate, or is inappropriate, to assess knowledge claims and explanations.[2] It does not matter that the authoritarianism is not deliberate. Whenever there is massive socialization toward intellectual dependence, how are students suddenly to become thoughtful, responsible citizens who habitually question and exercise their reasoning powers with respect to knowledge claims, explanations, and decisions? It is in giving serious consideration to that kind of question that the manner of teaching can be seen as a potential link between the here-and-now of the science classroom and the long-term value that democratic societies accord to responsible citizenship.

CHAPTER 9

Analyzing Discourse About Controversial Issues in the Science Classroom

ARTHUR N. GEDDIS

THIS CHAPTER DEVELOPS AND illustrates a conceptual framework for analyzing features of science classroom discourse within what Roberts has called the
Science, Technology, and Decisions curriculum emphasis (see Chapter 1 in this
volume). In a grade 10 classroom, the teacher has combined the scientific meaning of acid and base chemistry with a companion meaning developed from controversy over the sources of acid rain in the Canadian province of Ontario. I was
a participant observer in the classroom. The teacher and I discussed two lessons,
for which I had prepared verbatim transcriptions to accompany my notes about
the classroom events.

Because the focus is on controversy, the conceptual framework draws on a
view of reasoned debate that has at its core the need to justify one's own position
in a manner that takes contrary points of view into account. Such a stance is not
simply a matter of decorum. It is justified precisely because it requires of us a
reasoned examination of the reasons and evidence pertinent to the issues in dispute. This sort of view Green (1968) terms an *enabling belief* because of the manner
in which it enables critical discourse to proceed.

I do not want to imply that attention to the epistemological issues of reasons
and evidence is sufficient for dealing with controversy. Obviously, other concerns
related to the affective tone of the classroom are also of central importance. As Fine
(1993) points out, it is important to construct an atmosphere of relative trust and
safety if students are to be able to deal with the heated and difficult discussions that
emotionally charged social and political issues engender. In what follows I will
assume such an atmosphere, hoping in any event, along with Fine, that "students
are more resilient and able to handle disagreement than is often believed" (p. 412).

The chapter illustrates how the sophistication of classroom discourse about controversial issues can be increased by explicit attention to (1) the defensibility of more than one position, and (2) the relationship between protagonists' interests and the positions they adopt. Such a strategy helps address two pitfalls that may subvert the efforts of teachers to develop decision-making skills in their students: (1) ignoring the limitations of science and technology, and (2) adopting a narrow view of rationality in decision making, which gives a low priority to "the values and ideologies that guide . . . rational decisions" (Aikenhead, 1985, p. 470).

I begin the chapter with a clarification of what is intended by "*quality* of classroom discourse" with regard to controversial social issues. This is a normative matter, of course. What counts as quality in the discourse will have to be stipulated, and once this has been done it will define for my purposes the substance of the companion meaning that is of interest here. This stipulation will draw heavily on issues of knowledge and control and on the way power is distributed in the classroom (cf. Munby & Roberts, Chapter 8 in this volume). Next I describe a conceptual framework based on the companion meaning and outline the manner in which the items of the framework can help to understand teaching episodes in which a controversial issue is debated. The final portion of the chapter immerses the reader in the interactions of a grade 10 science class discussing acid rain and the discussions between me and their teacher.

QUALITY OF CLASSROOM DISCOURSE

The manner in which controversial issues are handled in school programs has long been the concern of social studies education. Despite its development 2 decades ago, the Canadian Public Issues Project (Bourne & Eisenberg, 1978) still appeals to me on the basis of its principles and substance. The authors reject attempts to foist ethical positions on students as violations of "the very human autonomy upon which ethics is based" (p. 11). Since Socrates's time, the need to subject traditional ethical positions to rational criticism has been the driving force behind ethical inquiry. The mere adoption of ethical conduct has been rejected as insufficient. Individuals need to understand the rational basis for their action, and for this to occur they have to work their own way through issues "until they arrive at a consistent, acceptable position which can be defended persuasively and which takes other points of view into consideration" (p. 11).

Intellectual Independence as a Goal

When students learn the norms, skills, and background knowledge to grasp the rational basis for decisions and actions, they are learning to be "intellectually independent" *of their teacher as an authority figure*. Munby (1973) stipulated such a meaning for intellectual independence as a pedagogical construct, in the context of teaching about knowledge claims within science. Teaching that honors such an aim

> make[s] provision for pupils to have the resources necessary for judging the truth of knowledge claims independently of others. Thus, an individual judging the truth of a claim on the basis of all assumptions, evidence and arguments necessary for the judgement is exercising intellectual independence. (p. 12)[1]

The Bourne and Eisenberg approach is precisely parallel, when the context is having students develop intellectual independence about debating controversial issues.

How Power Is Distributed in the Classroom

By contrast to the ideals expressed by Munby and by Bourne and Eisenberg, in two classic studies we find that it is the teacher rather than the students who gets to practice doing the thinking required to develop intellectual independence when judging scientific knowledge claims. In a study of 50 Australian secondary classrooms, Young (1980) noted that the teachers exercised an almost complete monopoly on higher-order intellectual acts. Teachers did almost all of the generalizing, specifying, hypothesis testing, and the like. Edwards's (1980) examination of a number of British classrooms revealed, similarly, that in those classrooms students were not "likely to be socialised into ways of constructing future knowledge for themselves" (p. 244).

I want to construe this as a matter of how power is distributed in the classroom: whether students are encouraged (or allowed) to engage in higher-order thinking has a direct bearing on the possibility that they will learn to become intellectually independent of their teachers. Of more particular concern regarding the companion meaning associated with defensible decisions is my sense that many science teachers are not taught the necessary skills to deal with situations in which scientific knowledge informs practical decision making. (Schwab, 1974, has pointed this out in striking terms.) That is, science teachers—even those who are conscientious in articulating the basis for their scientific knowledge claims—often have not been taught to teach in a manner that respects the need for evidence and rational argument when discussing issues such as acid rain, the extinction of species, or the fuel crisis. I want to suggest that teachers who lack such background are probably prone to hold on to the power of the classroom, not distribute it.

The distribution of power in the classroom is unquestionably affected by the fact that one adult is responsible for directing the learning of 30 to 40 students. Unfortunately, the need to maintain classroom discipline can militate against teachers' efforts to promote the development of intellectual independence. This is particularly noticeable in situations where teachers control students with power moves that masquerade as moves to validate knowledge claims. Such situations obscure the epistemological moves required to do the validating and hence undermine efforts to promote intellectual independence. In an earlier work (Geddis, 1988), I developed a number of perspectives on the concept of knowledge and the manner in which power is employed in the classroom, in the context of teaching scientific meaning. These perspectives are now modified as a means of illuminating problems associated with teaching about controversial issues in the science classroom. Concepts focused on issues of knowledge and control seem to be most relevant. In order to develop a conceptual framework for analyzing teaching, I have grouped these into three clusters dealing with (1) *knowledge as ideology*, (2) *the ideology of teaching*, and (3) *the intellectual transparency of teaching*.

THE CONCEPTUAL FRAMEWORK

Knowledge as Ideology

The *knowledge as ideology* cluster is directed at uncovering the interests that may underlie the contexts of knowing and teaching. Habermas (1971) has argued persuasively against the positivist's claim that knowledge is morally and politically neutral. Even if one does not completely accept Habermas's specific identification of knowledge and human interests, it is clear that his principle holds: Knowledge claims are indeed used ideologically. This points to a need to consider the interests underlying knowledge claims and the teaching of them, in light of their congruence with the knowledge and interests of students. When dealing with controversial issues, it is centrally important to uncover how particular knowledge claims can serve the interests of different claimants. If students are to be able to take other points of view into account in developing their own positions on an issue, they need to learn how to unravel the interplay of interests that underlie these other points of view.

For the conceptual framework, this cluster of concepts generates three questions:

- Whose knowledge is this, and whose interests might it serve?
- How is it in these students' interest to learn this?
- Does the teaching ignore or deny "knowledge" the students already have?

Ideology of Teaching

The *ideology of teaching* cluster consists of three dimensions intimately connected with the concept of knowledge itself. The *authority dimension* is taken from Russell

(1983), who based it on Peters (1967); it deals with the kind of authority used to substantiate knowledge claims. At one end of this dimension is what Russell calls traditional authority, which teachers have by virtue of their position in an institutional hierarchy. Thus, teachers can (and often do) "get away with" *not* giving reasons and evidence for knowledge claims, and students generally accept what teachers say without demanding further justification. At the other end of the dimension is rational authority, which teachers employ when they *do* supply reasons and evidence for knowledge claims. Rational authority derives its force from the teacher's expertise in the discipline being taught. When teachers employ rational authority, they make provision for students to "have good reasons" for believing knowledge claims. It is through the use of rational authority that teachers provide for the development of intellectual independence.

The *argument dimension* of the ideology of teaching relates to the concept of teaching itself, and in particular to Green's (1968) distinction between instruction and indoctrination. Here the central idea is that of a conversation of instruction—in which reasons are given and arguments advanced, not just to persuade but rather, in a spirit of inquiry, to learn. As Scheffler (1965a) puts it, instruction relies on such a conversation in which the teacher submits "his own judgement to the critical scrutiny and evaluation of the student" (p. 12). In indoctrination, on the other hand, the main concern is with the transmission of "knowledge." Arguments and evidence are used not in a spirit of inquiry, but to convince students of the "truth." The way in which argument is used—whether *to persuade* or *to inquire*—is an important dimension for reflecting on the provision made for intellectual independence in teaching.

The *view of reality dimension* addresses the degree of skepticism with which a view of reality is held. At one end of the continuum is the position of the "naive realist," for whom thinking is basically "a passive activity involving the reconstruction of the order of things as they basically are" (Nadeau & Désautels, 1984, p. 17). Reality is singular and fixed, in this view, and our task is to apprehend it objectively. At the other end of the continuum is the position that views of reality are constructed by individuals with particular interests and intentions: Knowledge is always knowledge from a particular social and historical perspective. Because views of reality are by their very nature limited, in this view, our task is not to determine "how we might arrive at a non-perspectivistic picture [of reality] but how, by juxtaposing the various points of view, each perspective may be recognized as such and thereby a new level of objectivity attained" (Mannheim, 1936, pp. 296–297). From this position, the advantages and disadvantages of different views of reality can be considered, and the strength of one can be used to supplement the weakness of another. However, when we see only *one fixed view of reality*, the possibility of such critical scrutiny is pre-empted. When considering controversial issues in the classroom, it is important to maintain the critical stance made possible by accepting *multiple perspectives on reality*.

Thus, the ideology of teaching cluster contributes to the conceptual framework under development the following questions about the dimensions along which teaching can be characterized:

- What kind of authority does the teaching project?

  TRADITIONAL .... RATIONAL

- What is the purpose of the argument(s) being made?

  TO PERSUADE .... TO INQUIRE

- What view of reality does the discussion project?

  SINGLE .... MULTIPLE
  FIXED .... CHANGEABLE

Intellectual Transparency of Teaching

Rounding out the conceptualization of knowledge and control is a third cluster of concepts, which I have called the *intellectual transparency of teaching.* "Transparency" here refers to the provision made by a teacher for students to "see" two kinds of features: epistemological and pedagogical.

The *epistemological features* dimension is intimately related to both the authority and argument dimensions identified above. However, it provides its own distinct focus, which has proven valuable in uncovering problems associated with making provision for intellectual independence. Kilbourn (1982) conceptualized this dimension as having epistemological "flatness" and "richness" at its extremes. In a lesson that is epistemologically flat, such statement types as observations, inferences, theories, speculations, and judgments all have the same status because no context is provided to show how they go together epistemologically. (Everything is a "fact," and is the same kind of "fact.") The important issue for me is that the more explicit the teacher is about epistemological features, the better the provision for intellectual independence.

The *pedagogical features* dimension has to do with the form, sequence, intent, and other aspects of the instruction. If students' intellectual integrity is to be respected, they need to know the function of particular components of the lesson and the way in which the teacher sees them fitting together to accomplish his or her aims. Presumably, students are in a better position to know about these features if the teacher makes them explicit. Yet, Young (1980) has noted that in many classrooms students often have little idea either of what will happen next or of the intended function of what they are doing presently. Such a situation leaves them dependent on the teacher and potentially decreases the meaningfulness of what they are learning—encouraging the learning of disparate "facts" and discouraging the overall search for integration and coherence. Similarly, in a comparison of an experienced science teacher's lesson to the lessons of two novice science teachers, MacDonald (1995) found that "a prominent feature of the experienced teacher's lesson [was] a sense of plot or drama in the sequence of events" (p. 185). He coined the term "pedagogical suspense" (p. 185) to capture the sense that students are provided with a reason to be involved with the lesson. The two novice teachers' lessons, on the other hand, were missing any such feature, being "strongly characterized by simple, linear 'and then, and then' sequencing, the only point of which seems to be to push through and 'unfold' the subject matter topics" (p. 186). Clearly, students would have no idea about what was coming next in the "and then, and then" sequence, even if they knew the topic that was coming.

Kilbourn and Roberts (1984) conceptualized this dimension of teaching as having pedagogical "flatness" at one extreme and "richness" at the other. For my purposes, that distinction is operationalized by considering the extent to which the teacher is explicit about his or her pedagogical moves.

Here, then, are the two questions that this cluster of concepts suggests for the conceptual framework:

- How transparent are the epistemological features of the lesson?

  IMPLICIT .... EXPLICIT

- How transparent are the pedagogical features of the lesson?

  IMPLICIT .... EXPLICIT

Communicating About Reasons, Control, and Power

In this section I have argued that certain features of teaching distinguish "high-quality" classroom discourse, when science teachers teach students to debate and discuss controversial issues. There are two noticeable aspects of the questions and dimensions of this conceptual framework and their articulation of companion meanings about knowledge and control. One is that explicitness is favored over implicitness, when it comes to communicating about epistemological and pedagogical features of a lesson. The other is that high-quality discourse is associated with such matters as giving reasons, taking another person's viewpoint into consideration, acknowledging that claims have interests behind them, and recognizing multiple realities. Thus, high-quality discourse is associated with students' intellectual independence from the teacher's authority, by virtue of the fact that students are taught how to do for themselves many of the "power-ful" actions teachers have at their command (e.g., attaching reasons and evidence to knowledge claims, anticipating pedagogical moves, and sensing where the other is coming from in the discourse). It is in that sense that power is distributed in the classroom, rather than being controlled by the teacher.

So the questions and dimensions that make up the conceptual framework constitute a scheme for analyzing teaching in science lessons that incorporate controversial issues. In the following section, we are immersed in the complex reality of two lessons. The conceptual framework was the basis for discussion about the lessons between me and the teacher, Tom Campbell (a pseudonym). We used the framework deliberately to analyze his first lesson on the topic of acid rain and to plan his second. My comments on the lessons are intended to exemplify the components of the framework, as they are illustrated by classroom events.

HOW IT LOOKS IN THE CLASSROOM

Tom Campbell and I had worked together for a long time, so we were both aware of the general teaching context at his school. Tom filled me in on details about this group of students and how his teaching of them had proceeded to this point. We planned to tape-record one lesson—which I would then transcribe so that we could analyze it individually before discussing it—and plan for a second lesson that also would be tape-recorded, transcribed, analyzed, and discussed.

Six girls and 15 boys made up Tom's grade 10 science class. We decided to test the conceptual framework on two lessons that occurred near the end of a unit on chemical change, at a point where students were expected to incorporate the scientific meaning of acid and base chemistry into understanding the nature of acid rain, the problems it poses for the environment, and the debate about who or what is responsible for it.

What Happened in Lesson I

Analysis of the transcription of Lesson I revealed that Tom had made a number of factual claims based solely on his traditional authority—that is, without providing reasons or evidence. What struck me forcefully was a claim he made not once, but twice, which was quite central to the lesson: "The majority of the acid rain falling in Ontario originated from the power plants in the Ohio Valley." At that time, students were being exposed almost daily to media reports in which this claim was disputed by the American government. Tom did not mention these, nor did he attempt to employ rational authority by engaging students in discussion of what would be needed to substantiate or refute such a claim. By presenting the claim as established "fact," Tom had effectively preempted critical scrutiny by the students.

The following points about this controversial knowledge claim surfaced for me, through the view afforded by the conceptual framework I had been working on:

- The "Canadian viewpoint" would somehow have to take account of the reasons behind the "American government viewpoint"—and vice versa. That is, there must be some explanation for the conflict.
- Students needed to understand how the protagonists argued their cases. This was a golden opportunity to teach them how to see the possibility of a number of legitimate perspectives on an issue and to examine the bases for competing perspectives.
- What appeared to be a fairly complicated, multifaceted issue had been presented in the classroom as a simple, single-cause event. Single, fixed reality needed to be replaced by multiple, changing reality.
- A fruitful place to look for the reasons behind the conflict in the two claims might well be to ask, "Whose knowledge is this, and whose interests might it serve?"
- Overall, there was a sense that Tom was concerned primarily with persuading students rather than inquiring into the claim itself.

Our Discussion of Lesson I

During our discussion, it was Tom who drew attention to the fact that he had used traditional authority in making the claim linking acid rain in Ontario to power plants in the Ohio Valley. He mentioned that a filmstrip he had shown the day after Lesson I repeated the claim and claimed as well that "governments are very hesitant to act until they have full direct scientific knowledge." Both statements were based simply on traditional authority; the latter was depicted as a position taken by the American government. We discussed the apparent contradiction between the two claims and I suggested we consider them in terms of the self-interests of the groups making them. Tom seemed intrigued by the idea, but less than convinced of the viability of the teaching strategy it would require. (In what follows, "Art" refers to me.)

> ART: This is where I wondered if the concept of "Whose knowledge is this?" is perhaps useful to look at. Because, while there are some people claiming one thing . . . for example, that the pollution is coming from the Ohio Valley, . . . there appear to be people who would disagree.
>
> TOM: Yeah, but it is interesting. "Whose knowledge is this?" opens up a whole new thing that is very interesting for the kids to look at. . . . Like, who's claiming what, and what is their basis for making that claim. But wow, to try and get that information [across]. Especially for a class like this, to . . . understand each person's position, and the basis for that claim. Wow.

ART: Well, I mean if we do identify claims like that, as claims that some groups would make and others would not, then are you saying . . . that this is the stance that should be taken with them?

TOM: It would be a very good stance to take. Uh, it would be very difficult to do though, very difficult to pull off because you would have to get the information: What is the Acid Rain Coalition saying? What do the spokesmen for those hydro plants say? What is the basis for their position? To get that information in a form that can be presented and understood by the kids would be very difficult.

Following this, Tom and I tried to unpack what might be required to substantiate the claim that the American power plants were responsible for Canadian acid rain. We quickly gave up, however, when it became apparent that neither of us was familiar enough with the relevant research. Later investigation revealed that at that point in time there was no complete causal mechanism linking the gaseous pollutants from the Ohio Valley with the environmental damage observed in Canada (Henry, 1984, p. 12).

The final outcome of our discussion was that Tom decided to teach a second lesson that would attempt to present both the Canadian and American viewpoints on this acid rain controversy, so that his students might better be able to arrive at their own positions.

Multiple Perspectives on a Controversy: Lesson II

In Lesson II Tom wanted to present both "the Canadian viewpoint" and "the American government viewpoint" about acid rain in Ontario, in such a manner that students would be able to see that both positions could be held by reasonable people. He distributed an article from the weekend paper (Miller, 1984), in which William Ruckelshaus of the U.S. Environmental Protection Agency pointed out that the U.S. Clean Air Act of 1970–71 had brought about significant reductions in emissions from both automobiles and coal-burning power plants. In the same article Ruckelshaus repeated American claims that "scientists still do not know what causes the problem," and reiterated the U.S. Administration's resistance to taking any immediate action.

Tom began class discussion by directing student attention to the main points made in the article. After students noted the more stringent U.S. control standards for automobile exhaust emissions, he questioned them further on why these standards had been enacted. By connecting more stringent standards to the smog problem that plagued Los Angeles, he was able to point out the interests behind the knowledge and action, namely, American concern with an American problem.

Partway into the lesson, Tom began to set up the tension between the American view, as expressed by Ruckelshaus, and what I have been calling the Canadian view, as expressed both in the film strip and in some articles the students had read. In the discussion that followed, Tom continued to press the issue of how the two protagonists could hold such divergent views and to challenge students to explain how the Americans could continue to claim that they didn't know the cause of acid rain. In my analysis of the student responses to his challenge, I was able to identify three categories of response:

R1. The Americans are wrong, or stupid.

R2. The Americans are just stalling to avoid the cost of paying for the damage they've caused.

R3. Evidence is never totally conclusive, and because the Americans' cost of further restricting sulfur dioxide emissions is extremely high, they quite reasonably want a higher degree of certainty than Canadians do.

These three classes of response display an increasing acceptance of both multiple realities and the effect of self-interest on knowledge claims. R1 reflects a very rigid view of a single, fixed reality. As Fred expressed it (below), the Americans must be "morons." This stance is almost inevitable for someone who "knows" that there is a single cause of acid rain. After all, if the emissions from the Ohio Valley power plants "cause" acid rain, then Ruckelshaus has to be wrong or stupid to claim otherwise.

In response to this extreme view, Tom tried to make room for a more sophisticated perspective by pointing out that both sides in the dispute had access to the same scientific studies. He continued to stress this point while implying that there must be some reasonable explanation for the divergence of the two views. R2—the reflection of selfish self-interest—also embodies the assumption of a single, fixed cause of acid rain. It does, however, widen the context from a singularly theoretical concern with *cause*, to the broader practical concerns of remedying the problem. This stance is taken by both Pam and Fred at different points in the discussion. (The numbers on the speeches are for convenient reference only; all student names are pseudonyms.)

1 PAM: . . . or they're just trying to delay it so they won't have to bother with it.

2 FRED: He's a moron. He don't want to bother doing anything. He's just spilling out these big words . . . ah, yeah, yeah, yeah, for sure like next year.

Category R3—acceptance of legitimate perspectives on the problem—seemed to start to emerge with Bill's response in interchange 3.

3 BILL: It's like there are two different stories—the Canadians say it's from the States, and the States' guys say that you don't know where it's coming from.

4   Tom: But . . . how do they get those two different conclusions based on
           the same observations?
5   Bill: They're two different countries . . .

Tom countered this with a statement that appears to reflect a fairly extreme view
of the existence of a single, fixed reality.

6   Tom: But they're scientists, and scientists should be people who look at
           the facts rather than look at the . . . you know, other things. They
           should be basing it on the facts.

Here, Tom implies that facts are unproblematic—uninfluenced by interests
or theoretical stance. From such a perspective, the scientist apprehends the facts
directly and simply reconstructs reality as it basically is.

In contrast to Tom's stance in interchange 6, the discussion that followed
seemed to reflect a determined effort by Karen to search out a broad perspective
that could account for more of the relevant factors.

7   Karen: Sir, the people in the United States, they don't want to give the
            impression that they're the ones who make the acid rain. And they
            give the Canadians . . .
8   Barb: They're lying.
9   Tom: Okay, but . . . yeah, I agree, there's a lot of pressure to do that. But
           how can they claim that they don't know where it comes from? How
           can they claim that?
10   Karen: They don't even know . . . well, they do know, but it . . .
11   Tom: Listen . . . all right, keep going. No, no . . . keep going, you're on
           the right track.
12   Karen: Okay, there's the United States, they know that they are making
            it, right? And the Canadians know that too, but they are just saying
            that they're not because . . .
13   Tom: Are they lying?
14   Karen: Probably. I think so. Well, not really, they're not lying, they're
            just trying to cover up until they really know what . . . what acid rain
            is really about, and then they can do something.

This interchange displayed a general shift in Karen's position from R2 to R3.
Up to interchange 12, she seemed to be maintaining that the United States was
primarily attempting to stall for time, even though the Americans know that they
are the main cause of the Canadian acid rain. In interchange 14, however, she appeared to reappraise her view of American moral culpability and to take the stance
that the U.S. position was legitimate. Interchange 11 displays a rather incongruous

use of traditional authority by Tom. In this interchange—where Karen appeared to be attempting to independently come to grips with the issue of the morality of the U.S. position—the bestowal of Tom's approval seemed at the very least to be condescending.

At this point in the lesson, Tom moved to a short discussion apparently aimed at bringing out the ideas that scientific knowledge is never completely certain and that this degree of uncertainty needs to be considered when deciding how to act. He reminded the students of their study of Sabine's discovery of the oral polio vaccine, during which they had had to consider the quandary they would have been in, had they been asked to be Sabine's first human subjects. Tom used this example to point out that the number of experiments supporting a particular scientific fact establishes our degree of confidence in it, and that different degrees of confidence may be required to justify different courses of action. To some extent here, the epistemology interacts with the interests of the stakeholders. The cost to the Americans of drastic cutbacks in sulfur oxide emissions would be considerable, and so they, quite legitimately, would demand a high degree of certainty before acting. The cost to Canadians is considerably less, and they stand to gain more if the claim is correct. Consequently, Canadians would be satisfied with a lower degree of certainty before demanding action from their American neighbors.

15   TOM: I know, but go back to the Americans. You're right. Now, if I'm a Canadian and I look at the observations and I say, "Okay, good enough for me . . . it's coming from the States, it's coming from sulfur." Why does the guy in the States say, "Hey, that's not good enough"?
16   BOB: They don't want to get screwed up.
17   PETER: Cause we're going to shut down all their plants.

Tom continued with a discussion of the way in which the interests of various groups affect the degree of corroboration considered necessary—that is, how interests affect what is to be accepted as knowledge. He used the article to point out that the same conflict in interests existed between New Englanders and midwesterners in the United States, resulting in similarly conflicting stances on acid rain. (The primary difference is that New Englanders were concerned with the impact of acid rain on forests more than on lakes, because most of their lakes are buffered effectively by limestone.)

Comments: Lesson II and the Conceptual Framework

The classroom discourse in Tom's second lesson certainly exhibits a more refined sense of what it means to debate controversial issues than did Lesson I. I was especially impressed with students' movement in the direction of rationally defending a position with arguments that take other points of view into consideration. Tom made effective use of the understanding of companion meanings about knowledge and control provided by the conceptual framework. He assisted students to identify the manner in which the interests of the protagonists could be seen to influence both their knowledge claims and the degree of certainty they demanded before taking action. The *view of reality* dimension was particularly helpful in uncovering a general progression of student responses from a single, fixed view of the controversy to a multifaceted, more flexible perspective.

In using this example to illustrate the conceptual framework, I've assumed that the "cause" of acid rain is indeed controversial. At some point in the future this may cease to be the case, and a single perspective would then be justified. The very nature of a controversial issue, however, is that more than one defensible position can be taken about it. That certainly is illustrated by this situation at the time it occurred.

The first two clusters of concepts (*knowledge as ideology* and *the ideology of teaching*) were most illuminating in this look at Tom's classroom. Older students with greater explicit knowledge of the manner in which claims can be supported might be encouraged to go a step further. They might consider the epistemological features of the arguments of each of the protagonists and the manner in which individual interests can influence the choice of epistemologies. A provocative example of this sort of connection can be found in the reluctance of tobacco companies to take seriously the mounting correlational evidence for a link between smoking and lung cancer, given the absence of a causal mechanism. The industry's use of a mechanistic causal epistemology in the debate contrasts sharply with the public health community's use of a pragmatic epistemology.

One final comment about the conceptual framework has to do with the pedagogical features of the lesson. It is interesting that the contrast between "Canadian" and "American" viewpoints created "pedagogical suspense" (MacDonald, 1995, p. 185), but *only* in light of the need to explain the difference. That, in turn, was prompted by Tom's attention to the matter we discussed, namely, trying to formulate a reasonable account of the self-interests behind the opposing points of view. Without that, the interchange would have been pedagogically flat because of the abundant opportunities for R1-type assertions.

CONCLUDING REMARKS

If a selected companion meaning is taken seriously as part of science curriculum, attention must be paid to its substance and to teaching it well (Roberts, 1995a). There is a subtle combination of explicit and implicit communication in the development of any companion meaning. The discussion of science-related controversial issues can be particularly tricky because students already have a significant amount of untutored experience with controversy and with how to "settle" it. Their habits of thought and argumentation are influenced by all manner of models of confrontation, destruction of one's opponent, sarcasm, and degeneration into a chaotic volley of R1- and R2-type statements of the sort that emerged initially in Tom's classroom.

It is such a daunting task to teach students to deal rationally with controversial issues in a science course that it is tempting to off-load the responsibility onto social studies. And yet, the very close conceptual connection between the scientific meaning and the companion meaning, in the case of acid rain, makes it very plausible to address the controversy in a science classroom. One of the most problematic aspects for science teachers, as I have discussed in general terms elsewhere (Geddis, 1996), is the need to learn new "subject matter." Tom and I found this to be a significant barrier for both of us, in our initial discussion.

Despite the problems, it is difficult to conceive of education in a democracy without teaching students to deal rationally with controversy. Indeed, as Fine (1993) puts it, "one cannot possibly avoid bringing into the classroom issues over which society is still divided because students themselves are well aware of these issues and hungry to discuss them with their peers" (p. 432). It may be that if we ignore such issues in science education, we confirm in the minds of many students the irrelevance of science to the increasingly complex real world in which they find themselves. Willinsky suggests as much about the irrelevance of biology teaching to students' lived experiences of racial tension (Chapter 6 in this volume). Or perhaps we implicitly condone the confrontational and other irrational means of "settling" controversy about which students are taught so effectively by television and on the street.

Controversial issues, however, bring both ambiguity and conflict with them. By assisting students to engage social, moral, and political issues, we help them come to grips with both ambiguity and conflict,

> not by denying conflict through positing an unproblematized, homogeneous ideal, but by helping students to take well-thought-out stands and to listen carefully to each other. Hopefully, by doing so they will learn to tolerate more fully the conflicts they will inevitably encounter in the world beyond the classroom. (Fine, 1993, p. 433)

It is to be hoped as well that they will learn to appreciate the role that science can play in resolving these conflicts.

PART III

Behind the Scenes

As suggested by the title, the four chapters in Part III focus on matters that are in the background of science curriculum. Graham Orpwood addresses in Chapter 10 the matter of how "science curriculum talk" can be understood, with a view to seeing options as considerations for curriculum planners to weigh and deliberate over. The alternative, which is very common, is to see such options as constructivism, or science-technology-society, or history and philosophy of science, as general and universal solutions to what their proponents perceive to be generally and universally wrong with science education. On a similar note, Rodger Bybee examines in Chapter 11 another perceived general and universal solution to the problems of science education, namely, "curriculum standards." He points out how these can be used as a basis for an increased professionalization of curriculum design rather than, for example, as a simplistic expression of an assessment basis for purposes of global comparisons.

There are many other aspects of school science curriculum that go on behind the scenes also. In Chapter 12, Joan Solomon presents some results from a very interesting study of science curricula in Europe. She makes a number of links to cultural features of different countries and identifies several companion meanings that are of interest because they seem to occur in many settings. Peter Fensham, in Chapter 13, explores the power politics of science curriculum debate, which is somewhat different from the analysis undertaken by Orpwood in Chapter 10. In particular, the process of legitimating and marginalizing different companion meanings for school science—in which academic scientists usually have a disproportionate amount of influence—is illustrated with three Australian case stories.

The Logic of Advice and Deliberation: Making Sense of Science Curriculum Talk

GRAHAM ORPWOOD

EDUCATION IN SCIENCE BY DEFINITION comprises the systematic acquisition of knowledge and skills drawn from the domain of science—in the language of this volume's authors, "scientific meanings." In addition, we have argued here, an education in science consists of an equally systematic acquisition of other knowledge, skills, and values that have been called "companion meanings" because of the close contextual relationship they hold to the scientific content. Furthermore, while the science content of an education is usually explicit and evident, the companion communications are often hidden or implicit, requiring sophisticated analyses if they are to be revealed.

Other authors in this volume have discussed the implications for students of the presence or absence of particular sets of companion meanings within a science curriculum. All of these analyses start from the principle that education is a moral enterprise, whose components, whether curricular or instructional, must be defensible in terms that are acceptable in a democratic society committed to equity and excellence for all. Östman and Roberts (1994), for example, have pointed out that "companion meanings are objects of choice in science curriculum policy development just as surely as science subject matter content topics are" (p. 3). Accordingly, this chapter turns from the context of the classroom and the discourse of the science curriculum itself to the context of curriculum policy development and discourse *about* science education—in particular, to an examination of arguments that bear on the inclusion of companion meanings.

Like companion meanings themselves, these arguments are often buried deep in other discourse, take forms that are not readily identifiable, and resist easy analysis or appraisal. However, if teachers and others responsible for the choice of companion meanings in science are to defend these decisions, then they must be able to think systematically about not only the discourse *of* science curriculum and instruction but also the discourse *about* science curriculum and instruction, a discourse I call here "science curriculum talk."

In this chapter I intend to demonstrate that there is a systematic logic to science curriculum talk that permits its analysis and critical appraisal; it follows that there can be a defensible basis for systematic improvement of the quality of curriculum debate and deliberation. This basis in logic contrasts with the all-too-common characterizations of science curriculum talk that close off analysis and discussion almost before they can begin. Three such frameworks (I hesitate to use the word *conceptual*, as they all represent escapes from serious conceptualization) come readily to mind:

- Bland relativism—whatever you are comfortable with
- Raw empiricism—whatever works in my classroom
- Mere politics—it all depends on who wants it

My argument is (1) that deliberating over the science curriculum and its companion meanings need not be left just to backroom power plays or individual matters of opinion; (2) that, like any area of politics, it can be done well or badly; and (3) that the interests of defensible science programs in a democratic society require that such deliberation be done as carefully and as well as possible.

First, however, I wish to distinguish this line of inquiry from another important and growing area of research focused on what often is referred to as "teacher knowledge." In a recent review of research in this field, Fenstermacher (1994) discusses epistemological issues surrounding teachers' knowledge claims and researchers' inferences about teachers' knowledge. At the heart of this work is the concern with clarifying the complex relationship between teachers' actions in classrooms and their knowledge, either propositional or practical. Such a clarification is of critical importance to the task of teacher education.

My own research interests have focused less on this relatively private knowledge and action of individual teachers concerning what takes place in their own classrooms and more on the relatively public discourse that takes place when a group of educational stakeholders discuss what ought to take place in classrooms. Thus, in what follows, "science curriculum talk" refers to discourse among varieties of people about the goals and content of the science curriculum, discourse that is intended to influence the future directions of science teaching, rather than personal reflections on past and present experience.

EXAMPLES OF SCIENCE CURRICULUM TALK

Science curriculum talk comes in a variety of forms that sometimes mask the logical and political character of the utterances. Three examples can serve to illustrate some of this variety: the first, a hypothetical but (I believe) plausible situation faced by a teacher new to a school, and the second and third, drawn from actual instances of public debate over companion meanings in the science curriculum.

Example A: Advice to a New Teacher

Imagine the following statement being communicated to an inexperienced teacher, new to a school:

> You should teach this science topic so that students understand how it affects their own community.

This statement can be analyzed logically, so that we can assist the teacher to understand what it means from a syntactical perspective. But consider the differences between the statement being uttered by, say, a textbook salesperson (who just happens to have a book that links science topics to community applications), the school principal (who is evaluating the work of this new teacher for conformity to official program policy), a parent (whose child is bored with science and who is threatening to complain), a friendly university professor (who is encouraging teachers to incorporate different curriculum emphases into their teaching, an idea the new teacher is intrigued by), and a helpful colleague (who has been asked by the young teacher for advice on coping with a difficult class). In these different political lights, the same statement takes on completely different hues.

In reality, of course, situations like these are much more complex in that these several "advisors" may all be offering different and possibly conflicting advice. The companion meanings urged by one may be at odds with the companion meanings another favors. The consequences of accepting one person's advice may be costly if it means that another's is ignored, and so on. What the teacher needs to think about is both the logical basis for each piece of advice and the political context in which the advice is given. This tension between logical and political force is the subtext throughout this chapter as we consider science curriculum talk.

Example B: Science Curriculum Policy Making in Alberta

Another example, this time drawn from the more public arena of science curriculum policy making in a Canadian province, illustrates this tension once again. In Alberta a few years ago, arguments hit the newspapers over a proposal to develop a new sequence of integrated science courses at the senior high school level. Alberta Education, the provincial ministry of education, proposed a common integrated course (Science 10) for all grade 10 students, replacing three separate science courses that had been taught at that level. Two further integrated courses in grades 11 and 12 (Science 20 and 30) were added to provide an alternative for students not interested in taking specialist courses in biology, chemistry, and physics in those grades. A pilot version of the proposed courses was issued for review. (For a detailed account of the program development, the reader may refer to Panwar & Hoddinott, 1995.)

The new courses downplayed the traditional emphasis on science content to allow development of a set of companion meanings that stressed the relationship of both science and technology to Alberta's changing economic orientation; to agriculture, oil, and gas; and to medical research. The goal of the new program was the creation of a more scientifically literate society, based partly on Alberta's reading of the (then) recently published report of the Science Council of Canada (1984), which urged educators to pay greater attention to science, technology, and society (STS). In many respects, Alberta Education took the report more seriously and acted more rapidly than did other provinces.

However, the price of this departure from tradition was high. Critics of the new program from both universities and high schools characterized the new courses as representing a "dumbing down" of high school education (MacDonald & Byfield, 1989, p. 28). The Minister of Education, Jim Dinning, argued on behalf of the new courses that they met the needs of all students, not just the 30% who go on to postsecondary education. The university science community responded with claims that the new program represented a reduction of real science content, and expressed the fear that this would threaten the quality of Alberta science, a position the Minister characterized as "self-serving resistance to change," adding, "Remember that the university interest is not the only one in achieving scientific literacy for 100% of high school students" (MacDonald & Byfield, 1989, p. 29). The public debate continued for several months before the Minister eventually backed away from the confrontation, appointing a special advisory committee and (6 months later) issuing new draft courses that "focus[ed] on fundamental science concepts and their application" (Alberta Education, 1990).

In this confrontation, arguments in favor of companion meanings based on STS were countered with arguments in favor of excellence, equated with companion meanings oriented toward mastery of specialist sciences. For example, a column in the *Calgary Sun* reported that science faculty members at the University of Alberta described the proposed science course in the following terms:

> The proposed Science 10-20-30 is not a good general science curriculum. It is largely devoted to a selective technological application of science and the current social issues of this technology. The result is social science masquerading as science. (Byfield, 1989, n.p.)

At issue here is not whether the university scientists were right or wrong, but the type of arguments they used and the force of those arguments in the deliberative context. In general, the university community had a prominent role (they were generally backed by the high school science teachers), and in the Alberta debate they had the added threat of refusal to accept Science 10-20-30 as a sequence of courses acceptable for university admission. This threat actually was issued and can be considered as possibly an overriding consideration in the Minister's decision to back off from his previous support of the new courses. Similar situations are described by Fensham in Chapter 13 in this volume.

Example C: Test Development in TIMSS

The third scenario is a much more recent case and concerns the development of science and mathematics tests for the Third International Mathematics and Science Study (TIMSS). A full account of the test development is described in the TIMSS Technical Report (Garden & Orpwood, 1996). However, one incident during the process shows how deliberation over the content of a test is as much a case of science curriculum talk as is curriculum planning or provincial policy development and also can have a bearing on the selection of companion meanings.

The occasion was the selection and editing of items for a mathematics and science literacy test for school leavers (Population 3 in TIMSS jargon). One purpose of this part of TIMSS was to determine the extent to which school leavers, both those who continued to study mathematics and science and others, still recalled the key science concepts they were taught earlier in school. For that reason, several test items from the Population 2 (13-year-olds) test were selected.

However, during a meeting of one of the TIMSS advisory committees, one of the members—a senior science educator with international standing in the field—commented that the items were "boring," that they were too much like school science, and that they failed to test what students needed to know as they entered the "real world." What was required, he continued, was that all these test items be "contextualized" into realistic or authentic contexts. In other words, the items in a literacy test should assess not only whether the students learned the scientific meanings of what they had been taught but also the companion meanings, the ways in which the science content related to technology and to solving real-world problems. In the resulting deliberation, the latter proposal outweighed the former, and the tests were redesigned to ensure that as many items as possible were "contextualized" into practical situations.

ADVICE AND DELIBERATION:
TYPES OF SCIENCE CURRICULUM TALK

The examples just discussed include instances of both science curriculum advice and deliberation. This type of discourse involves recommendations concerning what educators ought to do, and it can be general or specific in relation to its recipients.

General advice is typical of that found in science teacher education programs, in the prefaces of science textbooks, in the setting of science teachers' conferences or professional development workshops, and in the more general pronouncements of business groups or other educational stakeholders. Typically, such advice draws on research findings or other beliefs concerning learners, the nature of subject matter, the social context of education, or other sources as the basis for proposing a course of action. Implied, of course, in any piece of general advice for someone to act in a particular way is the caveat, "other things being equal." As every teacher knows only too well, other things rarely are equal, making the simple taking of general advice hard to justify. A process linking the advice to the specifics of a situation needs to intervene, and this process is what we call deliberation.

One example of general advice is found in the products of curriculum development projects or in textbooks. In analyzing this form of curriculum development, Walker (1971) coined the term "platform" to denote "the system of beliefs and values that the curriculum developer brings to his task" (p. 52). In justifying the curriculum emphases (Roberts, 1982a, 1982b) or companion meanings to be incorporated in a particular set of curriculum materials, one needs to refer to or discover the platform underlying a curriculum document.

Specific advice is advice to act in a particular way *in a specific context* and as such it tends to be much more useful than its general counterpart. Once the actual context is specified and is known by both the advisor and the advisee, then many (although not all) of the problems of general advice disappear. Science curriculum *policies*—whether for a class, a school, or an entire jurisdiction—constitute instances of specific advice because a policy necessarily relates to a specific context of practice.

Whether advice is heeded depends on a variety of factors, including its source, its timeliness, and also the reasons on which it is based. In the Alberta case cited earlier, the source of the advice to reduce the STS component of the new curriculum in favor of more science content—the university science faculty—appears to have been very influential (although I have no direct evidence for this). In the case of the TIMSS test development, the power of the argument concerning the nature and purpose of a literacy test—vis-à-vis the place of science in the real world— was clearly an overriding consideration. In both of these cases, one can see that a deliberative process is required to weigh all of the relevant considerations.

Advice, in whatever form it comes, always serves as an input to the process of deliberation through which all relevant considerations are brought to bear in order to make a decision concerning a course of action. While advice, as I have noted, can be general or specific, deliberation is always focused on a specific context. People do not deliberate about action in general terms (except perhaps in an academic debating context). The end result of deliberation is action: the teacher's choice of companion meanings, the Alberta policy on secondary school science, the TIMSS test item selection. In reaching the decision, deliberators will receive all kinds of advice that must be weighed and considered. Advice and deliberation are therefore closely related aspects of science curriculum talk—the logic of which is the next topic.

CONCEPTUALIZING SCIENCE CURRICULUM TALK

The argument of this chapter is that science curriculum talk, whether in the form of advice or deliberation, involves *arguments*, which are *practical* in nature and which can be analyzed for their *logic*, both in their final form and in the process of their development. Furthermore, since science curriculum talk is explicit and amenable to empirical investigation, an analytical framework that takes into account the nature of this somewhat specialized logical character is required if the discourse is to be adequately interpreted and critically appraised.

To illustrate the use of the framework for analysis, I will introduce another example of science curriculum talk, this time drawn from the deliberations of a science curriculum committee in a school district, Trillium, in the Canadian province of Ontario. ("Trillium" is a pseudonym, as are the names "Mr. Fleming" and "Jack," used in the example. A detailed account of these deliberations can be found in Orpwood, 1985.) At issue was the topic of energy and how it was to be taught in grades 9/10. An optional unit called "Wise Use of Energy" had been presented in the Ontario Ministry Curriculum Guideline for science at that level, a unit that combined scientific meanings about energy with companion meanings having to do with conservation of energy. (The guideline dated from 1978, a period when energy use—locally, nationally, and internationally—was very much on people's minds.) However, energy as a science topic traditionally had not been linked with companion meanings of this type. Rather, it traditionally had been taught in the context of the development of the concepts of force and work, and of companion meanings having to do with the value of performing calculations and solving "problems" in physical science.

The deliberative context was a meeting of teachers representing both elementary and secondary schools, chaired by Mr. Fleming, the science coordinator of the school district. Mr. Fleming began by introducing a proposal to include the unit on the basis that it ranked high in a survey, conducted by him earlier, of teachers' preferences of units to be taught. Separately, the secondary school science department heads, in a counterproposal, suggested that it not be included as a unit on its own but that the ideas be incorporated into other units. Mr. Fleming discounted this proposal on the grounds that "it just won't happen." The committee agreed that the ideas contained in the new unit—that is, the companion meanings— were very important to society and supported his proposal.

The proposal then went to a larger meeting of teachers for further discussion. Here, one teacher argued that it was undesirable for science courses to incorporate units that contained what he characterized as "an advocacy stance." Other participants suggested that students needed to have a "good grounding in the fundamentals" of energy before moving on to a consideration of its wise use, and backed the counterproposal not to include the unit. Another teacher tried to support Mr. Fleming by declaring that science courses at this level should be more "user-oriented." At this point, Jack, one of the science heads who had been opposed to the unit from the start, stood up and said, somewhat aggressively:

> I'd just like to summarize the opposition to Wise Use of Energy. I understand that the science heads have passed a resolution against the present program. I notice around the room here that at least half of us are more against than for it. I know my own teaching staff have severe misgivings about certain items in grade 9. I get the feeling that we have raised some questions, but that perhaps by sheer momentum it might still find its way into the program come September, and I wonder just how much opposition has to be recognized or perceived before it can be removed from this draft and be actually dumped.

Mr. Fleming responded, "You mean, how do you tell when a palace revolt is effective? Because obviously if the group won't have it, it would be foolish of me not to take into account the feeling of the group." The unit subsequently was dropped.

This was an interesting situation where arguments having to do with the acceptability of the unit among a certain group of teachers clearly had more weight than other, more substantive considerations such as the user-orientation of the course or the social importance of the companion meanings involved. The contest at one level was between proposals to include the unit and to drop the unit. At another level, however, it was between the benefits to students of certain types of companion meanings, on the one hand, and the need to accommodate the views of a powerful group of teachers, on the other.

The challenge for analysis is to find a framework for disentangling the issues, for analyzing what is at stake, and for discovering a basis on which one might counsel Mr. Fleming on a defensible way to manage the deliberative process. What arguments were used in this deliberation and how did they function in the deliberative context? Did the process itself have a logic that can be laid out? How did the process itself relate to the defensibility of the outcome? And how, if one were in Mr. Fleming's place and the deliberations were to take place again, could one improve on the process that was undertaken in Trillium? These are the issues with which a conceptual framework of science curriculum talk must grapple.

Analyzing Practical Arguments

While logic is a branch of philosophy going back many centuries, Stephen Toulmin, in his classic work *The Uses of Argument* (1958), has argued that the rules of formal logic are not helpful in analyzing arguments in substantive fields. He points out that the criteria for sound reasoning in specific areas are "field dependent" (p. 14) and must be elucidated through empirical rather than formal inquiry. He described an analytical framework that can be used for elucidating the field-specific characteristics of arguments from different fields of discourse; such a framework can therefore be a useful starting point for this inquiry. For a detailed account of the elements of Toulmin's argument pattern, the reader must refer to his original work. For present purposes, Figure 10.1 shows the configuration of the four most important elements, Data, Conclusion, Warrant, and Backing.

The first three elements of the argument pattern (Data, Warrant, and Conclusion) correspond to the elements of an Aristotelian syllogism. The data and conclusion of an argument are, of course, the specific elements of the argument. The warrant provides the (usually) principled basis for linking the two. Figure 10.2 displays a portion of an example given by Toulmin. In this case, the backing for the warrant comprises the statutes and other legal provisions on which the warrant is based. Because the argument is from the legal field, the nature of this backing is in law. The backing provides an answer to the question, "What is the basis for believing this warrant?" It is thus epistemological in nature and depends

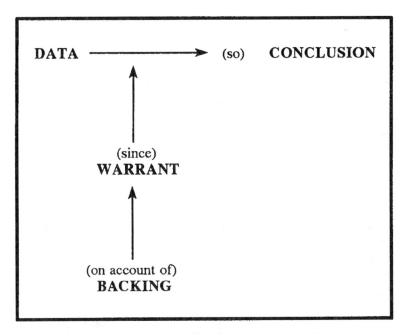

FIGURE 10.1. Basic Structure of Toulmin's Argument Pattern

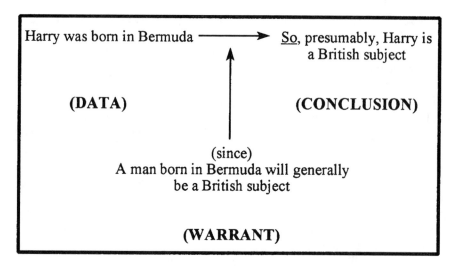

FIGURE 10.2. Sample Toulmin-Form Argument. *Source*: Toulmin, 1958, p. 102.

on the field from which the argument is derived. This is a point to which we will return once the nature of warrants in science curriculum talk becomes clear.

Schwab (1970) has reminded the educational community of the essentially "practical" nature of curriculum talk as distinct from the "theoretic" character of formal disciplines such as science or history. In so characterizing curriculum discourse, he does not echo the practice–theory dichotomy so beloved by some practitioners as a way to discount the value of "theory." Rather he revisits a fundamental Aristotelian distinction that separates formal knowledge from action. He goes on to describe the process by which decisions about how to act are made not through formal reasoning but through deliberation, a process that we will consider in more detail later. One of the characteristics of science curriculum talk is that it is always aimed at affecting somebody's actions rather than (merely!) a person's understanding. Consequently, arguments that are aimed at changing practice also must be treated as instances of "practical reasoning" and be analyzed in those terms.

Gauthier's (1963) account of practical reasoning is useful here, particularly as it maps well onto Toulmin's argument pattern already described. Gauthier is concerned specifically with arguments in which reasons are advanced for some action. His adaptation of the Aristotelian syllogism can be summarized as consisting of three parts:

- *Situational premises*—"statements concerning the situation in which the agent must act, his capacities, the probable and possible effect of attempt-

ing the various actions open to him in the situation" (p. 44), corresponding to Toulmin's "data"
- *Premises with practical force*—"statements containing desirability-
characterizations of the objects of the agent's wants" (p. 43), corresponding to Toulmin's "warrants"
- *Practical judgments*—"statements derived from the premises and specifying
the actions to be done" (p. 44), corresponding to Toulmin's "conclusions"

Two points should be noted in passing here. First, Gauthier shares with Schwab
an emphasis on the importance of a practical situation or context for the conclusions of a practical argument. While theoretic arguments state conclusions that
obtain regardless of specific situation—that is in the nature of theory—practical
arguments never do. A practical argument only has meaning if it is intended to be
applicable to a specific situation, such as a school, a classroom, even a province
or state, and the characteristics of that situation are always relevant in an effective
practical argument. Second, Gauthier's model of practical reasoning always includes a premise expressing a value position. Practical arguments, arguments about
what a person *ought to do*, must be based in part on premises concerning what is
desirable, worthwhile, or valuable. Frankena (1970) called these premises "basic
normative premises" in analyzing various philosophies of education.[1]
    Appraisal of practical advice consists then of clarifying and examining the
premises making up the argument, determining whether the situation is characterized adequately in the data, considering the normative warrants and the backing that
exists for them, and finally examining the reasoning that links all these together.
Using this framework, we can analyze the main arguments in Mr. Fleming's deliberations over the grade 9/10 program, as shown in Figure 10.3. It should be noted
that the warrants or normative premises of the arguments often are not stated explicitly, which is why this analysis becomes important as a tool to appraise the overall
process. In addition, what makes the analysis even harder is that the need for it rarely
occurs when a teacher is in a quiet situation in which careful reflection on a written
argument can be carried out. Instead, it occurs in the heat of a discussion about what
to do—in a department meeting, in a curriculum committee, in the context of designing an exam, or in a similarly dynamic rather than static context. To understand
the dynamic aspect of science curriculum talk as well as its final logical form, we
must examine the nature of "deliberation"—what Schwab (following Aristotle) calls
the "method of the practical."

Analyzing the Deliberative Process

While deliberation, like practical reasoning, is an Aristotelian concept, Aristotle
made little distinction between the two in his treatment on the subject (*Nichomachean Ethics*, trans. 1990). Gauthier (1963) points out that deliberation, the

	Situational Premises (Data)	Premises with Practical Force (Warrants)	Practical Judgments (Conclusions)
Argument 1	"Wise Use of Energy" contains companion meanings having to do with the impact of science on society	It is desirable for students to learn about the impact of science on society	"Wise Use of Energy" should be included in the grade 9 program
Argument 2	The science department heads do not want "Wise Use of Energy" to be included in the grade 9 course	It is unwise to include a unit against the express advice of the science heads	"Wise Use of Energy" should not be included in the grade 9 program
Argument 3	"Wise Use of Energy" is oriented toward users (consumers)	A user (consumer) orientation to science is desirable in grade 9	"Wise Use of Energy" should be included in the grade 9 program
Argument 4	"Wise Use of Energy" adopts an advocacy stance	It is undesirable for science courses to contain advocacy stances	"Wise Use of Energy" should not be included in the grade 9 program

FIGURE 10.3. Main Arguments in the "Wise Use of Energy" Deliberations

process people engage in when trying to determine a course of action, does not take place by analysis of practical syllogisms (p. 26). Rather it is a much more confusing process in which many ideas, facts, proposals, and principles all get tossed into the arena and worked over until a conclusion is reached.

Vickers (1965) describes the process as being parallel to navigating a ship in which the automatic steering collects information, weighs it against norms or standards, and selects an appropriate response. Vickers's contribution to the understanding of deliberation is that he emphasizes the continuing nature of the enterprise. He uses the term "appreciation of the situation" (p. 39) to capture the need to change directions in midstream rather than plot a new voyage.

Kaplan (1964) provides another helpful insight in recognizing a systematic if unarticulated method at work when people deliberate about what to do. This method he calls a "logic," pointing out that the term can be used to denote both the conduct of an activity and the study of its conduct. We say that a person is planning logically and also that there is a "logic of planning." Kaplan refers to the former as a "logic-in-use" and the latter as a "reconstructed logic," drawing attention to the fact that the two may not correspond exactly. He illustrates the distinction with reference to the practices of scientists as studied by sociologists of science—their logics-in-use—and the reconstructed logics of scientific method as described by philosophers of science. "Logic," Kaplan notes, "deals with what scientists do when they are doing well as scientists" (p. 8).

We can see that the Toulmin–Gauthier framework presents a reconstructed logic of the products of deliberation, while not addressing the intellectual "moves" that constitute the deliberative process, the logic-in-use of those who debate science curriculum meanings. In Kaplan's words, it "presents the denouement (of the drama) but we remain ignorant of the plot" (p. 10). More seriously, it can present the practical reasoning to justify the conclusion as a conclusive argument as though that were the only argument considered (cf. Barry, 1965, p. 32), and in so doing misrepresent the complexity of the deliberative process. To capture this complexity and to facilitate analysis of the deliberative process, we must add the conceptual contributions of yet another philosophical analysis.

Baier (1958) is concerned with the gradual development of an argument during the course of deliberations. He distinguishes two stages of activity:

> The first stage consists of a survey of the facts for the purpose of drawing up a list of those that are relevant considerations; the second, of the weighing of those considerations, of the pros and cons, with a view to determining their relative "weight" and so deciding the course of action supported by the weightiest of reasons, the course that has the weight of reason behind it. (p. 93)

The reader will note the parallel with Vickers's "appreciative judgment" referred to earlier. Baier, however, suggests a process in which the various elements of the argument change in status as the deliberative process develops. The process (see Figure 10.4) starts with "contributions," which may include facts, general principles, and specific proposals. Initially all data (Toulmin's term is used deliberately here) may be described as "facts," but following the first stage, some of these may be discarded as irrelevant. Those remaining are called "considerations," and the second stage involves the weighing of these and determining what eventually become "reasons" for action. Of course, not only data about the situation may be weighed for relevance and priority, but also general normative principles and specific proposals for action. All types of "contributions" to the deliberation may become "considerations" and eventual "conclusions," as shown in the figure. It is important to note that any of these may be entered into the deliberative process at any time. In practice, several considerations may be in the process of being weighed together when new facts or proposals emerge that change the balance entirely. Deliberation is far from being a linear process, and the frameworks described here are means for analyzing what is taking place—not guides for conducting the process.

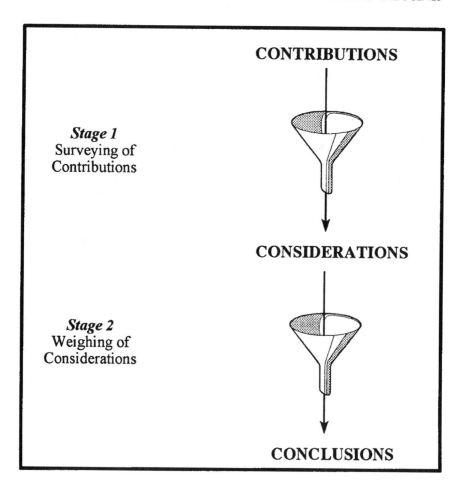

FIGURE 10.4. Baier's Stages of Deliberation

At the first stage of deliberation, one selects contributions—facts, principles, or proposals—that may become considerations later. Thus, for example, when I deliberate about whether to go skiing next weekend, the fact that there is presently good snow on the slopes is likely to be admitted as a consideration, while the equally true fact that it is my father-in-law's birthday may not be. At stake here is the relevance to the problem at hand of all the myriad facts available. In admitting some contributions as considerations and excluding others, we apply "rules of relevance" or, as Baier describes them, "consideration-making beliefs" (p. 24).

At the second stage of deliberation, relevant considerations are weighed to determine which are the most important and which, therefore, are to constitute grounds or reasons for acting. At the beginning of this stage any consideration is a potential or prima facie reason for acting in some way. We say that we will do X, "other things being equal," when we have a prima facie reason for doing X. It means that we are in possession of facts that, in the absence of other consider-ations, would constitute adequate reasons for doing X. Whether we eventually do X depends on the results of our weighing all the considerations and developing "reasons on balance" for doing X. This phase of deliberation involves the appli-cation of further rules—Baier (1958) calls them "rules of superiority" (p. 99)—to rank different considerations.

In the case of the Trillium deliberations, the reader would need to study the entire transcript of the meeting to appreciate the full flow of the meeting but, in general, all the arguments analyzed earlier in this chapter were accepted as meet-ing the rules of relevance, thus becoming considerations in the second stage of the deliberation. However, the conclusion (eliminating the "Wise Use of Energy" unit) showed which of these considerations were seen to carry the most weight. Argument 2, which invoked the opinion of the science heads, clearly carried the day over any substantive arguments concerning the claimed benefits for students. In this case, Mr. Fleming saved face by withdrawing his proposal in order to forge a consensus at the meeting and, because the unit made no further appearance, no further argument was required by way of final conclusion.

Overall Analytical Framework

A well-reasoned conclusion to deliberation is one in which an argument has force as well as validity. Analysis using the Toulmin–Gauthier framework helps one to know whether an argument is valid, rational, or defensible. But analysis of the argument's force—its relative weight over other arguments—is also needed. Neither analysis is adequate on its own; the two dimensions—force and validity—require combination into a single framework. The two-dimensional framework shown in Figure 10.5 illustrates the dual task of deliberation: It is a process that leads to a *conclusion of a rational argument* (the horizontal dimension) and to a *resolution of the practical problem* (the vertical dimension). In practice, all nine elements shown here may not be evident but they are certainly implicit. Analysis of the parts can show just what has and has not been taken into consideration and can assist in assessing what more may be needed to complete the deliberative task effectively and defensibly.

Before concluding, a word about the backing for warrants in science curricu-lum talk is in order. The Trillium deliberations exemplified an interesting situa-tion where arguments having to do with the (political) acceptability of the unit among a certain group of teachers clearly had more weight than other, more sub-

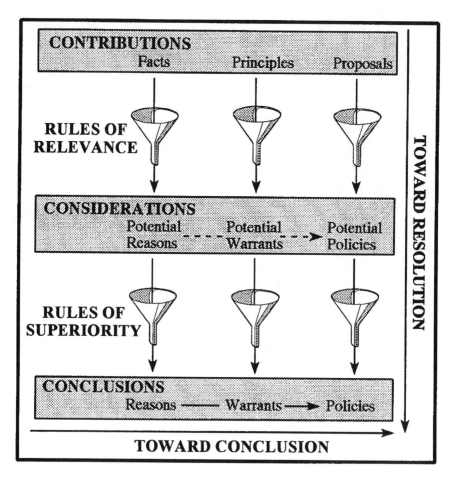

FIGURE 10.5. Two-Dimensional Framework for Analyzing Force and Validity

stantive considerations such as the user-orientation of the course or the social importance of the companion meanings involved. The contest at one level was between *alternative conclusions* to argument 1 (to include the unit) and argument 2 (to drop the unit). At another level it was between *alternative warrants* (concerning the benefits to students of certain types of companion meanings, on the one hand, and the acceptability of the change in orientation to a powerful group of teachers, on the other). These alternative warrants are backed by fundamentally different views of the basis for constructing a science curriculum. The backing for warrants supporting argument 1 has to do with the curriculum as being related to the needs of students and society, and the backing for warrants supporting argument 2 is concerned with the curriculum as a political compromise between factions. Thus, the analysis enables one to grapple with two fundamentally different views of curriculum making at the same time as understanding the process by which conclusions can be reached. The Alberta instance of curriculum policy making also can be understood in similar terms, given the analytical power of this framework.

This is not the place to discuss the merits of alternative backings for arguments in science curriculum talk, although that is indeed a subject worth of further study. One cannot simply assume that substantive arguments concerning students will automatically outweigh the more political arguments involving the stakeholders in education, since education is *both* a moral and a political enterprise. Nevertheless, the examples of deliberations cited here show how arguments concerning companion meanings in science education can be treated in a deliberative context. It behooves those who desire to see these meanings changed to consider carefully the arguments they mount in support of change and to understand the nature of the deliberative process through which the arguments must pass before change is effected.

CHAPTER 11

National Standards, Deliberation, and Design: The Dynamics of Developing Meaning in Science Curriculum

RODGER W. BYBEE

DURING A RECENT VISIT to the National Gallery of Art in Washington, DC, I overheard a conversation about a painting by Jackson Pollock, an Abstract Expressionist. A group was asked what they saw in the painting. The replies varied—an aerial photograph, a forest, a misty morning. One individual said he did not like the painting because he thought it had no content. The discussion reminded me of comments one sometimes hears about science curriculum. As a person who has designed curriculum materials, I am always interested in what individuals see in the curriculum and the basis for their interpretations. One person may see in a given science curriculum a focus on "the processes of science," another on the "big ideas" of science. Others may describe the same curriculum in terms of instructional strategies such as "hands-on" or "use of cooperative groups." When some individuals do not see enough of what they identify as scientific content, like the person who did not like the painting, they express a negative judgment about the curriculum.

The temptation to focus on what one recognizes immediately, to single out the familiar, is a matter of some concern when a nation produces standards for something as complex as science education. The point of developing and publishing *National Science Education Standards* (National Research Council, 1996) in the United States is to stimulate and assist the work of the science education community not only by recording the outcomes of widespread consultation on standards, but also by developing a broad, systematic framework of matters to which standards should apply. It is anticipated that school districts and states will develop a variety of science curricula, tailored to their needs, yet it is also expected that the *Standards* will have influence. No procedures are included for translating the *Standards* into curriculum materials, nor was that the intention in developing them. How, then, can professionals responsible for science curriculum appraise materials, and develop their own, in a way that respects local autonomy and still capitalizes on the very substantial amount of work incorporated in the *Standards*?

Just as the ability to interpret an abstract painting lies in some appreciation of the artist's intent and some understanding of basic design principles in art, so too the ability to appraise science curriculum—to understand differences in curricula and appreciate their value—depends on systematic considerations. In this chapter I develop the concept of *design* as a basis for systematic discussion of the creation and interpretation of curriculum materials. I find the design concept in both art and engineering to be a useful and appropriate way to think about the process of developing school science materials and to understand how individuals interpret and react to them.

I will draw on a decade of curriculum design experience at the Biological Sciences Curriculum Study (BSCS) and develop my ideas from the perspectives of curriculum materials and curriculum development. I acknowledge the broader, more inclusive perspectives of curriculum policy and curriculum theory. However, for the purpose of elaborating the idea of design, I will place materials and development in the foreground in order to make some connections between artists and engineers and the products of their work, on the one hand, and curriculum developers and their products, on the other.

This discussion provides an opportunity to examine how design affects the meanings that are expressed in a science curriculum—both scientific meanings and companion meanings, to use the terminology of this volume. I want to examine two kinds of decisions in this regard. There are decisions about *intents* or *purposes* of curricula, for instance, about which scientific concepts and which companion meanings should receive most attention in classrooms for different groups of students. Such decisions are the focus of deliberative processes in policy formulation (Orpwood, Chapter 10 in this volume). There are also technical matters associated with anticipating how such intents and purposes might materialize—and these matters are the focus of design decisions. Factors to be taken into account include the way teachers will perceive the materials, how students will understand them, how assessment of students will be oriented, and how the materials will fit with the milieu of a given school, community, and classroom. By calling attention to both deliberative decisions and design decisions, I intend to provide a conceptualization of curriculum materials and curriculum development that is sufficiently comprehensive both to respect the realities of science education practice and to give substance to the broad array of issues attended to in the *Standards*.

The remainder of the chapter has three sections, the first of which is an elaboration of the reasons why I see translating the *National Science Education Stan-*

dards into curriculum as a design problem. This information is presented as background against which to make the argument that a comprehensive, systematic view of science curriculum is needed if one is to avoid the temptation to seize on any one, or a few, of the components of the *Standards* as the sole basis for a curriculum. (Scientific subject matter is the most obvious candidate.) The concept of design in art and engineering is elaborated, with reference to the analogous application to science curriculum development. Next, there is a summary and discussion of the *Standards* themselves, presented in the context of considering the design opportunity their publication presents. Finally, the importance of deliberation as a precursor to design is presented in light of the significance of commitment by professionals to the spirit of the *Standards* and how they bear on the improvement of science education.

A DESIGN PROBLEM: TRANSLATING STANDARDS TO SCIENCE CURRICULUM

Why a Design Concept Is Important

Publication of *National Science Education Standards* will not of itself achieve the goal of improving science curriculum, classroom practices, and ultimately student achievement. As important and challenging as development of the *Standards* was, their publication and dissemination represent only the first step in the progress of standards-based systemic reform of science education. One of the steps to follow is particularly important, namely, translation to science curriculum materials.

The changes implied by the *Standards* present a complex array of interdependent factors, organized into six areas: content, teaching, assessment, professional development, school science programs, and systemic reform. It is important to grasp these as an integrated set of potential policy matters, even if one does not have much experience in thinking about curriculum development this way and the integration is not immediately obvious. It is important also to go beyond one's habitual and comfortable views of science curriculum and classroom practices, to suspend one's disbelief if the spirit of the *Standards* is contrary to such views. This is especially important for teachers, since views of curriculum and teaching often are sustained through consistent expression by commercial publishers, school boards, administrators, and communities.

Such factors reflect the systemic character of the science education enterprise. Indeed, the *Standards* are based on a systemic view of change in science education. It follows that the temptation to see the content standards as the sole basis for a curriculum framework—or worse, an actual curriculum—is misguided. Yet this is a common perceptual barrier to comprehending what is involved in changing science education. Incorporating the content standards into curriculum materials will have to respect the teaching standards and assessment standards as well. There will be implications for professional development, school science programs, and system reform, so these standards will have to be respected also. The commitment to move science education in a direction suggested by the *Standards* will have to develop through deliberation among the professionals and other stakeholders in various educational jurisdictions. Exemplars are needed as well, to bring the standards to life, to demonstrate their use, and to provide a basis for understanding and dialogue about these matters.

A design concept is important for implementing the *Standards* precisely because the components of the science education system cannot be considered in isolation. As suggested earlier, I find that design principles in both art and engineering are helpful in fashioning a design concept for curriculum. The attention to form, function, and meaning in art informs the task of making materials, teaching, and assessment consistent and meaningful. The attention to purpose and constraint in engineering informs the work of considering implications for professional development, links to the rest of the school program, and the need for systemic support. While numerous scientists and artists have discussed connections between science and art (see, e.g., Kepes, 1965), to my knowledge no one has developed the connections between art and curriculum. Similarly, despite discussions of the different characteristics of the science curriculum in terms of its components (see, e.g., Fensham, 1992; Roberts, Chapter 1 in this volume), I am not aware of any elaboration of the potential of artistic and engineering design concepts in the context of curriculum materials and development.

Design in Art: Form, Function, and Meaning

Different responses to art provide an introduction to ideas associated with design. Individuals who discuss paintings, for example, often reveal their understanding of art and their visual literacy. While viewing Impressionist paintings of such artists as Claude Monet, Pierre Auguste Renoir, and Camille Pissarro, one might hear the following comments: "What a beautiful picture," "I like the light and color," and "The scene is so peaceful." On the other hand, in listening to comments about Abstract Expressionist paintings by such artists as Jackson Pollock, Mark Tobey, Robert Motherwell, and Mark Rothko, one is likely to hear comments such as: "What is this?" and "This does not make sense, why is this art?" and "Anybody could do this!"

Impressionist painters concentrated on the form of the work, highlighting techniques that emphasized color, light, and atmosphere. They often used everyday scenes of people and nature. The meaning of Impressionist art for the viewers in my example lies in the beauty and scenes. In general, individuals view such art as they view photographs. That is, they identify the realistic content of the painting. Abstract Expressionists were less interested in representing scenery and people realistically and more interested in evoking emotional responses through their use of action painting or color fields. They used color, of course, but Abstraction was a way to achieve their primary goal of engaging the viewer in the making of meaning.

Rather than digressing into the history of art and issues of technique, my point goes to the different kinds of meaning that various art forms have for the artist and viewer. Abstract Expressionist art has little meaning of the photographic sort. Its significance lies in the intellectual activity and emotional response the artist engenders in the viewer. This, in fact, may be exactly the intention of Abstract Expressionists. When we compare the Abstract Expressionists to the Impressionists, we are considering the meaning of art more than its isolated elements, such as subject matter or technique (cf. Kilbourn, Chapter 3 in this volume). The two "schools" of artists approach meaning quite differently.

The concept of *design* in art is completely tied up with meaning, but it also refers to the arrangement, composition, and combination of shapes and forms—that is, the formal organization of the artist's work (Grillo, 1960). Design comprises all the elements the artist uses in creating art, including lines, shapes, values (lightness or darkness), textures, and colors. A person considering the design of a painting asks the question: "How did the artist use these elements to determine the final appearance of the work of art?" (Ocvirk, Bone, Stinson, & Wigg, 1962).

Wong (1993) relates these technical points to the artist's meaning by defining design as "a process of purposeful visual creation." Embracing other contexts in which the term is used, he continues: "A good design is the best visual expression of the essence of 'something' whether this be a message or a product. The designer has to look for the best possible way the 'something' can be shaped, produced, distributed, used, and related to the environment" (p. 41).

Two points suggest to me the usefulness of a design concept in art for understanding the interpretation and creation of science curriculum materials: (1) the need to understand a curriculum developer's intentions, and (2) a viewpoint that respects the way in which meaning is created and conveyed by the form and function of elements in the materials and related teaching and assessment procedures. Regarding the first point, it would be more productive for the improvement of science education if scientists, science educators, and science teachers would reserve judgment when they confront curricula that have emphases and meanings different from the ones to which they are accustomed. For example, an abundance of attention to scientific meaning often is perceived as *good* science curriculum, while emphasis on such companion meanings as those of science-technology-society, inquiry, or history of science are viewed as *bad* or *meaningless* curriculum. Like the (stereotyped) responses to Abstract Expressionist art, such responses do not honor the developers' different intentions and the different meanings embodied in the materials. Such responses also fail to honor the scope of the *Standards*, as discussed later.

Regarding the second point, a design concept permits one to view a science curriculum as a "something" (Wong's term) that results from a process of purposeful creation. It has to fulfill a practical need and it has to be shaped, distributed, adapted, used, and related to the school environment. Every science curriculum, then, has an inherent design.

Design in Engineering: Purpose and Constraints

Engineers use the term *design* with a problem-solving orientation. In general, designing involves recognition of a problem and identification of possible solutions; consideration of criteria, constraints, and trade-offs; evaluation of models; and finally presentation of a solution. The resultant design can be embodied in either a process or a technological device.

The essence of engineering has been described as "design under constraint" (American Association for the Advancement of Science, 1989, p. 41). In engineering, constraints include physical laws such as conservation of energy, and properties of materials such as flexibility, conductivity, and friction. Other constraints arise from social, economic, ecological, and ethical matters. Whether designing paper clips, computers, or skyscrapers, engineers must account for constraints in their designs.

In accommodating constraints, engineers often recognize that there are different solutions to a problem and that they will have to make trade-offs in selecting one design over another. Testing has a significant role as part of this problem-solving process (Ferguson, 1993; Rowe, 1992). Both processes and technological devices that result from design have control mechanisms based on feedback that can activate change. Technologies have side effects, often unintended ones, and technological devices eventually fail—as a result of failure of parts, mismatch of parts, or inappropriate use. Such matters have to be considered in design as well.

The design concept in engineering is helpful for understanding some further features of science curriculum development. Constraints that affect the design of a curriculum include, for example, criteria set by states or provinces or nations; developmental appropriateness of concepts for students; feasibility, usability, and manageability of the materials and content for teachers; and availability of resources for new equipment and for professional development. Feedback systems (e.g., assessments) are associated with curriculum materials. Often there are unintended side effects that emerge in the variety of interactions among students, teachers, and the materials. So design in curriculum is like design in engineering as well as design in art.

THE DESIGN OPPORTUNITY

In this section I present an overview of the U.S. *National Science Education Standards* and use design concepts from art and engineering to discuss how the standards have coherence and relevance in the process of developing science curricula. First, three categories of standards (content, teaching, and assessment) are associated with the design concept in art because they are closely related to the production of meaning. Then the other three (professional development, school programs, and system support) are linked to the design concept from engineering because they illustrate the constraints that have to be anticipated in curriculum development.

Given the preceding discussion of design, I propose that one can think of a science curriculum as a *system of constructed relationships* among such elements as science concepts, cognitive abilities, manipulative skills, and companion meanings (i.e., understandings and values about science). There is a compelling analogy to the work of an artist who constructs relationships among the forms and functions of line, color, and so forth, that give meaning to a painting. There is also a compelling analogy to the work of an engineer who constructs a process or device with an eye to the constraints under which it has to function, the feedback that will change it, and its systemic implications. The coherence and relevance of the *National Science Education Standards* thus can be viewed in two clusters with respect to the two analogies to science curriculum development.

In the United States, national efforts to improve education include legislation, such as the Goals 2000: Educate America Act, and development of national standards for school subjects. The National Committee on Science Education Standards and Assessment (1993) reminded the various groups working on *National Science Education Standards* of the challenge facing them:

> In the United States, there is a pervasive attitude that science is a difficult, somewhat exotic, and impractical area of study, pursued by an elite with a natural gift for it. Even some very influential people can be heard to say that they got by in life very well without a knowledge of science. . . . It is therefore extremely important in preparing for presentation of the standards to refine and hone both understandings of and convincing arguments for why science is so important in the education of all students today, why all students and eventually all adults should be and can be "scientifically literate." (p. 8)

The vision of science education expressed by the *Standards* thus accommodates the historically important broad purpose of science education that usually has been called scientific literacy (see, e.g., Agin, 1974; American Association for the Advancement of Science, 1989; Bybee, 1993; Murnane & Raizen, 1988; Pella,

1976; Uno & Bybee, 1994). Because of the widespread agreement and support for this goal, the design of contemporary science curricula should contribute directly to making the vision of scientific literacy a reality in terms of student achievement.

It should be noted that "national" in this context means a nationwide agreement, not a federal mandate, on what constitutes successful science learning and the school practices that optimize the learning of science. National standards do not define a national curriculum and are not a form of national standardization. Options are open for the design of science curricula, but the intent of the *Standards* is to guide the science education system in the direction of the broad overarching goal of scientific literacy.

The Standards for Content, Teaching, and Assessment

Three sets of standards are best approached with a design concept based on art. The elements in the content standards give meaning to a science curriculum, and the teaching and assessment standards are closely linked to realizing this meaning in classrooms. The summary of the *Standards* in this section and the next is necessarily only a sketch. In every case the standard presented is a category identifying a factor or area that is important to take into account when professionals deliberate and plan curricula for their own settings. More information is available in the published *Standards* document itself (NRC, 1996); page numbers refer to the document, and italics have been added.

The content standards set forth eight curriculum elements:

> The *science content standards* outline what students should know, understand, and be able to do in the natural sciences over the course of K–12 education. They are divided into eight categories:
> - Unifying concepts and processes in science
> - Science as inquiry
> - Physical science
> - Life science
> - Earth and space science
> - Science and technology
> - Science in personal and social perspective
> - History and nature of science. (p. 6)

The first category is common to all grade levels. "This standard describes some of the integrative schemes that can bring together students' many experiences in science education across grades K–12. . . . [It] should always be closely linked to outcomes aligned with other content standards" (p. 104). An example is "change, constancy, and measurement." The remaining seven categories are presented in a progressive, developmental sequence for grade levels K–4, 5–8, and 9–12.

The second category, the inquiry standard, highlights the ability to do inquiry and the fundamental understandings *about* scientific inquiry that students should develop. This standard goes beyond the "processes of science" and emphasizes students' critical thinking and scientific reasoning as they use evidence and extant knowledge to construct scientific explanations.

The third, fourth, and fifth categories—standards for physical, life, and earth and space science—express the historically important disciplines and subject matter of science. In the language of this volume, these standards focus on the science concepts, principles, and theories that are fundamental to the disciplines and therefore constitute the scientific meanings students are to develop if they are to be considered scientifically literate.

In the final three categories, the idea of content is broader and decidedly nontraditional. There is content derived from three major sources of companion meanings, approximating the curriculum emphases Roberts has called Science, Technology, and Decisions, Everyday Coping, and Structure of Science (Chapter 1 in this volume). The science and technology standard establishes useful connections between the natural world and the designed world and presents the opportunity for students to develop decision-making abilities. The standard on science in personal and social perspectives establishes connections between students and their world: understandings about health, populations, resources, environments, and natural hazards that will enable them to fulfill their obligations as citizens. The standard on the history and nature of science includes an understanding of the nature of science and uses history in school science programs to clarify different aspects of science in society, the human aspects of science, and how scientific advances occur.

In the concluding section of the chapter, I will take up the matter of blending scientific meanings from each of the third, fourth, and fifth standards with companion meanings expressed by each of the last three. Like an artist crafting meaning in a painting, the curriculum designer develops an artistic blend to create a system of constructed relationships among the elements that constitute the content of curricula. At this point, it is very important that all of the categories be seen as appropriate content for a science *curriculum*. Sometimes content is equated exclusively with discipline-based subject matter, while other potential content is seen to be content-free or, more pejoratively, as "fluff." Like the example of viewing art, this is a value judgment that precludes the acceptance of curriculum materials that have differing emphases and meanings. Such judgments present considerable hurdles to the development of understanding and acceptance of different systems of constructed relationships in science curricula.

It is natural to have begun this section with content, since it is one of the most compelling features of a science curriculum. However, anyone developing curriculum materials has an eye on both teaching and assessment procedures. Hence the system of constructed relationships applies to the actual materials, the teaching, and the assessment of students. In the case of curriculum materials, the system of constructed relationships is evident in such features as the table of contents or scope and sequence for the program, the selection of scientific meanings to be developed, and the companion meanings to be emphasized in the various units of study. Because they have their own views of science and pedagogy, teachers using the materials superimpose other systems of constructed relationships as they engage students using various instructional practices, strategies, and methods. Science teachers have to respond to the unique events of the classroom, so they have to adapt curriculum materials to emerging situations. They have to adapt as well to students' cognitive constructions and prior knowledge. Hence the *Standards* document includes a set of standards about teaching, reflecting the kinds of capabilities teachers will need if their adaptations of materials are to be creative and profitable:

> The *science teaching standards* describe what teachers of science at all grade levels should know and be able to do. They are divided into six areas:
> * The planning of inquiry-based science programs
> * The actions taken to guide and facilitate student learning
> * The assessments made of teaching and student learning
> * The development of environments that enable students to learn science
> * The creation of communities of science learners
> * The planning and development of the school science program. (p. 4)

Assessment of students always conveys a clear message about the most valued scientific and companion meanings in a given science curriculum. The view of assessment in the *Standards* document thus goes far beyond the ordinary sense of testing. It includes not only the familiar classroom tests, but also a range of strategies for collecting and interpreting information about student achievement, teacher performance, and the work of educational institutions. Assessment standards are not tests and they do not describe a single strategy to judge student learning or a school science program:

> The *assessment standards* provide criteria against which to judge the quality of assessment practices. They cover five areas:
> * The consistency of assessments with the decisions they are designed to inform
> * The assessment of both achievement and opportunity to learn science
> * The match between the technical quality of the data collected and the consequences of the actions taken on the basis of those data
> * The fairness of assessment practices
> * The soundness of inferences made from assessments about student achievement and opportunity to learn. (p. 5)

The standards for content, teaching, and assessment represent a framework of elements parallel to the elements with which an artist works. Like the design used by an artist to give meaning to a painting, the design of curriculum involves the interplay of a variety of considerations. The *Standards* are intended to systematize the considerations, but the artistic work of curriculum materials development remains to be done.

The Standards for Professional Development, School Programs, and System Reform

A design concept from engineering is proposed as more appropriate for the remaining three sets of standards. Even the most meaningful curriculum materials will not be successful if teachers currently in the schools cannot teach from them, if the school's program is inconsistent with them, or if there is no systemic support for them. These three areas constitute constraints that the curriculum developer must take into account:

> The *professional development standards* present a vision for the development of professional knowledge and skill among teachers. They focus on four areas:
> - The learning of science content through inquiry
> - The integration of knowledge about science with knowledge about learning, pedagogy, and students
> - The development of the understanding and ability for lifelong learning
> - The coherence and integration of professional development programs. (pp. 4–5)

The constraint represented by these standards is associated quite clearly with the abilities and skills of currently employed teachers who would be using the materials. That is why there is a need for a category other than the teaching standards, although the two obviously are related. This need is met by the standards for school science programs:

> The science education *program standards* describe the conditions necessary for quality school science programs. They focus on six areas:
> - The consistency of the science program with the other standards and across grade levels
> - The inclusion of all content standards in a variety of curricula that are developmentally appropriate, interesting, relevant to students' lives, organized around inquiry, and connected with other school subjects
> - The coordination of the science program with mathematics education
> - The provision of appropriate and sufficient resources to all students
> - The provision of equitable opportunities for all students to learn the standards
> - The development of communities that encourage, support, and sustain teachers. (p. 7)

The program standards refer to internal and external constraints that have to be considered. For example, the program is to be broad and diverse enough to accommodate science instruction for all students. There are also administrative specifications and requirements for coordination across subjects.

Standards for the science education system guide the policies that must be implemented and the alignment of elements within education that policy makers and others must pursue to support science learning described in the standards. System standards also address the essential functions that serve to build and sustain the capacities demanded by the standards of teachers and school communities:

> The science education *system standards* consist of criteria for judging the performance of the overall science education system. They consider seven areas:
> - The congruence of policies that influence science education with the teaching, professional development, assessment, content, and program standards
> - The coordination of science education policies within and across agencies, institutions, and organizations
> - The continuity of science education policies over time
> - The provision of resources to support science education policies
> - The equity embodied in science education policies
> - The possible unanticipated effects of policies on science education
> - The responsibility of individuals to achieve the new vision of science education portrayed in the standards. (p. 8)

Other Design Considerations

Contemporary recommendations for science curriculum typically include decreased reliance on textbooks, increased use of computer technologies, and greater emphasis on laboratory investigation and cooperative learning. It is important not to make design judgments based on analysis of individual elements in this way. One cannot derive a sense of the meaning of a curriculum exclusively from, say, the extent of computer usage, or the incorporation of cooperative learning, any more than one can get the meaning of a work of art entirely by an analysis of such visual devices as lines, shapes, textures, and colors. Granted, the lines, brush strokes, and use of colors reveal something, but a given painting would have a different form and function had the artist used a different technique (Grillo, 1960). It is the final appearance of the total work of art that engages our intellectual and emotional response.

So it is with the science curriculum. Curriculum developers attempt to assemble the various components so that they work together in a meaningful way, that is, in a manner that creates a unity of form and function. Traditionally, those who discuss curriculum development address form and function through such principles of organization as concepts, skills, and values (Tyler, 1949); subject matter, learners and learning, teachers and teaching, and the educational milieu (Schwab, 1962); and chronological, developmental, or thematic orientations (Posner, 1988). In the language of design, these principles of organization result in the balance, rhythm, domination/subordination, and harmony of the curriculum. Science curriculum materials have many parts; thoughtful design and implementation bring unity.

CONCLUSION: THE SIGNIFICANCE OF DELIBERATION

At this time, the science education community in the United States is poised between the completion and publication of *National Science Education Standards* and the development and revitalization of science curricula designed to enhance students' opportunities to achieve scientific literacy. The standards are "criteria to judge quality [and] progress toward a national vision of learning and teaching science in a system that promotes excellence." On the other hand, "a hallmark of American education is local control, where boards of education and teachers make decisions about what students will learn" (NRC, 1996, p. 12). Local control implies legitimate variation in science curricula, depending on the deliberations and decisions of professionals and other stakeholders about what is most appropriate for their unique situations. Local control also means local responsibility, of course.

I recommend beginning the design and/or appraisal of materials in local situations with a period of deliberation and dialogue based on *National Science Education Standards*, as well as *Benchmarks for Science Literacy* (American Association for the Advancement of Science, 1993). Use of the latter "by state framework committees, school and school-district curriculum committees, and developers of instructional and assessment materials complies fully with the spirit of the content standards" (NRC, 1996, p. 15). Standards and benchmarks incorporate conceptions of learners, teachers, science, and society that are theoretical and general. These need to be discussed and debated, if they are to be considered seriously in making deliberative decisions about the various curriculum emphases needed in programs that will satisfy the theme "Science for All" that underlies the contemporary reform (cf. Roberts, 1995b).

Such a theme represents a general education approach, as opposed to a narrow and specific approach geared strictly to the education of scientists. The difference is expressed in the specific referents of science for *citizens* and science for future *scientists* (see, for example, Boyer & Levine, 1981; Harvard Committee, 1945). Both must be addressed. This is a very important area for deliberation by local school personnel, and to avoid one-sidedness in the direction of future scientists the debate should be refocused from time to time on a question I have asked before (Bybee, 1993): What should the scientifically and technologically literate person know, value, and do—as a citizen? The curricular questions are not new: What is the balance of inquiry and subject matter? What are the trade-offs between science concepts and other content such as history and nature of science, or science in personal and social perspectives? How will teaching and assessments change?

A Possible Pitfall: The Rush to Closure

Given the need for debate and discussion about such matters, it would be most unfortunate if curriculum developers and textbook publishers were to embrace the standards in a superficial way as the basis for new programs claimed to meet, or exceed, the recommendations. Unfortunately, such development may be driven by personal or market needs instead of a larger, more thoughtful conception of science education, the goals of contemporary reform, and the changes implied by the standards and benchmarks. Such a response can be aided and abetted when school personnel seek quick and easy solutions that bypass a period of study, re-flection, dialogue, and debate. The combination of curriculum developers and publishers who use standards and benchmarks to their personal or economic ends and school personnel who unknowingly support such efforts creates a cycle that can be broken if local professionals and other stakeholders insist on a period of deliberation before proceeding to decisions and designs for their science curricula.

Another Possible Pitfall: Narrow View of Content

After 10 years of experience developing science curriculum at BSCS and 4 years of experience working on national standards, I am convinced that most individuals who use standards and engage in reform efforts will place content in the foreground of their deliberations. This is understandable, given that one does not have a cur-riculum unless one has content. However, sometimes the focus of deliberation is narrowly on scientific meanings within a specific discipline and grade level. In-terest can center on what Ziman (1980) calls "valid science" in the curriculum emphasis Roberts calls Correct Explanations (Chapter 1 in this volume).

The definition of content in the *National Science Education Standards* and *Benchmarks for Science Literacy* is broader than "valid science" and Correct Explanations. To be sure, there is traditional content associated with physical, life, and earth science, but content is defined to include also the nature of science, tech-nology, history of science, inquiry, and science in personal and social perspec-tives. If deliberation about content becomes restricted to the traditional type, the deliberation can be shifted by posing questions such as, "What content is implied in a conception of scientific literacy?" Also, the idea of a companion meaning should be injected into the discourse, by pointing out that the standards dealing with traditional content can be combined with the standards that refer to content of companion meanings, in a blend that will accomplish both kinds of content objectives. (Cf. Östman, Chapter 5 in this volume.)

Such a blend applies directly to the structure of goals and the curriculum (Bybee, 1993; Bybee & DeBoer, 1994). Using generic terms for broad goals to be attained (e.g., science knowledge; science methods, including inquiry and nature of science; and personal and social applications, including STS), one can imagine several different forms of curriculum depending on which goal is placed in the foreground. Here are four examples:

SCIENCE CURRICULUM 1

Scientific Terms
Scientific Inquiry (Knowing)
Social Applications

SCIENCE CURRICULUM 2

Scientific Inquiry (Doing)
Scientific Concepts
Social Applications

SCIENCE CURRICULUM 3

Social Issue
Scientific Inquiry (Doing)
Scientific Knowledge

SCIENCE CURRICULUM 4

Scientific Principles (Understanding)
Social Applications (Doing)
Scientific Methods

A Third Possible Pitfall: Losing Sight of the Classroom

Deliberation and development also must consider how the curriculum will function in the science classroom, in particular, how science teachers will adapt the materials to accommodate the needs of students and adapt their teaching styles to accommodate the materials. What provisions for these adaptations are the responsibility of curriculum developers and what are the responsibilities of science teachers? Developers do have a responsibility to make explicit their design and system of constructed relationships. Science teachers have a responsibility to adapt science curriculum to accommodate their students' needs and the strengths of their own teaching. Note that standards provide some guidance for the parameters of these responsibilities.[1]

Similarly, one has to consider assessment. Are the form and function of assessment consistent with the form and function of the science curriculum? Is the assessment component of the curriculum consistent with the valued outcomes of the developer and teacher? One significant feature of the national standards is their close connection between assessment and various dimensions of science content and science teaching.

A Fourth Possible Pitfall: Losing Sight of Constraints

The deliberations discussed thus far have largely to do with design of curricula from the point of view of their meaning—based on the design concept from art that I introduced early in this chapter. Other matters of concern arise when one recalls the design concept from engineering. These include the constraints under which the local system operates, for example, the cost implications for resources and professional development programs. These are matters that cannot be decided "in general" by reference to standards, but must be the subject of deliberation by the groups that have to find the resources.

Deliberation is thus a crucial part of standards-based science education reform. The *Standards* do not make the decisions; the professionals and other stakeholders do. Östman and Roberts (1994) put it this way:

> The informed involvement of teachers and other stakeholders, based on a thorough understanding of the choices being made—choices of both subject matter content and companion meanings—is vital to the conduct of education in democratic countries. The selection process has a moral character in that some consequences for students are being privileged over others, and the moral responsibility for making the choices is shared among all stakeholders in the curriculum development process. Hence, the need for all stakeholders to understand. (p. 3)

In this chapter I have emphasized the importance of thoughtful involvement by professionals and others, primarily by considering what is involved in the intended results of materials development and/or appraisal, namely, meaningful and defensible science curriculum for all students.

The Science Curricula of Europe and the Notion of Scientific Culture

JOAN SOLOMON

WHAT IS TAUGHT IN SCHOOL is, quite simply, the stuff of our future culture, whether it teaches what good literature or music is like, or what constitutes a scientific experiment. That is not to suggest that it will be the whole of culture. We add to that what we learn and appreciate all our lives, but often we build that upon the foundations of knowledge and attitudes learned at school.

We are rapidly approaching the position in Europe and North America where there will be science education of some sort for all children from 5 or 6 years of age to 18. Thus the scientific component of common culture—and what that means will be discussed later in this chapter—may be expected to become more salient. The problems that face those of us who design syllabi and curricula are what science should be taught, or could be taught, and in what ways, so that it may serve for a lifetime as a foundation upon which to build. It needs to be an invitation to participate and enjoy science. In the newly emerging European Union (EU) there is also an operational aim: to construct a scientific culture uniform enough for ideas to travel from country to country as freely as they did, by all accounts, in the days of Erasmus. What might constitute that scientific culture—its scope and meaning—is the central concern of this chapter.

The incentive for writing the chapter is a large collaborative project, set in motion by the European Commission (EC), to examine "school science and the future of scientific culture in Europe." While the EC in Brussels is interested in the scientific culture of the future citizens of Europe for both political and economic reasons, the Treaty of Rome, which began the slow process of building the new Europe, contains a strong recommendation to respect the "linguistic and cultural diversity" of European countries. This produces a substantial dilemma for those who might like to see scientific culture as an unfractured whole across the continent. From the start of this project, diversity was expected, but what kind of diversity and how important it might be, was part of the brief to be explored. The research program, established in 1993, commissioned national reports from a wide range of European countries, not all of which were already in the EU, and then it used the data about science education in these different countries to guess at what the future of scientific culture might be for citizens of the new Europe. At the end of the first phase of this project the EC asked for recommendations for educational policies that might enrich this subtle future commodity.

The sections that follow describe some of the very interesting diversity found during the project. Two senses in which one can speak of scientific culture are explored. The more familiar sense of the term, here called "academic" scientific culture, coexists with a sense of "common" or "popular" or "public" scientific culture. Clarification of the distinction is supported by examining school practice in the various member states of the EU, some ideas from cultural anthropology, and the "companion meanings" concept used as a common thread in this volume. Discussion of the implications of different, often implicit views of scientific culture for the lives of students leads, finally, to the position that whatever else is meant by the concept, it must be comprehensive enough to accommodate and integrate the two important senses in which it is used. In other words, it needs to refer to "something" to which all citizens have access, regardless of whether they are professional scientists.

CULTURAL DIVERSITY AND THE SCHOOL CURRICULUM

If the foundations for scientific culture stem from school science, then they derive from a mixture of intentions of governments, programs within schools, how teachers in different countries perceive science and science education, and how much of this they manage to convey to school students. At this level the cultivation of students' attitudes depends on several very broad factors:

- The perceived *purposes* of science education
- The *contents* of a national curriculum for science
- The national attitude toward how *school science education* should be carried out
- The national attitude toward *science as an academic system of thought*

The first item should have set the scene for the whole project. However, it seems almost impossible for any country to define its science education ideology so clearly and uniquely that everything else follows from it. For example, the contents of a nation's curriculum might be expected to reflect both the national, economic, and technological purposes science education is thought to serve, and the nature of scientific thought. However, national curricula rarely stipulate how science is to be taught in schools, and this colors young people's perceptions so vividly that it is crucial to the formation of their attitudes toward science. The conduct of lessons is affected, for example, by teachers' perceptions of the nature of science as a system of thought (e.g., Brickhouse, 1990)—as abstract and mathematical or empirical and technical. It also will depend on educational traditions, such as whether children should be positively encouraged to cooperate in their study (very strong in the Scandinavian countries) and what is a suitable activity for a school teacher to perform (quite different in, for example, Switzerland and the United Kingdom).

The fourth factor on the list above may seem surprising. Science, much more than literature, for example, might be expected to possess an academic commonality across different member states, in terms of both content and philosophy. At least since the Scientific Renaissance of the sixteenth and seventeenth centuries, it has been common to speak about the universal invisible college to which all scientists belong by virtue of their common study. This aspect of science is referred to by the influential American sociologist of science, Robert Merton (1942), as the norm of "universality." However, this scientific norm does not necessarily produce complete uniformity. There have been notable and even scandalously chauvinistic controversies within Europe about scientific matters (the nature of light or the invention of the calculus); there are other, deeper differences as well.

The cultural diversity within European thought may be denser and richer than that in any other comparable continent. The evolution of different streams of European thought is far too vast a subject to be treated here (see Durkheim, 1977; McClean, 1995). Nevertheless it is impossible to describe the differences in school science education, its purposes, delivery, and reception, without being struck by the effect of these different modes of thought. One finds quite general differences that affect broad personal and institutional factors in all education, such as national and political attitudes toward—

- Standardization and uniformity (e.g., France)
- Efficiency and market forces (e.g., United Kingdom)
- Personal autonomy and moral education (e.g., Scandinavia)

In addition, there is variation in what we might call the preferred "regulative principles of thought," which affect all education, and science in particular. These might include—

- Humanism
- Rationalism
- An inductive/heuristic/empirical approach to knowing
- A deductive/abstract/mathematical approach to knowing

There can be no doubt that such differences are present and that they are an integral and valued part of each national culture.

Science is a comparative newcomer to the school curriculum. It has been received in a different spirit in the different countries. In Italy, for example, science education is still fighting for status against the classics, a battle fought and won nearly 40 years ago in some other European countries. Over 30 years ago C. P. Snow (1965) showed how scientific thinking may be respected for its rigor, and yet still form a separate culture within the educated community. A country that "sees" that separateness as highly significant will rely more on traditional learning in general education and consider science as a mere optional extra. In the United Kingdom, school science was just that, essentially a matter of personal choice, until the imposition of the country's first mandatory national curriculum in 1987.

If scientific culture is to have a viable future in Europe, science should be linked deeply and thoroughly into all educated thought. The essay of Jegede (1994b) on the effect of scientific education on the indigenous African cultures shows most valuably how hard it may be to create such links between very different ways of thinking. The problem in Africa is highlighted because Western science is so clearly a foreign import, yet it is instructive for the situation within Europe. Even though Europe may pride itself (too much) on being "the cradle of modern science," academic science similarly may be a "foreign" subject in the context of the culture of our modern schoolchildren. (See Aikenhead, Chapter 7 in this volume.)

One basic but unexpected cultural difference between the science curricula in the different European countries is their quite different school discipline boundaries. In France, science includes mathematics. In Italy and to some extent Greece, where the classics still maintain the cachet they used to have in the United Kingdom, science is taught along with business studies and economics. In Portugal, school science includes history, geography, and the social sciences. Only in the United Kingdom are laboratory investigations mandatory in science lessons at all ages. "Natural science" may mean "natural philosophy" in the grand German sense of *Naturwissenschaften*, as Isaac Newton also used the term to encompass all the sciences, or else it may be just "nature study" or observational biology. These demarcations cannot fail to affect how students see the place of science within knowledge and hence its wider cultural significance.

Education also is becoming more of a political hot potato in European countries. The school budget, specifying salaries and the cost of resources, including computers and laboratory equipment, often figures in party manifestos. Thus students are exposed to a public view of the perceived importance of science in the organization of their education: its funding, its local standing and relevance, and the social status accorded to their science teachers. These economic and sociological aspects of science education, as well as the contents of the different national curricula, were included in the data from which the project compiled its final report (European Commission, 1996).

POPULAR AND ACADEMIC SCIENTIFIC CULTURE

Whatever we mean by "scientific culture," it is clear that communications of all sorts move far more surely within a culture than across cultural frontiers. Indeed this freedom of movement may be taken as the simplest test of cultural commonality, a point that is central to the definition of a culture. Two very different conceptions of scientific culture are explored in this section. One, "popular" scientific culture, refers to the concerns of the public, so important within their own local culture and often having a scientific and technological basis. Against that, a culture of academic science is much more restrictive.

Popular Scientific Culture

The STS courses that now constitute an internationally recognized aspect of reform to the curriculum (Solomon & Aikenhead, 1994) have popular scientific culture as one of their objectives. They began during the 1970s and 1980s in the United Kingdom and the Netherlands and have spread quite widely in Europe, although apparently avoiding the curricula of France and Belgium until the present day. A novel chemistry course in the upper secondary school in France shows the first crack in the almost impregnable cultural defense of the abstract and deductive in science education.

This gives us an instructive example of the diverse thought traditions existing within Europe—the Latin countries emphasizing the rational and abstract, while the northern countries are more empirical and heuristic. The United Kingdom has a tradition of choosing content with reference to its moral value for children; in Sweden it is almost an overriding criterion. France gives precedence to mathematical content and still confines entrance to its prestigious *Grandes Écoles* to those who have passed the scientific and mathematical baccalaureate.

In STS teaching, discussions using moral positions and value judgments take place within the science classroom, thus creating an element of full-blooded popular communication with all its moral and political elements of argumentation. Environmental and other science-based issues are controversial precisely because they do not exist just within the confines of a system of logical thought. They connect with other areas of our lives where the controversy is about local values and social responsibility.

Academic Scientific Culture

Academic science itself bids to be a culture of quite another kind, one common across the invisible college that unites professional scientists from around the world. Within Europe, and most countries of the world, the scientific content of the published national curricula, at least at secondary school level, is almost identical. Ohm's Law,

Newton's Laws of Motion, the function of photosynthesis—all of these and many others familiar to the reader—are parts of the cultural heritage of all children and figure in all national curricula. However, learning the scientific meaning of such topics requires a considerable period of effort and acculturation; Schutz and Luckmann (1973) call it a "secondary process of socialization." In a scientific meaning system, such words as *energy* and *life* have specialized meanings that differ from what they more vaguely imply in daily conversation (cf. Säljö, Chapter 4, and Östman, Chapter 5, in this volume). Scientific meanings are precise and lack the common ambiguity that fathers both poetry and puns in other contexts. Academic science is serious about its methodology, and also about its explanations. Originality may be praised in an Einstein, but it is suspect in a student.

Another reflection of the general functions of a culture can be seen in the requirements for scientific communication. Research papers need to be clear, unambiguous, and understandable across different language frontiers. They are to contain neither poetry nor puns. Unfortunately, we have tended to expect the same of our school science students. Science is a strict knowledge culture prescribing the meanings of words, experimental design, the form of explanations, and even the methods of publication of its practitioners. For our students it is a whole new world of thought. Coming to feel comfortable within this new territory is, for most of our young students, as long and slow a process as joining a new tribe might be. To make it even more difficult, the students find that while they learn, their own culture of everyday life and meanings continues to intrude on every side.

Operating in these two different domains of thought (Solomon, 1984) is essential if students are to become professional scientists. The problem is that not many of the young people in our classes are going to be scientists in this sense, so educationalists have been debating whether they need to tread the difficult track of full enculturation with all their students. This curricular discussion has been going on for a considerable time and lately with greater urgency (Aikenhead, 1994; Duschl, 1988; Solomon, 1987). Can science be taught so that it connects with attitudes, personal values, and political issues? This would indeed make science a part of popular culture. But would it still be science?

WHAT IS A "CULTURE"?

What Europeans would call *la culture scientifique* is similar to, but also subtly different from, both "Public Understanding of Science" in the United Kingdom and "Scientific Literacy" in North America. At first sight it may not seem surprising to find the term "culture" emphasized in this concept. The European nations pride themselves on their long history of prestigious knowledge. It includes such venerable subjects as philosophy and the arts, without which a person in previous ages might not have been considered fit to take an honorable place in educated discourse. Culture, in this sense, holds a more elitist place in general estimation than does literacy.

However, alongside this prestigious knowledge the term "culture" also can refer to popular attitudes, knowing, and doing. In the contemporary scene, anthropologists have begun to conceptualize culture as so fragmented that it can apply to every group of people and every type of living. From this perspective Clifford Geertz (1983), writing about local knowledge and attitudes, summarizes the meaning of the term in his pithy comment, "We are all natives now!" That includes students and their teachers, as well as parents and their parliaments. Every person and every group "has" a culture, in this sense. An earlier anthropological tradition confined the meaning of culture to the codes of conduct that people learn by imitation and that could, more or less, be written down by a visiting anthropologist. More recently anthropologists have come to see that there is also a tacit cultural understanding about how things are, or how they should be—what Bourdieu (1977) called "the habitus"— which continues to exist alongside the encoded culture.

What constitutes a culture was defined in an early seminal work by Geertz (1973). He argued, with a host of examples, that culture is not a self-contained reality with forces and purposes of its own. This already constitutes an important warning to the science education community, governments in general, and the EC in particular. Scientific culture can be uniform with respect to neither general outcome nor popular intention. Thus we cannot educate precisely for a culture that will accept or reject new genetic technology. All we can do is to teach scientific knowledge about genetics in such a way and with such illustrations that it sets up links in the students' minds with other spheres of living and feeling. This cross-linking is the essence of the view of culture being developed here. From it follows a description broad enough to encompass both the popular and academic senses of scientific culture:

> Believing, with Max Weber, that man is an animal suspended in webs of significance he himself has spun, I take culture to be those webs. (Geertz, 1973, p. 5)

The linked meanings that constitute these webs thus become the focus of the study of scientific culture and of the school curriculum.

COMPANION MEANINGS AND WEBS OF SIGNIFICANCE

What Primary School Science Can Mean

One of the recent innovations in school science education, and probably the most potent for making links to everyday meanings, is the introduction of science into primary schools. Almost all European countries now have this in their national curricula or are about to introduce it. Since young children are more likely than older ones to rush home to parents to tell about what they have learned and to ask questions, there is a possibility of two-way linkage here. Parents whose own education lacked any formal science content may be pleasantly surprised to find that this apparently arcane and forbidding subject can be made easy enough for their young children to study. They may even find it interesting enough to want to participate in simple family activities or visits to a science museum. More unfortunately, other parents may convey to their children a personal view of the difficulty or unpleasantness of learning science. In this and many other ways, aspects of primary science can become embedded, for good or ill, in the mini-culture of the home (Solomon, 1994b).

Most European countries have decided that "the environment" is the most suitable topic for primary science. Sometimes, indeed, it seems to be all that is taught, and in countries such as Norway, Sweden, and Spain, voices from the educational establishment are questioning whether just *feelings* for animals and *enjoyment* of the countryside might not be swamping scientific learning. At one level this kind of teaching may even point the finger at science, implicitly or explicitly, as the villain of all our environmental problems. Renate Bader (1993) has written about the adult public perception of science in Germany in the following terms:

> Ecology is not necessarily seen as a science, but as a new holistic approach to all aspects of life and nature. It is precisely those most disenchanted with and critical of traditional research and its applications who are drawn towards the "Greens". Science for them equals risk; ecology is the saviour. (p. 49)

If that companion meaning is communicated by science teaching, it might be enough to build a lifetime of anti-science attitudes. Even if the hostile link is not forged deliberately, it can be reinforced implicitly if primary science curricula omit all physics and chemistry and concentrate only on biology, as they often do. Indeed it is only in the United Kingdom that physics and chemistry content (e.g., connecting simple electric circuits and making solutions) is specified for primary-age pupils.

The Epistemology of Science

The debate on including the history and philosophy of science in science lessons and science curricula is still unresolved. The United Kingdom launched its first National Curriculum with a compulsory Attainment Target on "the nature of science," which included stories from history; but within 2 years this was almost completely dropped from the curriculum. In France the philosophical component in education, once compulsory until 18 years of age, has been greatly reduced. That country is now more of a leader in the Interactive Science movement than in natural philosophy. The evidence on how companion meanings about epistemology get through to students points more to the teacher than to the particular science topics of the curriculum.

One way to incorporate history and philosophy of science in the curriculum is to make links between what the student learns in science and in history. This serves not only to embed science more securely in the culture, but also to place ideas and theories in the human context of their discoverer. Students may find the abstract mental modeling that is demanded by physics and chemistry very difficult to learn; human modeling—such as working out how it might feel to be a scientist on the brink of a new discovery—is far easier for many people.

Another way is to teach the processes of hypothesis making and testing through practical work in the laboratory. In most European countries there are official exhortations to teachers to do just this. The general opinion, however, is that this advice is mostly ignored. In the United Kingdom, "Scientific Investigations" is enshrined in the curriculum, but attempts to organize nationwide standardized tests to support and evaluate its teaching had to be abandoned. It remains in the curriculum and is assessed by teachers, however. It would be an interesting project to find out how far classroom practice has actually been changed by this formal inclusion in the curriculum.

Gender, Choice, and Difficulty

There are common perceptions within Europe about the difficulty of science. These are moderated with respect to gender and type of science discipline. Although it is widely held that physics is not only a male subject, but also inherently difficult and widely disliked for this reason alone, it might be wise to pause before attributing this to some actual difficulty in the subject itself. In almost all the Interactive, Hands-on Science Centers, a large majority of the exhibits are related to physics. Small children may love cuddly animals, but they are also fascinated by experiments with mirrors, magnets, and colors. So indeed are most adults, women as well as men. It has always been a matter of some surprise that these are so emphatically not the topics most taught in school or given prominence in the physics curricula of most countries.

The designation of physics as a boy's subject and biology as a girl's subject is widespread and has been the object of much discussion, especially in feminist circles. However, it is not a uniform designation across Europe. The division scarcely exists at all in Portugal, Spain, and most Eastern European countries. It is strongest in the United Kingdom, Sweden, Italy, and the Netherlands, where the problem has been both perceived for several decades and tackled with some vigor, in the same way as it has been in the United States and Australia. Clearly, then, it is a cultural artifact, but one produced in ways that are still basically mysterious.

One dilemma for this Europe-wide project was that a study of national curricula can provide numerical data on students' preference for science only if there is room for student choice of subject. In Belgium, the Netherlands, and Germany, selection at about the age of 12 into different schools may effectively force pupils into "science or nonscience" options. In Belgium it also affects whether practical work is available for pupils. Where this choice or selection does not exist, students may not be at all clear about gender stereotyping or about which of the sciences they prefer. Data about girls' and boys' actual enjoyment of science is much more difficult to obtain. What is needed is more action research rather than questionnaire data, where responses so often are evoked by the question rather than revealing genuine preferences. Not only is choice of subject by gender *illustrated* by the statistics provided where the possibility for choice exists, but the figures may actually be *generated*, or at least emphasized, by the provision of choice. There is evidence from both the British and Australian experiences (Byrne, 1993) that the gender preferences become more accentuated when students are allowed to choose which science to study or permitted to opt out of studying science altogether. This is not just a question of the number of females taking science, but the actual enjoyment of those that do.

Another factor that may be important is the prominence of mathematics in the science being learned. Potential employers often use mathematics or physics as a criterion for selection to well-paid jobs in commerce and banking. So do many universities such as the prestigious *Grandes Écoles* in France. It could be argued that this practice serves to keep up a level of difficulty in mathematics and science in general that is not helpful for their public image. The science considered to be the most difficult, physics, is, of course, the one involving the highest level of mathematics. It is also the science in which there is most gender differentiation.

SCIENTIFIC CULTURE AND SCHOOL SCIENCE

Companion meanings of the sort just discussed have to be taken seriously in considering how citizens develop their sense of what scientific culture is. Students are caught up in webs of their significances, and curriculum policy makers and developers have control over some, but not all, of the sources of significance within school science curricula. The messages of many of the companion meanings noted here are communicated by the way science is taught. Yet, in some cases they can be components of curricula; whether history and philosophy of science are present or absent is a matter of choice, for example. But what of the issues of gender and perceived difficulty? The broad sense of scientific culture insists that we heed all such issues, that they are part of the significances attached to science by our young people who will become our future citizenry.

"Academic" scientific culture also must be cultivated so that the whole edifice of scientific knowledge is accessible by those who may become the next generation of science scholars. It is only through such transmission that our young students can, in the words of Isaac Newton, "stand on the shoulders of giants" and carry out valuable new research. That process requires some practical work, and an historical dimension, but it also needs a very high level of abstract and mathematical capability, which, as we have noted, is difficult and discouraging for most students.

There are aspects of vocational preparation in science-related fields other than those of pure research science, of course—for example, engineering, medicine, and computer technology. It is harder to identify these with any particular "kind" of school science program. Of course, practical work is essential for such students, but so also are core transferable skills that include communication of many kinds, familiarity with information technology, some mathematics, and a sound conceptual understanding of science. For these students, as indeed for most citizens, science education should include some familiarity with science in its industrial setting.

"Popular" scientific culture is just as significant an educational requirement: the promotion of a wide scientific and technical culture as discussed in this chapter. It is a process brought about by an attitude and a willingness to learn more science as innovation presents it. Science needs to be learned in order that everyone can appreciate new developments and can evaluate them for their own and others' styles of living. This requires, as we have seen, linkage with other areas of thought as well as moral sensibility, and simple enjoyment.

Are there conflicts among the requirements for these three purposes for school science education? Perhaps the two kinds of vocational preparation require more conceptual science teaching in secondary schools than does education for the broader sense of scientific culture. All three purposes require more engagement between the students' ideas and hypotheses and their laboratory activities. All three types of education could benefit from more awareness of industrial science, and more historical links.

Only in one respect is there a substantial problem in the formulation of a school science curriculum that can serve all three of these societal purposes. The challenge seems to be how to teach valid and relevant science in the largely comprehensive schools of Europe without coming up against the barrier of mathematical and conceptual difficulty. The cautionary note in backing away from that challenge is that the broader sense of scientific culture will be distorted into one of its narrower meanings, as the term "culture" once implied, or else that success in school science could become a trademark for the intellectuality of a small minority of research boffins.

This chapter makes no attempt to specify curriculum content appropriate to the task, for the task has more to do with companion meanings than with content. Indeed, the data from Europe suggest that content is likely to be common in most respects in most countries. However, the argument does insist that scientific culture, in Europe as in other countries, must by its very nature embrace all citizens and not remain the preserve of any intellectual or mathematical elite.

CHAPTER 13

The Politics of Legitimating and Marginalizing Companion Meanings: Three Australian Case Stories

PETER J. FENSHAM

THERE IS SOMETHING REMARKABLE about changing the science curriculum for upper secondary school courses. Often students' achievement in these courses is the major criterion for their selection and entry into university and other tertiary courses of study that involve science and technology. The individual and societal significance of these transitions makes curriculum debate at this level quite different from the debate about science that occurs at lower levels of schooling. At the lower levels also there is much argument and discussion about the content of the curriculum and how it should be taught, but the key players tend to be within the school sector. When the upper secondary science curriculum is in contention, other, outside players are added. Among these "extras" are academic scientists who, historically, have had the lead or starring roles in this periodic drama.

In the Australian state of Victoria, the lead by academic scientists was definitive, while the final levels of schooling were essentially for students who intended to study at one of the universities in that state—that is, until the early 1970s. The University of Melbourne, founded in 1856, until the 1960s was the only university. In that decade it was joined by Monash and Latrobe Universities, as the student population of Victoria burgeoned—with immigration supplementing the baby boom after the Second World War. (The states and territories of Australia control their education systems individually.)

Since 1975, full secondary education steadily has become a mass phenomenon. Chronic youth unemployment forced participation by many students in addition to those who traditionally enrolled in the upper secondary years. The tertiary education scene also changed as many vocational colleges were established, and former teachers colleges and senior technical institutes became universities. Despite these considerable changes in the composition of grade 12 students and in the educational sector beyond school during the past 2 decades, the dominant voice heard in discourse about the upper secondary school science curriculum has continued to be that of scientists at the University of Melbourne—although now they are supported to a degree by their academic colleagues elsewhere.

In this chapter, three "case stories" are presented as a basis for exploring the remarkable dominance of the academic scientists' voice in this discourse. The term "case story" is used in the sense given it by Biddle and Anderson (1986, p. 238), to identify relatively brief, descriptive accounts to be used for illustrative purposes rather than for extensive analysis. The case stories are one person's interpretation (the author's), which inevitably will suggest that these events were simpler social situations than they were in fact. The various players in each of the dramas might write different accounts. Perhaps they would not agree on the significance of events in each chain of happenings; the contributions made by groups and individuals certainly would be valued differently. Nevertheless, it is the author's view that a significant role is being played by academic scientists in these cases, with respect to the politics of legitimating and marginalizing specific "companion meanings" as part of what students will learn in science courses.

The remainder of the chapter is structured in three sections. Following some historical background, the cases are presented as a group. The final section is an analysis and reflection on the dynamics of the interaction in these cases and in similar situations.

HISTORICAL BACKGROUND FOR THE CASES

In 1944 the Education System in Victoria moved away from the Scottish model that had been such a strong influence on its origins in the late 1800s. Instead of the grade 11 Leaving Examination, a grade 12 (Sixth Form) was added to secondary schooling and its examination became the basis for matriculation to study at the only university in the state at that time, the University of Melbourne. Approximately 10% of the age cohort were in school in grade 12 to take the Matriculation Examination. Among the 27 subjects that were available for study were five science subjects: agricultural science, biology, chemistry, geology, and physics.

Soon afterward, a general science course (officially referred to as science) became the form of science study in grades 7–10. Its content in each year was made up of topics drawn from biology, chemistry, geology, physics, and astronomy. This left grades 11 and 12 as the period during which students were expected to undertake further study of separate science subjects for matriculation purposes. In 1969, the external Leaving Examination at the end of grade 11 was abolished, and a number of school-based curriculum initiatives began to appear. However, little change occurred in the five science subjects, three of which (biology, chemistry, and physics) by then were strongly based on NSF-supported curriculum projects in the United States.

By 1975, nearly 30% of each age cohort continued to grade 12. The number of subjects offered in the Higher School Certificate (HSC) Examination had risen to 57, but there were still only the original five science subjects. Most students studied five subjects in grade 12, and university entrance was based on a student's "best four" results. Biology was the most popular subject, apart from compulsory English, and girls dominated its enrollment. Chemistry and physics were still in the top 10 subjects for enrollments. However, both had lost substantially in the proportion of grade 12 students they attracted, compared with the early 1960s when about half of the grade 12 students studied them and the two advanced mathematics subjects (the "golden four" as they often have been called). Chemistry was slightly biased toward boys, and physics was very strongly so. Geology and agricultural science had few students, being offered by only a few schools, although the latter had something of a revival when it was redefined in 1980 as environmental science.[1]

Retention to grade 12 increased more rapidly after 1975 as high unemployment (particularly among early school leavers) became a chronic feature of the Australian economic and social scene. In response, the schools invented a number of alternative curricula for the final 2 years, some of which were recognized for tertiary entrance by Colleges of Advanced Education (tertiary institutions developed since the 1980s from primary teachers colleges or vocational senior technical colleges). The universities resisted such recognition, and alternative science subjects were not part of these new curricula, except for a radical one that was based on a negotiated and balanced program of integrated studies in which science was to have a place. (Science in this program was very elastically defined and not usually in terms of traditional content.) Not surprisingly, the proportion of this expanding student body studying chemistry and physics (the two "gateway" prerequisites to so many university science- and technology-related courses) continued to decline.

In 1984–85 Dr. Jean Blackburn conducted a major review of what was termed "postcompulsory education" (grades 11 and 12). Her diagnosis (1984) of the issues, in which access and equity loomed large, was well received, and her suggestions that detailed work should be undertaken on curriculum, credentialing, and the structural aspects of school programs were implemented. The ensuing report (Blackburn, 1985) was received with much less unanimity, but the state Labor Government adopted most of its recommendations. A new body, the Victorian Curriculum and Assessment Board (VCAB), was charged with designing a totally new overall curriculum for these 2 years of study to lead to a Victorian Certificate of Education (VCE). The VCE was to serve a number of purposes, including the traditional one of providing the basis for university preparation and selection.

Fourteen Fields of Study were defined. Field of Study Committees (FOSCS) were established for each, having very wide representation from all sectors of education and including for the first time the vocational sector. Teacher unions were strongly represented, along with nominees from the wider trade union movement and from the key industrial or commercial bodies. Science was just one of the Fields of Study so that, for the first time in Victorian education at this level, there was no Chemistry Committee, no Physics Committee, and so on. The interests of these hitherto powerful subjects were to be attended to by subcommittees of the overall Science Field of Study Committee, which, at least initially, had the widely representative character referred to above. The VCE was to be introduced in grade 11 in 1991 so that the administrative staff of VCAB had 3 years in which to deliver a very radical and unfamiliar model of a senior secondary curriculum. The detailed work in the Fields of Study was to be done by the voluntary committees mentioned above and a small number of persons employed as writers attached to each of the FOSCS. The case stories, presented next, need to be seen in the light of this brief historical sketch.

CASE I

The Setting

In the face of the declining popularity of the "golden four" subjects, a curriculum team was established in 1975 to develop a course of study and supporting materials for a single grade 12 subject in the physical sciences. Much had happened since the mid-1960s when local versions of NSF-sponsored courses from the United States had become the curriculum for chemistry and physics. There was now very strong recognition in Australia of the importance of environmental issues. The author (the new project's team leader) had been involved with others since 1973 in Australia's response to the UNESCO–UNEP challenge to contribute through schooling to issues of conservation and environmental quality (Linke, 1976). Australians knew of the world oil crisis, although its impact was relatively less than elsewhere because local oil had just come on line. Qualitative evidence from young people and the community suggested a wider disillusionment about science beyond the numerical evidence of a decline in the proportion of senior secondary students studying chemistry and physics.

The team, accordingly, viewed its task as extending the participation of students in the physical sciences—rather different from those who saw it simply as extracting some essential part of the content of existing physics and chemistry.

The developers were inspired conceptually by the phrase, "Man and the Physical World" (on a banner wrapped around a globe, it could also read, "Woman and the Physical World"). They used it as an abiding criterion for selecting the new course's content and emphasis. Existing physics and chemistry were seen as concerned with the conceptual outcomes of scientists' attempts to describe and explain physical phenomena. Physical science, on the other hand, was to be concerned with various aspects of the interaction between humans and the physical world. Thus, the processes whereby scientists investigate phenomena (including how concepts are invented), the interactions between science and society via technology, and the authority of the scientific community in society were to become content alongside the conceptual outcomes in the two sciences.

The Proposed Course

Academic and applied scientists who were consulted suggested several topics to include. One was a more realistic treatment of energy and the practical problems of its use, and accordingly two units, "Energy Transformations" and "Engines and Fuels," were developed. Another suggestion was recognition of the many exciting new materials coming into use, and this led to "Useful Materials," which included the study of polymers, wood, ceramics, and metals. Because of the well-known problems students have in relating the atomic- and molecular-scale representations in chemistry and physics to macroscopic systems, the team decided to restrict these representations to easily observable properties of the materials, such as hardness, elasticity, and electrical and thermal conductivity.

The units developed by the team were grouped under three broad topics: "Energy Use," "Materials," and "Change." Although some units dealt mainly with content that would be recognized as physics or chemistry, all of them drew from both sciences and in a number the integration of content went beyond such disciplinary identification. One unit about "Change," for example, considered the precision with which changes could be predicted when almost elastic collisions occurred between billiard balls, when chemicals reacted, and when new technologies entered society.

The Response

As these units were developed, criticisms began to emerge from academic scientists involved in chemistry and physics, particularly at the University of Melbourne. These took several forms. The "Energy" units were said to be inappropriate simply because the treatment of the concept of energy was not the same as the treatment in chemistry and physics courses. Some accused the very practical treatment of efficiency in energy transformations as an attempt to teach the Second Law of Thermodynamics—which should be left to the universities. The social, economic, and environmental associations with energy were said to be inappropriate for a course including the word *science* in its title. Again, the inclusion of types of materials (including metallic alloys) that were not in the existing physics and chemistry courses was objected to.

A professor of physics at the University of Melbourne who had, and still has, a strong interest in the teaching of physics at the school level approached the team members with an offer. He would support them if they would declare that the subject would be for "nonscience students" only. He would oppose them if they persisted with the original intention of offering an alternative means of studying the physical sciences for "would-be science students." Approval of the course to become a grade 12, matriculation subject required, at that time, the independent consent of the Academic Committees of the three universities in Victoria and of the Board responsible for the HSC and its examinations. By chance, the Board meeting was the same date and time as the meeting of Melbourne's Academic Committee. The main opponents from Melbourne's physics department chose to attend the Board meeting, where they lost the debate; meanwhile in their absence the Melbourne Academic Committee approved the course.

This approval did not mean the end of the opposition, and the subject was shackled in a number of ways throughout the next 15 years of its life. It was not listed by any of the universities as either a recommended or a prerequisite subject for any faculty. Despite this silence, it could be studied and counted in students' selection for the Science Faculty of each university and for several other technical faculties. Its opponents did, however, persuade the Board that it could not be taken with physics or chemistry, despite their argument earlier that its content was inappropriate because it deviated from these subjects. This latter constraint, together with the fact that chemistry was a prerequisite for the two Medical Faculties in Victoria (as physics and chemistry were for the Engineering Faculty), meant that small schools with few academically oriented students dared not offer it, lest they forego the prospect of retaining an academic reputation. When physical science came up for reaccreditation, the University of Melbourne made another attempt to discredit it along with two other subjects. This move was aborted, probably because one of the other subjects—human development and society (an evolution in the 1970s of home economics)—had very strong support from a prestigious private girls school!

Nevertheless, physical science was offered each year from 1977 through 1991. Enrollment ranged from 100 to 200 students, in six to 15 schools. During this period, the core of the curriculum in all subjects was externally assessed, while optional components were internally assessed. The examiners for the subject, accordingly, did develop great expertise and experience in assessing what was perhaps the first STS science course to be a mainstream alternative to the study of the prestigious disciplinary sciences of chemistry and physics (Thomas, 1987). The subject pioneered relations with industry by having applied scientists on the committee and as advisors. In 1982, when STS began to be used as the slogan for more inclusive and socially relevant school science, the name of the subject was changed to Physical Science, Technology, and Society.

CASE II

The Setting

A number of curriculum policies of the VCAB stemmed directly from the tenor of the Blackburn Report of 1985. The postcompulsory curriculum was to (1) promote inclusive participation, (2) be challenging and worthwhile for all students, (3) balance theory and application, (4) relate knowledge to its social context, reflecting the Australian experience, and (5) encourage links across the disciplines.

A number of the new representatives on the Science FOSC (including environmental science, vocational education, and "the McClintock Collective" for more gender-inclusive science) believed that their goals for school science education would not be achieved if the traditional sciences continued to define the subjects. Very early in the FOSC's life there was a major debate on the issue of disciplinary and nondisciplinary science subjects. Six members favored no disciplinary sciences at all, four (who included representatives from the University of Melbourne and two elite private schools) favored only disciplinary sciences, and nine opted for a mix. The representational presence of the traditional sciences thus was very much reduced in the Science FOSC at this stage.

The First Proposal

Following this debate, the Committee proceeded to work on the basis of the disciplinary/nondisciplinary compromise, the only structure able to command majority support. A common study of science was proposed for the first semester of grade 11, to be followed by branching sequences for three semesters of study in each of the four traditional disciplinary sciences and in science (a contemporary inheritance from physical science in Case I) and environmental science. This structure could be, and was, argued for most strongly on the grounds of VCAB's policy on inclusiveness, but it was also consonant with the policies on substantive merit, social/Australian context, and cross-disciplinary links.

Response to the First Proposal

The Executive Committee of VCAB suddenly intervened in May 1987, during a 3-month period the Board had declared for discussion and comment about its initial plans for the VCE. It notified the Science FOSC in a stormy meeting that it was recommending to the next meeting of the full Board that "branching structures based on a common, identical or compulsory semester unit across several studies within a field will not be acceptable" and that "all studies will be prepared in at least two-unit sequences" (Hart, 1995, quoting from the Executive minutes). In other words, the disciplinary/nondisciplinary compromise was unacceptable.

Most members of the FOSC, which had seemed to be a strongly unified working group, were very angry. Through external pressure (the University of Melbourne representatives being the obvious source), a small minority opinion in the FOSC's own debate had gained the approval of the Executive, none of whose four members had a science background. In the days before the Board meeting, an intense lobbying effort was undertaken by FOSC members, to explain to the Board members the equity and other bases for the FOSC's plan. The Executive's recommendation won by a vote of 10 to 9. (One proxy vote from the vocational sector was ruled inadmissible.) Salt was rubbed into the wounds of the FOSC when the Chief Executive Officer stated that "while specifically excluding the common compulsory gateway unit of Science, the Board was nonetheless supportive of the FOSC's resolve to address problems relating to participation, gender balance and flexible access in science and to the development of a broader view of science" (Hill, 1987, p. 1).

The Second Proposal

Quite soon after this, two women on the FOSC—one from the McClintock and one from vocational education—resigned and were replaced by teachers with more traditional views. Gradually the composition of the FOSC became very different from the group that had so strongly supported the common science unit. Nevertheless, the FOSC, including the opponents of the common unit, readily accepted the principle that the content of all the science studies should include the nature of science and its relation to technology and society. In support of this STS principle, the FOSC developed the following "Introductory Statement" to begin each of its six sets of studies:

> The six studies (in the Science Field) have been developed by a single Field of Study Committee . . . to a common framework drawn from VCAB policy and research findings in science education. . . .
> Science serves economic and environmental purposes as well as cultural and personal ones. Scientific research often extends across disciplines in its social impact and in the way research is conducted. The science studies recognise the interdisciplinary aspects of science as part of problem solving, application and the context of science.
> The studies emphasise:
> - theoretical knowledge and the processes scientists use to develop and test the knowledge
> - technology and the solution of practical problems in technological development and environmental management

- the relationships between science and society, the way science proceeds, the values which guide scientific activity, and the influences of scientific discovery on values and beliefs in society.[2]

Response to the Second Proposal

The six subcommittees set about their tasks of developing sequences of curriculum units, reporting regularly to the FOSC as a whole on their efforts to reconstruct six subjects that all had form and content, with the emphases referred to in the "Introductory Statement." Not surprisingly, some were more successful than others. For both physics and chemistry, as the two sciences from which the greatest concern about the common gateway proposal had come, substantial changes were suggested, and writing to support them continued through 1988 and 1989.

The FOSC thus was quite unprepared when, late in 1989, a VCAB administrative committee, coordinating and editing the materials from the 14 FOSCs, decided without consultation that "the *Statement* is unsuitable for use in the study designs" (Hart, 1995, quoting from Science FOSC minutes of November 21, 1989, p. 3). Thus was begun the whittling away of the agreement to an STS orientation in these senior science studies.[3]

CASE III

The Setting and the Initial Proposal

A related proposal surfaced during the debate about the common, or "gateway," unit of science for all students entering the final 2 years of secondary school. The intent of the proposal was to give students an opportunity to reflect on their 12 years of studying science, in the fourth-semester units of these 2 years, and to help them identify features of science as a way of knowing about the natural world, while they learned about the content of some of the really big questions scientists had been asking for hundreds of years.

Under pressure from the universities and from the conservatism of many disciplinary science teachers to include as much of their previous content as possible in the new STS framework, the subcommittees for biology, chemistry, geology, and physics could do very little about this proposal. The subcommittee for science did, however, put a lot of effort into devising such a unit. "Changing Views of the Origin of the Earth" and "Changing Views of Life on Earth" were the two big topics that were chosen to be the basic content of *Changing Views of the Universe*, Unit 4 of science. The unit was developed with suggestions for a number of "Work Requirements" (learning experiences that teachers should ensure students undertake during the semester, from which their assessment in the unit would be derived). One of these became notorious as "Work Requirement 7." It related to the general intention of having students reflect on the whole of their school science learning. The requirement read as follows:

> Purpose: to assist students to appreciate the way in which their understanding of scientific ideas has taken shape and the general nature of the development of scientific ideas.
>
> Description: Students should prepare a brief statement explaining their understanding of a scientific concept or natural phenomenon before and after a period of study. The statement should include comment on influences which led to change in their original views.
>
> This could involve:
> - listing knowledge and explanations before and after a period of investigation
> - commenting on processes involved in changing the student's views, which are similar to or different from processes occurring in the development of scientific ideas
> - preparing concept maps of the student's ideas prior to and after completing the period of study
> - keeping a diary which notes significant changes in the student's understanding of the scientific concepts studied.
>
> Students should provide an account of the effects of the learning activities on their original views.[4]

The Response

This proposed activity was not at all surprising to those on the science subcommittee who were familiar with, or interested in, the constructivist approaches to science learning that had been presented prominently for a decade to science teachers in Victoria by researchers such as Osborne of New Zealand and Gunstone and White of Monash. After all, numbers of these teachers were using regularly "Predict–Observe–Explain" and other cognitive conflict strategies as a regular part of their teaching. In Victoria the research of Baird and White, as early as 1982, had publicized the keeping of a learning diary by students as a useful pedagogical technique. The subcommittee strongly favored Work Requirement 7, but its new staff writer was not comfortable with it. By various devices, internal to VCAB, he and other VCAB bureaucrats stalled its inclusion in the proposed study details, referring it back to the subcommittee and ensuring that it was debated at length in the FOSC, which at this time was much more traditionally represented with new members unfamiliar with the original interest in the idea of a reflective and summative unit.

As Work Requirement 7 became a cause célèbre, academic concern was again evident. The discussion and debate in the FOSC produced a number of contradictory and bizarre arguments against it. The University of Melbourne scientist said it was too difficult and that he would be unable to do what was required. One of his usual allies among the more traditional teachers, on the other hand, argued that it was trivial and below the rigor and level of learning that should be expected in grade 12 sciences. Another argument was that its real intention (despite the explicit study-related suggestions above) was to push students to reveal their underlying religious and other belief systems.

Work Requirement 7 did survive in the FOSC itself. However, by the time other general review committees of VCAB had carried out what had become a regular sanitizing of the Science FOSC's units, it was hard to recognize in it the notion of reflecting on one's learning of science.

DISCUSSION

In each of the cases, academic scientists (1) advocated a very narrow view of the curricular purpose of school science, and (2) exercised considerable political influence to legitimate their view and marginalize any others. In fact, their influence on the VCE bureaucrats was so powerful that it outweighed what Orpwood calls all other "contributions" and "considerations," in his model for analyzing science curriculum talk (Chapter 10 in this volume). Furthermore, their view was the most narrow of all of the "curriculum emphases" identified in North American science education history (Roberts, Chapter 1 in this volume).

Neither the view nor the extensive influence of such a view is a surprise to anyone who works in science curriculum. Nonetheless, this final section of the chapter explores some aspects of what seems to lie behind the events that occurred. While one might be tempted to consider the cases as sources of data from which generalizations can be made about science curriculum change, or about academic scientists as a group, this discussion will move in another direction of analysis. The point of what follows is to try to understand.[5]

What Doesn't Count

A number of assertions are listed below, about what seemed to be the core of resistance to the innovations discussed in the three cases. Where appropriate, these have been labeled (in parentheses) in terms of Roberts's curriculum emphases; three other categories have been added (Fensham, 1994) that capture companion meanings in some more recent curriculum developments: Science for Nurturing, Science in Applications, and Science in Making. So in this first analytical step, we are considering which curriculum emphases and companion meanings stand a good chance of being marginalized. Innovation in secondary school science, particularly in the senior years, seems to be a risky business for—

- A science course, as in Case III, that acknowledges the tentative character or socially constructed nature of scientific knowledge in the science community or by individuals learning it (Structure of Science; Self as Explainer)
- A science course, as in all three cases, that draws in an integrated way its content from a number of scientific disciplines (Science for Nurturing; Science, Technology, and Decisions)
- A science course, as in Cases I and II, that includes social, political, and economic aspects of the STS relationships as content rather than as mere motivation (Science, Technology, and Decisions; Science for Nurturing; Science in Applications)
- A science course, as in Cases II and III, that includes historical and sociological aspects of the nature of science as content (Structure of Science; Self as Explainer)
- A science course, as in Cases I and II, that derives some of its content from applications of science, from technology, and from environmental issues (Science in Applications; Everyday Coping; Science, Technology, and Decisions; Science for Nurturing; Science in Making)
- A science course, as in Case I, that claims to be an alternative basis to prepare students for entry into science-based courses at the university level—especially if more able students are attracted to it

ACADEMIC SCIENTISTS AS GUARDIANS

Three of the curriculum emphases do not appear in these assertions. Solid Foundation, Correct Explanations, and to a lesser extent Scientific Skill Development were the priorities of the academic scientists and some of the more academic teachers in all three cases. Layton (1973) has referred to the role academic scientists play as "guardians of the disciplines," and some recent work by De Vos, van Berkel, and Verdonk (1994) and van Berkel (1994) in the context of chemistry has helped to elaborate what this means. They identified as one of the main tasks of its guardians, the "demarcation" of school chemistry (1) from common sense, (2) from physics and other sciences, and (3) from technology.

The first of these demarcations is concerned with changing conceptions like "stuff" for materials into more rigorously defined "substances." The second decrees, for example, that chemical changes are distinct from physical ones, and the third sets out to avoid such confusions as that between "pure water" in a research laboratory and "pure water" in society. These demarcations are served most easily by denying the existence in the curriculum of the alternatives, and it is just these alternatives that the emphases associated with the assertions above would include in senior school science. This understanding of "guardianship" clarifies much of what occurred in the cases, each of which began with the curriculum developers assuming that interdisciplinary science and active learning in the interface zones between science, technology, and society were desirable pedagogically.

Alternative Student Motivations

An ascetic dourness in science curricula was expected by the academic scientists in all three cases. Changes in the curriculum—knowledge content or pedagogy and assessment—that were responsive to students' interests or to aspects external to the hierarchical education system were viewed with suspicion or disdain. Students were expected to find their motivation in the inherent neatness and power of the conceptual structure of the empirical disciplines (Correct Explanations and Scientific Skill Development) or in the reward that entry to a university course offered (Solid Foundation). The positive attitudes of Victorian students who had studied physical science were not seen as relevant, nor was the considerable evidence of negative attitudes among students studying chemistry and physics. Positive reports from elsewhere about student responses to STS-type science courses such as PLON physics (Science, Technology, and Decisions; Structure of Science; Science as Applications) in the Netherlands (Jorg & Wubbels, 1987) and "Chemistry from Issues" (Science in Applications; Science for Nurturing) in England (Harding & Donaldson, 1986), which inspired the protagonists in Cases II and III, meant nothing to the antagonists.

Exposing the Clay Feet

In their own domain of research, academic scientists accept and practice the provisional nature of science, are well aware of and skilled in the internal processes whereby science is developed and validated, and generally accept the limitations of science (and of themselves) in making judgments about socio-scientific issues. These are companion meanings that are developed in both Structure of Science and Science, Technology, and Decisions curriculum emphases. Aikenhead (1985), Fleming (1986), Millar and Wynne (1988), and Solomon (1988) have been advocating, since the mid-1980s, inclusion of these companion meanings in school science.

The academic scientists in Cases I and III were opposed to inclusion of such companion meanings. It was as if sharing the existence of these socially constructed procedures with a neonate or nonscience audience would undermine an authority about their knowledge that these academics have a responsibility to protect. Bingle and Gaskell (1994) have pointed out how this power and authority of science is threatened by the complexity of real-life environmental situations, for which a totally scientific analysis is impossible. Science educators tend to take a very different view of this matter, and their emergence as another group of academics is significantly shifting the debate about the school science curriculum, as I have discussed elsewhere (Fensham, 1992). There is perhaps a major issue about distribution of power here, as discussed by Geddis (Chapter 9 in this volume).

Behind the Cases

This discussion of these cases could easily go too far in the modernistic direction of assuming that curriculum change is only a matter of laying bare the competing claims and needs, and of meeting them with a rational compromise. To counter that assumption, I will conclude by discussing the cases at quite a different level.

If science in school is to become an important knowledge field for all students as future citizens, as well as for the small minority who go on to become scientific professionals, it needs to become a process of empowerment for living, rather than an inevitably incomplete induction into one or more of the scientific disciplines. It seems also, if empowerment is to be sensed, that students need to be studying science at the highest level of their schooling, but with more and more personal involvement in how they study it.

The practices of school-based curriculum determination that developed in Victoria in the 1980s provided a context in which this type of science study might be possible, even at the hitherto unaffected level of the senior secondary years. The initial curriculum policies of vcab referred to earlier were expressions of intent that this flexibility was to be built into the various study designs for science. In Cases II and III, the Science fosc set out to develop guides or frameworks for the science curricula rather than detailed, content-specified syllabi. The common science unit (Case II) and Work Requirement 7 (Case III) were intended specifically to offer students pedagogical experiences that would contribute to empowerment.

Such an educational paradigm in the high-stakes areas of the physical sciences turned out to be unacceptable to both the dominant group of academic scientists and the bureaucrats who were responsible for the whole of the vce. The latter became more and more concerned with the internal curriculum efficiencies that a prescribed set of conceptual learnings could provide, especially when these also would have the approval of the University of Melbourne. Facilitating the Science fosc's interest in trying to provide curricula that were "inclusive and challenging" took a decidedly lower priority.

Robottom (1983) concluded that school science, because of the dominance in its curriculum of positivist or modernist views, was an inappropriate vehicle for the recognition of contestation in knowledge claims and, instead, would seek to impose consensus meaning on its key concepts, thereby disenfranchising students to an instrumental role.

In Blades's (1994) account of the drama in developing Science 10-20-30 in the Canadian province of Alberta, the curriculum bureaucrats and the academic scientists played not dissimilar roles to those demonstrated in Cases II and III. The voices of students were not part of the discourse, and in Blades's allegorical story they are phantom figures who are not noticed by most of the participants. In his own encounters with them, he found, on the other hand, that they were informed critics and had a number of valuable ideas. The pressures to rein in the suggestions for new curriculum emphases were, Blades suggests, overwhelming on the individuals who, at various stages in the Alberta case, exercised decision-making power. Whether this applies in the Victorian cases is hard to tell since some of the key players who were present in Case I were still there in Case III, a decade later.

Both Blades and Robottom argue for a school science curriculum that gives primacy to dialogue, negotiation, and playing with paradox, rather than to amass-ing facts and conceptual propositions in what amounts to a foreign language. Such postmodernist views of senior school science will require much more of the "wres-tling" (Blades describes this so imaginatively) with ourselves as science teachers and science educators, and with our colleague scientists, before they become es-tablished in the search for what has come to be known as Science for All.

Not all academic scientists, however, disagree with such ideas. Hirschbach, a chemistry Nobel Laureate at Harvard, expressed his concern that

> students in school science typically have the sense that it's a question of mastering a body of knowledge that has been developed by their ancestors. . . . Particularly they get the impression that what matters is being right or wrong. I like to stress to my students that like research scientists we don't know how to get the right answer; we're working in an area where we don't know what we are doing. . . . Any way we can encourage students to see that, in science, it's not so important whether you are right or wrong. Because the truth is going to wait for you. (Swedish television inter-view, quoted in Fensham & Marton, 1992, pp. 119–120)

◯ Notes

CHAPTER 1

1. Fletcher's views on the matter, expressed later in that decade, can be found in Watson (1967).
2. Further to this point, see Wittrock (1994).
3. Zacharias and White (1964) present a very interesting account of just how deliberate this intent can be.
4. The work of Lemke (1990) is important in this regard, but our interest in this volume is broader than his. Östman discusses this point in Chapter 5.

CHAPTER 2

This chapter is based on a paper presented at the symposium "Didaktik and/or Curriculum" at the Institut für die Pädagogik der Naturwissenschaften an der Universität Kiel (IPN) in Kiel, Germany, October 1993. For a different version of the original paper, see Englund (1995).

1. Swedish educational research grew out of philosophy around the turn of the twentieth century, but the philosophical aspects have ended up in the background since then (Englund, 1992, 1996b). The main explanation for this is the dominance of scientific-technical rationality and the adjustment of education as a science to the demands of this rationality (cf. Säfström, 1994, 1996), educational research being reduced to psychology or sociology.

The development of schooling in Sweden has been analyzed from the viewpoint of educational philosophy by Englund (1986, Ch. 7), and the educational-philosophical characterizations used in that work—progressivism, essentialism, perennialism, and social reconstructionism (Brameld, 1950)—can be seen as one type of starting point for further analysis of the production of companion meanings.

2. My division of frame factor and curriculum theory into three stages with reference to sociologies of education was originally presented (Englund, 1989) at the International Sociology of Education Conference on the State, Curriculum and Schooling, held in Birmingham (see also Englund, 1996c).

3. For further analysis of traditional sociology of education from the standpoint of the new sociology of education, see Kallós and Lundgren (1979) (for a Swedish view) and Whitty (1985) (for an international perspective).

4. "Dahllöf's model explains and generates testable hypotheses about curricular determinants of achievement. As a research scholar, he does not propose ability-grouped or mixed-ability classes, but rather suggests the trade-offs anyone must accept in choosing one or the other. Neither is completely superior in his analysis, but he has shown that each has its distinctive pattern of results for students of different abilities. The scholar's role, in this case, is to investigate, describe in detail, and illuminate the choices for us. It is a form of scholarship that leans heavily on the empirical, scientific model of research. It is not critical and judgmental, nor does it advocate courses of action" (Walker & Soltis, 1986, pp. 62–63).

5. See Englund (1986, Ch. 3), for more details.

6. I will not deny the general success of that portion of research on learning subtitled "alternative conceptions, prior conceptions, and misconceptions," to refer to the ideas students hold about phenomena such as physical concepts prior to and sometimes after instruction. However, this does not mean that the transfer to didactics is unproblematic.

7. Roberts (1988) develops in his research on science education seven different "curriculum emphases" for this branch of education. These are used and elaborated by Östman (1996a) in an attempt to conceptualize different discourses within chemistry education in Swedish schools during the 1980s. By analyzing syllabi, texts, and textbooks in school science and trying to clarify their respective meanings, Östman (1995) seeks to develop different ways of looking at, and more explicitly systematizing, a didactic typology of this area of the curriculum.

8. This is said from a Swedish perspective. Generally the theory can be seen to stress the curriculum-making center. This perspective is developed in detail in Englund (1986).

9. See Englund (1986) and the research program "The Content of Socialization and the Dimensions of Citizenship" (Englund, 1991c, 1996c). For examples of recent studies, see Englund (1996c), Ljunggren (1996), Säfström (1996), and Östman (1996a).

10. I have dealt in more detail with the division of responsibilities for this process and tried to define the character of didactic competence in Englund (1991a); cf. Englund (1996a). As examples of the type of systematic knowledge that I am aiming for, see the "didactic typologies" in Englund (1986, Ch. 9), the "curriculum emphases" in Roberts (1988), and the "subject foci" and "nature languages" in Östman (1996a).

CHAPTER 4

The research reported here has been financed by the Swedish Council for Research in the Humanities and Social Sciences and by the National Agency of Education.

CHAPTER 5

1. Another central assumption that lay behind my perception of concept was that words refer directly to the "real" world and take on their meanings in that way. Säljö (Chapter 4 in this volume) gives some clarifying critique on this assumption, which belongs to the empirical theory of meaning—the pictural theory.

2. In the science texts I have analyzed, I have not found any instance of a biocentric line of reasoning.

3. Two other examples of subject focus found in my investigations are *Exploitation of Nature* and *Nature as a Precondition* (for human life and living, that is). Their meanings are relatively transparent, even though they are not illustrated in this chapter. If an instance of biocentric reasoning could be found, the subject focus could be labeled *Preservation of Nature*.

4. In my analysis of all the textbooks in lower secondary school biology and chemistry published in Sweden in the 1980s, the only epistemological view of science I found was a positivistic one.

CHAPTER 6

I wish to thank Denise Buchner, Peter Chin, Anne Hawson, Leif Östman, Edward Robeck, and Douglas Roberts for their helpful assistance with this chapter.

1. The larger study examines the educational legacy of imperialism in the disciplines of history, geography, science, language, and literature (Willinsky, 1998).

2. Although I place particular emphasis on the science of race in this chapter, it is worthwhile keeping Paul Gilroy's (1993) caution in mind, namely, that "science did not monopolize either the image of the black or the emergent concept of biologically based racial difference" (p. 8). He points out how science was part of a far broader racial determination of the true, the good, and the beautiful across the full range of Western intellectual interests, which in itself points out science's willing collaboration with the other disciplines in setting what is for Gilroy the cornerstone of modernity.

3. It is ironic that the considerable movement away from the viability of race as a concept should occur in physical anthropology textbooks. After all, the discipline originated, Lieberman and colleagues claim (citing Franz Boas), in the efforts of "zoologists in the 18th century to measure and classify human races" (1992, p. 305), so the concept should be an enduring one. They also report that the American Committee for Democracy and Intellectual Freedom (which Boas helped found in 1939) conducted a survey of prewar science textbooks; a majority carried prejudicial concepts of race and a fifth of them embraced forms of white racial superiority.

4. This is among the textbook instances cited by Lieberman and colleagues (1992, p. 311).

5. The interviews were conducted by Lynn Thomas.

6. In *The Descent of Man*, Darwin (1871/1905) allows that fertility between the races is no guarantee of a common species, especially among domesticated types, but points to three factors that speak to human races as constituting the same species: the easy association of the human races in places such as Brazil; the inconstance of so-called race characteristics within a given race; and, ultimately, the way in which the races "graduate into each other, independently in many cases, as far as we can judge, of their having intercrossed" (p. 232), an observation further borne out by disagreement among the learned over the number of races among humankind, which ranged in Darwin's day from Kant's four to Burke's sixty-three. Darwin's case is that humankind constitutes, from its origins,

a single species. It goes far toward undermining the reliability of race as a stable scientific category.

7. Philippe Rushton (1991), a University of Western Ontario psychology professor, has become well known for a remarkable 26-item table on "the relative ranking of races on diverse variables" (p. 30), comparing Mongoloids, Caucasoids, and Negroids on such questionable measures as cranial capacity, millions of excess neurons, IQ test scores, age of walking and first intercourse, size of genitalia, and state of mental health. While allowing for "numerous sources of error" in his data, he holds that its overall consistency guarantees his conclusions about the civilized superiority of Mongoloids compared with Caucasoids, who, in turn, are more advanced than the Negroid races. Rushton portrays himself as a victim of political correctness, blaming decolonization and the civil rights movements for forcing upon science ideologies of egalitarianism. For scientific critiques, see Weizman, Wiener, Wiesenthal, and Ziegler (1991) and Anderson (1991). For popular press coverage, see Dolpin (1989).

8. The Lieberman and colleagues (1992) study does make passing reference to reports on the decline of race in biology textbooks used in high schools. What is striking in their report on high schools are the studies that, while focusing on "social issues" (p. 303), fail to consider race as a category to assess.

The texts I examined are Barr and Leyden (1986), Biological Sciences Curriculum Study (1987), Creager, Jantzen, and Mariner (1986), Galbraith (1989), Gottfried and colleagues (1983), Heimler (1981), Kaskel, Hummer, and Daniel (1981), Levine and Miller (1991), Mader (1988), McLaren and Rotundo (1985), McLaren, Stastik, and Levering (1981), Oram (1983), Ramsey, Gabriel, McGurik, Phillips, and Watenpaugh (1986), Slesnick, Balzer, McCormack, Newton, and Rasmussen (1985), and Webster, Fichter, Coble, and Rice (1980).

9. A second valuable work in this vein, serving as a manual for teachers and educators, is *Race, Equality and Science Teaching* (Thorp, 1991). For additional work on multiculturalism in science education, see Bazin (1993); for reading and activities in multicultural approaches to math, science, and technology, see Alcoze, Bradley, Kashima, Kane, and Madrazo (1993).

10. Consider the white mythology that Leslie Roman (1993) has perceptively described as giving a seemingly "natural" invisibility to *being white*, a reassuring need not to be named in this racial way, which imitates, in effect, the privileged point of the disengaged scientific observer.

CHAPTER 7

An expanded version of this chapter appeared in *Studies in Science Education* (Aikenhead, 1996).

CHAPTER 8

Portions of this chapter are drawn from an earlier version (Munby, 1980). The material is reproduced here by kind permission of University Press of America.

1. *Editors' Note*. It is important to bear in mind that Munby developed the concept of "intellectual independence" in a pedagogical sense. It has to do with the prerogatives and developmental opportunities afforded students by the way the teacher controls discourse and hence distributes, or does not distribute, power. It does not have to do with somehow becoming independent of science and scientists, as Norris (1995) suggests. Unquestionably the teacher represents a particular view of reasoned discourse; hence both he or she and the students are dependent on science as a system of thought (as they are, indeed, on English as their language of communication, in this case). That being so, Norris's objection to the effect that no one can be truly and completely intellectually independent is acknowledged, and we are impressed with his alternative term "intellectual communalism." However, his objection that students and teachers can't be intellectually independent of *scientists* is baffling. Our view is that Norris has in some respects misinterpreted, even trivialized, the way "intellectual independence" is used by Munby and others who give it this power-distribution sense.

2. The concept of "learned helplessness," from cognitive psychology, is pertinent here (see Qian & Alvermann, 1995).

CHAPTER 9

This chapter is based in part on an article that appeared previously (Geddis, 1991). I am grateful to John Wiley & Sons for permission to make use of this earlier work in preparing the chapter.

1. *Editors' Note*: The points raised by Norris (1995) concerning Munby's concept of intellectual independence are discussed in Chapter 8 in this volume.

CHAPTER 10

1. In another study, I have shown how Frankena's and Gauthier's work can be used to characterize arguments in support of educational objectives (Orpwood, 1976, 1980).

CHAPTER 11

I wish to extend my appreciation and gratitude to Joseph D. McInerney and Janet Carlson Powell for their insightful comments and recommendations on this chapter.

1. *Editors' Note*: For an interesting and relevant analysis of this point, see Connelly's (1972) distinction between "external developers" and "user developers."

CHAPTER 12

Portions of this chapter are contained in *EuroScientia Forum, 1*.

CHAPTER 13

1. In important respects this redefinition parallels Goodson's (1987, Ch. 8) account of the development of environmental studies in England.

2. The statement is a one-page attachment to the *Minutes* of the Science FOSC for September 13, 1989. See also Hart (1995).

3. In a study about the case of physics, Hart (1995) has documented and discussed how this principle and the more general ones of VCAB as well were steadily eroded and deflected in the final stages of development.

4. Victoria Curriculum and Assessment Board (1990, February), p. 28.

5. There have been similar events, of course. For example, the case of Science 10-20-30 in the Canadian province of Alberta (Blades, 1994; Panwar & Hoddinott, 1995) is quite similar to Case I.

○ References

Agin, M. (1974). Education for scientific literacy: A conceptual frame of reference and some applications. *Science Education, 58*(3), 403–415.

Aikenhead, G. S. (1980). *Science in social issues: Implications for teaching.* Ottawa, ON: Science Council of Canada.

Aikenhead, G. S. (1985). Collective decision making in the social context of science. *Science Education, 69*(4), 453–475.

Aikenhead, G. S. (1991). *Logical reasoning in science and technology.* Toronto: John Wiley.

Aikenhead, G. S. (1994). The social contract of science: Implications for teaching science. In J. Solomon & G. Aikenhead (Eds.), *STS education: International perspectives on reform* (pp. 11–20). New York: Teachers College Press.

Aikenhead, G. S. (1996). Science education: Border crossing into the subculture of science. *Studies in Science Education, 27*, 1–52.

Alberta Education. (1990, January 26). News release.

Alcoze, T., Bradley, H. C., Kashima, T., Kane, I. M., & Madrazo, G. (1993). *Multiculturalism in mathematics, science and technology: Reading and activities.* Menlo, CA: Addison-Wesley.

American Association for the Advancement of Science. (1989). *Science for all Americans.* Washington, DC: Author.

American Association for the Advancement of Science. (1993). *Benchmarks for science literacy.* New York: Oxford University Press.

Anderson, J. (1991). Rushton's racial comparisons: An ecological critique of theory and method. *Canadian Psychology, 32*(1), 51–60.

Anderson, T., & Kilbourn, B. (1983). Creation, evolution, and curriculum. *Science Education, 67*(1), 45–55.

Andréasson, B., Bondeson, L., Forsberg, K., Gedda, S., Luksepp, K., & Zachrisson, I. (1986). *Biologi för högstadiet* [Biology for lower secondary schools]. Stockholm: Natur och Kultur.

Anyon, J. (1980). Social class and the hidden curriculum of work. *Journal of Education, 162*(1), 67–92.

Apple, M. (1979). *Ideology and curriculum.* London: Routledge & Kegan Paul.

Aristotle. (trans. 1990). *The Nichomachean ethics* (D. Ross, Trans.). New York: Oxford University Press.

Armstrong, R. L. (1980, January). A personal and philosophical memoir of Stephen C. Pepper. *Paunch,* no. 53/54, 214–217.

Bader, R. (1993). Science and culture in Germany: Is there a case? In J. Durant, & J. Gregory (Eds.), *Science and culture in Europe* (pp. 47–52). London: London Science Museum.

Baier, K. (1958). *The moral point of view*. Ithaca, NY: Cornell University Press.

Baird, J. R., & White, R. T. (1982). A case study of learning styles in biology. *European Journal of Science Education, 4*(3), 325–337.

Baker, A. O., & Mills, L. H. (1943). *Dynamic biology today*. Chicago: Rand McNally.

Baker, D., & Taylor, P. C. S. (1995). The effect of culture on the learning of science in non-Western countries: The results of an integrated research review. *International Journal of Science Education, 17*(6), 695–704.

Banton, M. (1977). *The idea of race*. Boulder, CO: Westview.

Barr, B. B., & Leyden, M. B. (1986). *Addison-Wesley life science*. Menlo, CA: Addison-Wesley.

Barry, B. (1965). *Political argument*. London: Routledge & Kegan Paul.

Barzun, J. (1937). *Race: A study in a modern superstition*. New York: Harper & Row.

Battiste, M. (1986). Micmac literacy and cognitive assimilation. In J. Barman, Y. Hébert, & D. McCaskill (Eds.), *Indian education in Canada: Vol. 1. The legacy* (pp. 23–44). Vancouver: University of British Columbia Press.

Bazin, M. (1993). Our sciences, their sciences. *Race and Science, 34*(4), 35–46.

Ben-Peretz, M. (1975). The concept of curriculum potential. *Curriculum Theory Network, 5*(2), 151–159.

Bernstein, R. (1986). *Philosophical profiles*. Philadelphia: University of Pennsylvania Press.

Biddle, B. J., & Anderson, D. S. (1986). Theory, methods, knowledge, and research on teaching. In M. C. Wittrock (Ed.), *Handbook of research on teaching* (3rd ed.; pp. 230–252). New York: Macmillan.

Bingle, W. H., & Gaskell, P. J. (1994). Scientific literacy for decision making and the social construction of scientific knowledge. *Science Education, 78*(2), 185–201.

Biological Sciences Curriculum Study. (1987). *Biological science: An ecological approach. Teachers' edition* (6th ed.). Dubuque, IA: Kendall Hunt.

Birdsell, J. B. (1972). *Human evolution: An introduction to the new physical anthropology*. Chicago: Rand McNally.

Birdsell, J. B. (1975). *Human evolution: An introduction to the new physical anthropology* (2nd ed.). Boston: Houghton Mifflin.

Blackburn, J. (1984). *Ministerial review of postcompulsory schooling: A discussion paper*. Melbourne: Ministry of Education, Victoria.

Blackburn, J. (1985). *Ministerial review of postcompulsory education* (Report, Vol. 1). Melbourne: Ministry of Education, Victoria.

Blades, D. W. (1994). *Procedures of power and possibilities for change in science education curriculum-discourse*. Unpublished doctoral dissertation, University of Alberta, Edmonton.

Boas, F. (1974). Anthropology: A lecture delivered at Columbia University in the series on Science, Philosophy, and Art, December 18, 1907 (New York: Columbia University Press, 1908). In G. Stocking (Ed.), *The shaping of American anthropology, 1883–1911: A Franz Boas reader* (pp. 267–281). New York: Basic Books.

Bondi, H. (1985). Society's view of science. In G. B. Harrison (Ed.), *World trends in science and technology education* (pp. 10–13). Nottingham, UK: Trent Polytechnic.

Borén, B., Moll, O., & Lillieborg, S. (1988). *No-kemiboken. Faktabok för högstadiet* [The chemistry book. Book of facts for lower secondary schools]. Stockholm: Esselte Studium.

Bourdieu, P. (1977). *Outline of a theory of practice.* Cambridge: Cambridge University Press.

Bourne, P., & Eisenberg, J. (1978). *Social issues in the curriculum: Theory, practice, and evaluation.* Toronto: OISE Press.

Boyer, E., & Levine, A. (1981). *A quest for common learning: The aims of general education.* Princeton, NJ: Princeton University Press.

Brameld, T. (1950). *Patterns of educational philosophy. A democratic interpretation.* New York: World Book Company.

Brickhouse, N. (1990). The teaching of the philosophy of science in secondary classrooms: Case studies of teachers' personal theories. *International Journal of Science Education, 11*(4), 437–449.

Bullard, J., Cloutier, F., Flood, N., Gore, G., Grace, E. S., Gurney, B., Hirsch, A. J., Hugh, D., Madhosingh, C., Millett, G., & Wootton, A. (1992). *Science probe 10* (2nd ed.). Toronto: John Wiley.

Bybee, R. W. (1993). *Reforming science education: Social perspectives and personal reflections.* New York: Teachers College Press.

Bybee, R. W., & DeBoer, G. E. (1994). Research on goals for the science curriculum. In D. Gabel (Ed.), *Handbook of research on science teaching and learning* (pp. 357–387). New York: Macmillan.

Byfield, M. (1989, July 11). APEGGA slams science course. *Calgary Sun,* n.p.

Byrne, E. (1993). *Women and science: The snark syndrome.* London: Falmer Press.

Chaiklin, S., & Lave, J. (Eds.). (1993). *Understanding practice: Perspectives on activity and context.* Cambridge: Cambridge University Press.

Cherryholmes, C. (1988). *Power and criticism: Poststructural investigations in education.* New York: Teachers College Press.

Cobern, W. W. (1991). *World view theory and science education research* (NARST Monograph No. 3). Manhattan, KS: National Association for Research in Science Teaching.

Cobern, W. W. (1994). Point: Belief, understanding, and the teaching of evolution. *Journal of Research in Science Teaching, 31*(5), 583–590.

Cohen, P. C. (1982). *A calculating people. The spread of numeracy in early America.* Chicago: University of Chicago Press.

Cole, M. (1991). A cultural theory of development: What does it imply about the application of scientific research? *Learning and Instruction, 1*(3), 187–200.

Connelly, F. M. (1972). The functions of curriculum development. *Interchange, 3* (2/3), 161–177.

Costa, V. B. (1993). School science as a rite of passage: A new frame for familiar problems. *Journal of Research in Science Teaching, 30*(7), 649–668.

Costa, V. B. (1995). When science is "another world": Relationships between worlds of family, friends, school, and science. *Science Education, 79*(3), 313–333.

Creager, J. G., Jantzen, P. G., & Mariner, J. L. (1986). *Biology*. New York: Macmillan.

Cross, R. T., & Price, R. F. (1992). *Teaching science for social responsibility*. Sydney: St. Louis Press.

Culler, J. (1992). In defence of overinterpretation. In S. Collini (Ed.), *Umberto Eco: Interpretation and overinterpretation* (pp. 109–123). Cambridge: Cambridge University Press.

Dahllöf, U. (1981). *Timplaneförändringar på grundskolestadiet i ett långtidsperspektiv* [Changes in the allocation of teaching time in Swedish compulsory schooling in a long-term perspective] (Report 43). Uppsala: Education Department, Uppsala University.

Dahllöf, U. (1989). Har det svenska pedagogikämnet någon identitet? [Does education as a science in Sweden have an identity?]. *Forskning om Utbildning, 16*(4), 4–20.

Darwin, C. (1905). *The descent of man and Selection in relation to sex* (2nd ed.). New York: Collier. (Original work published 1871)

De Vos, W., van Berkel, B., & Verdonk, A. H. (1994). A coherent conceptual structure of the chemistry curriculum. *Journal of Chemical Education, 71*(9), 743–746.

Dewey, J. (1934). *Art as experience*. New York: Minton, Balch.

Dewey, J. (1963). *Experience and education*. New York: Collier. (Original work published 1938)

Dewey, J. (1966). *Democracy and education*. New York: Macmillan. (Original work published 1916)

Dolpin, R. with W. McCann. (1989, February 13). Race and behavior: A theory outrages ethnic and other critics. *Maclean's, 102*(7), 44.

Driver, R., Asoko, H., Leach, J., Mortimer, E., & Scott, P. (1994). Constructing scientific knowledge in the classroom. *Educational Researcher, 23*(7), 5–12.

Driver, R., & Easley, J. (1978). Pupils and paradigms: A review of literature related to concept development in adolescent science students. *Studies in Science Education, 5*, 61–84.

Durkheim, E. (1977). *The evolution of educational thought: Lectures on the formation and development of secondary education in France* (P. Collins, Trans.). London: Routledge & Kegan Paul.

Duschl, R. A. (1988). Abandoning the scientistic legacy of science education. *Science Education, 72*(1), 51–62.

Eagleton, T. (1989). *Literary theory: An introduction*. Oxford: Basil Blackwell.

Edwards, A. D. (1980). Patterns of power and authority in classroom talk. In P. Woods (Ed.), *Teacher strategies: Explorations in the sociology of the school* (pp. 237–253). London: Croom Helm.

Eisner, E. W. (1992). Curriculum ideologies. In P. W. Jackson (Ed.), *Handbook of research on curriculum* (pp. 302–326). New York: Macmillan.

Eisner, E. W., & Vallance, E. (Eds.). (1974). *Conflicting conceptions of curriculum*. Berkeley: McCutchan.

Englund, T. (1984). *Didaktik—vad är det?* [Didactics—what is it?] (Report 84). Uppsala: Department of Education, Uppsala University.

Englund, T. (1986). *Curriculum as a political problem: Changing educational conceptions, with special reference to citizenship education* (Uppsala Studies in Education 25). Lund, Sweden: Studentlitteratur/Chartwell Bratt.

Englund, T. (1989, January). *State, curriculum and citizenship—Notes towards a citizenship sociology of education and curriculum.* Paper presented at the International Sociology of Education Conference, Birmingham.

Englund, T. (1990). På väg mot en pedagogiskt dynamisk analys av innehållet [Towards a dynamic analysis of educational content]. *Forskning om Utbildning, 17*(1), 19–35.

Englund, T. (1991a). Didaktisk kompetens [Didactic competence]. *Didactica Minima, 18–19,* 8–18.

Englund, T. (1991b, April). Rethinking curriculum history: Towards a theoretical reorientation. Paper presented at the American Educational Research Association Conference, Chicago.

Englund, T. (1991c). *Socialisationens innehåll och medborgarskapets dimensioner. Ett forskningsprogram* [The content of socialization and the dimensions of citizenship. A research program]. Uppsala: Department of Education, Uppsala University.

Englund, T. (1992). Pedagogik som vetenskap [Education as a science]. *Forskning om Utbildning, 19*(2), 4–15.

Englund, T. (1995). Narrow and broad didactics in Sweden: Towards a dynamic analysis of the content of schooling. In S. Hopmann & K. Riquarts (Eds.), *Didaktik and/or curriculum* (pp. 125–150). Kiel: Institut für die Pädagogik der Naturwissenschaften an der Universität Kiel.

Englund, T. (1996a). Are professional teachers a good thing? In I. Goodson & A. Hargreaves (Eds.), *Teachers' professional lives* (pp. 75–87). London: Falmer Press.

Englund, T. (1996b). Educational research in Sweden—historical perspectives and current trends. *Scandinavian Journal of Educational Research, 40*(1), 43–55.

Englund, T. (1996c). The public and the text. *Journal of Curriculum Studies, 28*(1), 1–35.

Englund, T., & Östman, L. (1992). Orienteringsämnenas framtid. En didaktisk betraktelse av läroplansbetänkandet [The future of the orientation subject sector. A didactic view of the curriculum committee report]. *KRUT Kritisk utbildningstidskrift, 67,* 32–40.

Englund, T., & Svingby, G. (1986). Didaktik och läroplansteori [Didactics and curriculum theory]. In F. Marton (Ed.), *Fackdidaktik* [Particular didactics] (Vol. 1, pp. 97–152). Lund, Sweden: Student litteratur.

European Commission. (1996). *School science and the future of scientific culture in Europe* (Report to the Commission). Brussels: Author.

Feinberg, W. (1989). Foundationalism and recent critiques of education. *Educational Theory, 39*(2), 133–138.

Fensham, P. J. (1988). Familiar but different: Some dilemmas and new directions in science education. In P. J. Fensham (Ed.), *Development and dilemmas in science education* (pp. 1–26). New York: Falmer Press.

Fensham, P. J. (1992). Science and technology. In P. W. Jackson (Ed.), *Handbook of research on curriculum* (pp. 789–829). New York: Macmillan.

Fensham, P. J. (1994). Progression in school science curriculum: A rational process or a chimera? *Research in Science Education, 24,* 76–82.

Fensham, P. J., & Marton, F. (1992). What has happened to intuition in science education? *Research in Science Education, 22,* 114–122.

Fenstermacher, G. D. (1994). The knower and the known: The nature of knowledge in research on teaching. *Review of Research in Education, 20,* 3–56.

Ferguson, E. S. (1993). *Engineering and the mind's eye.* Cambridge, MA: MIT Press.

Fine, M. (1993). "You can't just say that the only ones who can speak are those who agree with your position": Political discourse in the classroom. *Harvard Educational Review, 63*(4), 412–433.

Fleming, R. (1986). Adolescent reasoning in socio-scientific issues. *Journal of Research in Science Teaching, 23*(8), 677–687, 689–698.

Ford, J. (1990, July). Systematic pluralism: Introduction to an issue. *The Monist, 73*(3), 335–349.

Frankena, W. K. (1970). A model for analyzing a philosophy of education. In J. R. Martin (Ed.), *Readings in the philosophy of education: A study of curriculum* (pp. 15–22). Boston: Allyn & Bacon.

Fraser, S. (1995). *The Bell Curve wars: Race, intelligence, and the future of America.* New York: Basic Books.

Fuhrer, U. (1993). Behavior setting analysis of situated learning: The case of newcomers. In S. Chaiklin & J. Lave (Eds.), *Understanding practice: Perspectives on activity and context* (pp. 179–211). Cambridge: Cambridge University Press.

Gabel, L. L. (1976). *The development of a model to determine perceptions of scientific literacy.* Unpublished doctoral dissertation, Ohio State University, Columbus.

Galbraith, D. (1989). *Understanding biology.* Toronto: John Wiley.

Gallagher, J. J. (1991). Prospective and practicing secondary school science teachers' knowledge and beliefs about the philosophy of science. *Science Education, 75*(1), 121–133.

Garden, R., & Orpwood, G. (1996). Development of the TIMSS achievement tests. In M. O. Martin & D. L. Kelly (Eds.), *Third international mathematics and science study (TIMSS) technical report: Vol. 1. Design and development* (pp. 2-1–2-19). Chestnut Hill, MA: Boston College.

Gaskell, P. J. (1992). Authentic science and school science. *International Journal of Science Education, 14*(3), 265–272.

Gauld, C. (1982). The scientific attitude and science education: A critical reappraisal. *Science Education, 66*(1), 109–121.

Gauthier, D. P. (1963). *Practical reasoning: The structure and foundations of prudential and moral arguments and their exemplification in discourse.* Oxford: Clarendon Press.

Geddis, A. N. (1982). Teaching: A study in evidence. *The Journal of Mind and Behavior, 3*(2), 363–373.

Geddis, A. N. (1988). Using concepts from epistemology and sociology in teacher supervision. *Science Education, 72*(1), 1–18.

Geddis, A. N. (1991). Improving the quality of science classroom discourse on controversial issues. *Science Education, 75*(2), 169–183.

Geddis, A. N. (1996). Science, teaching, and reflection: Incorporating new subject matter into teachers' classroom frames. *International Journal of Science Education, 18*(2), 249–265.

Geertz, C. (1973). *The interpretation of cultures: Selected essays.* New York: Basic Books.

Geertz, C. (1983). *Local knowledge: Further essays on interpretive anthropology.* New York: Basic Books.

Giarelli, J. (1983). The public, the state and the civic education. In A. Bagley (Ed.), *Civic learning in teacher education* (Society of Professors of Education Monograph, pp. 33–36). Minneapolis: University of Minnesota College of Education.

Gill, D., & Levidow, L. (1987). *Anti-racist science teaching*. London: Free Association.

Gilroy, P. (1993). *The black Atlantic: Modernity and double consciousness*. Cambridge, MA: Harvard University Press.

Goodson, I. F. (1987). *School subjects and curriculum change: Studies in curriculum history* (Rev. ed.). London: Falmer Press.

Goodson, I. F. (Ed.). (1988). *The Making of curriculum: Collected essays*. London: Falmer Press.

Goodwin, C. (1998). The blackness of black: Color categories as situated action. In L. Resnick, R. Säljö, C. Pontecorvo, & B. Burge (Eds.), *Discourse, tools, and reasoning: Essays on situated cognition* (pp. 111–140). Heidelberg and New York: Springer-Verlag.

Gottfried, S., Madraso, G., Lamoine, M., Sinclair, P., Skog, G., Hampton, C. D., Hampton, C. H., & Leibel, W. (1983). *Prentice-Hall biology*. Englewood Cliffs, NJ: Prentice-Hall.

Gould, S. J. (1977). Why we should not name human races—A biological view. In *Ever since Darwin: Reflections in natural history* (pp. 231–236). New York: Norton.

Gould, S. J. (1981). *The mismeasure of man*. New York: Norton.

Green, T. F. (1968). A topology of the teaching concept. In C. J. B. Macmillan & T. W. Nelson (Eds.), *Concepts of teaching: Philosophical essays* (pp. 28–62). Chicago: Rand McNally.

Grillo, P. J. (1960). *Form, function, and design*. New York: Dover.

Habermas, J. (1971). *Knowledge and human interests*. (J. J. Shapiro, Trans.). Boston: Beacon Press.

Hannerz, U. (1992). *Cultural complexity: Studies in the social organization of meaning*. New York: Columbia University Press.

Harding, J., & Donaldson, J. (1986). Chemistry from issues. *School Science Review*, *68*(242), 48–59.

Harding, S. (Ed.). (1993). Introduction. *The racial economy of science: Toward a democratic future* (pp. 1–22). Bloomington: Indiana University Press.

Harré, R., & Gillett, G. (1994). *The discursive mind*. London: Sage.

Hart, C. (1995). *Access and the quality of learning: The story of a curriculum document for school physics*. Unpublished doctoral dissertation, Monash University, Clayton, Australia.

Harvard Committee. (1945). *General education in a free society*. Cambridge, MA: Harvard University Press.

Haste, H. (1994). *The sexual metaphor*. Cambridge, MA: Harvard University Press.

Hawkins, J., & Pea, R. D. (1987). Tools for bridging the cultures of everyday and scientific thinking. *Journal of Research in Science Teaching*, *24*(4), 291–307.

Heath, S. B. (1983). *Ways with words*. Cambridge: Cambridge University Press.

Heimler, C. H. (1981). *Focus on life science*. Columbus, OH: Merrill.

Henry, B. (1984). Watch on the rain: The atmosphere's acid toll. *Science Dimension*, *16*(2), 7–13.

Herrnstein, R. J., & Murray, C. (1994). *The bell curve: Intelligence and class structure in American life.* New York: Free Press.

Hill, P. (1987, May 29). Memorandum to Science FOSC members and writers. Melbourne: VCAB. (Quoted in Hart, 1995)

Hills, G. L. C. (1989). Students' "untutored" beliefs about natural phenomena: Primitive science or commonsense? *Science Education, 73*(2), 155–186.

Hirst, P. (1974). *Knowledge and the curriculum.* London: Routledge & Kegan Paul.

Hodson, D. (1993). In search of a rationale for multicultural science education. *Science Education, 77*(6), 685–711.

Hoeg, P. (1995). Fröken Smillas kännsla för snö [Smilla's sense of snow]. Stockholm: Norstedts.

Hopmann, S., & Riquarts, K. (Eds.) (1995). *Didaktik and/or curriculum.* Kiel: Institut für die Pädagogik der Naturwissenschaften an der Universität Kiel.

Hurd, P. D. (1969). *New directions in teaching secondary school science.* Chicago: Rand McNally.

Hutchins, E. (1995). *Cognition in the wild.* Cambridge, MA: MIT Press.

Hutchins, E., & Palen, V. (1998). Constructing meaning from space, gesture, and talk. In L. Resnick, R. Säljö, C. Pontecorvo, & B. Barge (Eds.), *Discourse, tools, and reasoning: Essays on situated cognition* (pp. 23–40). Heidelberg and New York: Springer-Verlag.

Jegede, O. J. (1994a). African cultural perspective and the teaching of science. In J. Solomon & G. Aikenhead (Eds.), *STS education: International perspectives on reform* (pp. 120–130). New York: Teachers College Press.

Jegede, O. J. (1994b, November). *School science and scientific culture: An African perspective.* Paper presented at the International Conference on Science in School and the Future of Scientific Culture in Europe, Lisbon.

Johansson, B., Marton, F., & Svensson, L. (1985). An approach to describing learning as a change between qualitatively different conceptions. In L. H. T. West & A. L. Pines (Eds.), *Cognitive structure and conceptual change* (pp. 223–257). New York: Academic Press.

Jorg, T., & Wubbels, T. (1987). Physics a problem for girls, or girls a problem for physics? *International Journal of Science Education, 9*(3), 297–307.

Kallós, D., & Lundgren, U. P. (1979). *Curriculum as a pedagogical problem* (Studies in Curriculum Theory and Cultural Reproduction 4). Stockholm: Stockholm Institute of Education.

Kaplan, A. (1964). *The conduct of inquiry: Methodology for behavioral science.* San Francisco: Chandler.

Kaskel, A., Hummer, P. J., & Daniel, L. (1981). *Biology: An everyday experience. Teachers' annotated edition.* Columbus, OH: Merrill.

Keller, C., & Keller, J. D. (1993). Thinking and acting with iron. In S. Chaiklin & J. Lave (Eds.), *Understanding practice: Perspectives on activity and context* (pp. 125–143). Cambridge: Cambridge University Press.

Kelly, G. J., Carlsen, W. S., & Cunningham, C. M. (1993). Science education in sociocultural context: Perspectives from the sociology of science. *Science Education, 77*(2), 207–220.

Kepes, G. (1965). *Structure in art and in science.* New York: George Braziller.

Kilbourn, B. (1974). *Identifying world views projected by science teaching materials: A case study using Pepper's* World Hypotheses *to analyze a biology textbook.* Unpublished doctoral dissertation, University of Toronto.

Kilbourn, B. (1982). Curriculum materials, teaching, and potential outcomes for students: A qualitative analysis. *Journal of Research in Science Teaching, 19*(8), 675–688.

Kilbourn, B. (1994). World views and curriculum. *Journal of Nordic Educational Research, 14*(3), 131–140. (Formerly published in *Interchange*, 1980/81 *11*(2), 1–10).

Kilbourn, B., & Roberts, D. A. (1984). *Science, society, and the non-academic student (Phase I) Final Report.* Social Sciences and Humanities Research Council of Canada. (Project #410–81–0726)

Kohlberg, L. (1966). Moral education in the schools: A developmental view. *The School Review, 74*(1), 1–30.

Komisar, B. P. (1968). Teaching: Act and enterprise. In C. J. B. Macmillan & T. W. Nelson (Eds.), *Concepts of teaching: Philosophical essays* (pp. 63–88). Chicago: Rand McNally.

Komisar, B. P. (1969). Is teaching phoney? *Teachers College Record, 70*(5), 407–411.

Lakoff, G., & Johnson, M. (1980). *Metaphors we live by.* Chicago: University of Chicago Press.

Layton, D. (1972). Science as general education. *Trends in Education, 25*, 11–14.

Layton, D. (1973). *Science for the people: The origins of the school science curriculum in England.* London: George Allen & Unwin.

Layton, D., Jenkins, E., Macgill, S., & Davey, A. (1993). *Inarticulate science?* Driffield, East Yorkshire, UK: Studies in Education.

Lave, J., & Wenger, E. (1991). *Situated learning: Legitimate peripheral participation.* Cambridge: Cambridge University Press.

Lemke, J. (1990). *Talking science: Language, learning, and values.* Norwood, NJ: Ablex.

Levine, J. S., & Miller, K. R. (1991). *Biology: Discovering life.* Lexington, MA: D. C. Heath.

Lieberman, L., Hampton, R. E., Littlefield, A., & Hallead, G. (1992). Race in biology and anthropology: A study of college texts and professors. *Journal of Research in Science Teaching, 29*(3), 301–321.

Lijnse, P. (1990). Energy between the life-world of pupils and the world of physics. *Science Education, 74*(5), 571–583.

Linke, R. (1976). *Education and the human environment.* Canberra: Curriculum Development Centre.

Livingstone, F. B. (1964). On the nonexistence of human races. In A. Montagu (Ed.), *The concept of race.* New York: Collier Books.

Ljunggren, C. (1996). Education, media and democracy: On communication and the nature of the public in the light of John Dewey, Walter Lippmann and the discussion of modernity. *Journal of Curriculum Studies, 28*(1), 73–90.

Luria, A. R. (1971). Towards the problem of the historical nature of psychological processes. *International Journal of Psychology, 6*(4), 259–272.

Luria, A. R. (1976). *Cognitive development: Its cultural and social foundations.* Cambridge, MA: Harvard University Press.

MacDonald, D. A. G. (1995). *What counts as teaching science?* Unpublished doctoral dissertation, University of Calgary.

MacDonald, P., & Byfield, V. (1989, June 19). "Dumbing down" high schools. *Alberta Report*, pp. 28–29, 32–34.

Mader, S. S. (1988). *Inquiry into life* (6th ed.). Dubuque, IA: W. C. Brown.

Mannheim, K. (1936). *Ideology and utopia: An introduction to the sociology of knowledge*. New York: Harcourt Brace Jovanovich.

Mannheim, K. (1968). *Essays on the sociology of knowledge*. London: Routledge & Kegan Paul.

Mårtensson, G., & Sandin, H. (1988). *Kemi försök & fakta* [*Chemistry experiments and facts*]. Malmö: Liber.

Marton, F. (1980). Phenomenography—Describing conceptions of the world around us. *Instructional Science, 10*, 177–200.

Marton, F. (1983). *Från utbildningsmetodisk till fackdidaktisk forskning* [From research about educational methods to particular didactics] (Report 100). Lärarutbildningen vid universitetet i Linköping.

Marton, F. (Ed.). (1986). *Fackdidaktik* [Particular didactics] (Vol. 1). Lund, Sweden: Studentlitteratur.

Mayer, M. (1984). Understanding the functioning of simple domestic appliances in relation to scientific concepts. In *Proceedings of the Third International Symposium on World Trends in Science and Technology Education* (Vol. 1, pp. 183–187). Mount Gravatt: Brisbane College of Advanced Education.

McClean, M. (1995). *Education traditions compared: Content, teaching and learning in industrialized countries*. London: David Fulton.

McLaren, J. E., & Rotundo, L. (1985). *Heath biology*. Lexington, MA: D. C. Heath.

McLaren, J. E., Stastik, J. H., & Levering, D. F. (1981). *Spaceship earth: Life science*. Boston: Houghton Mifflin.

Mendelsohn, E. (1976). Values and science: A critical reassessment. *Science Teacher, 43*(1), 20–23.

Merton, R. (1942). Science and technology in a democratic order. *Journal of Legal and Political Sociology, 1*, 115–126.

Millar, R., & Wynne, B. (1988). Public understanding of science: From content to processes. *International Journal of Science Education, 10*(4), 388–398.

Miller, G. A. (1956). The magical number seven, plus or minus two: Some limits on our capacity for processing information. *Psychological Review, 63*, 81–97.

Miller, J. (1984, May 26). U.S. is trying harder to lick acid rain than Canada, environmental chief says. *The Toronto Star*, p. A2.

Montagu, A. (1972). *Statement on race: An annotated elaboration and exposition of the four statements on race issued by the United Nations Educational, Scientific, and Cultural Organization* (3rd ed.). New York: Oxford University Press.

Moore, H. (1953–54). *Warrior with shield*. Bronze, 152.4 cm high. Toronto: Art Gallery of Ontario.

Munby, A. H. (1973). *The provision made for selected intellectual consequences by science teaching: Derivation and application of an analytical scheme*. Unpublished doctoral dissertation, University of Toronto.

Munby, H. (1980). Analysing teaching for intellectual independence. In H. Munby, G. Orpwood, & T. Russell (Eds.), *Seeing curriculum in a new light: Essays from science education* (pp. 11–33). Toronto: OISE Press.

Munby, H. (1986). Metaphor in the thinking of teachers: An exploratory study. *Journal of Curriculum Studies, 18*(2), 197–209.

Munby, H., & Russell, T. (1983). A common curriculum for the natural sciences. In G. Fenstermacher & J. Goodlad (Eds.), *Individual differences and the common curriculum* (pp. 160–185). Eighty-second Yearbook of the National Society for the Study of Education. Chicago: University of Chicago Press.

Murnane, R. J., & Raizen, S. A. (Eds.). (1988). *Improving indicators of the quality of science and mathematics education in grades K–12.* Washington, DC: National Academy Press.

Nadeau, R., & Désautels, J. (1984). *Epistemology and the teaching of science.* Ottawa, ON: Science Council of Canada.

National Committee on Science Education Standards and Assessment. (1993, February). *National science education standards: An enhanced sampler.* Washington, DC: National Research Council.

National Research Council. (1996). *National science education standards.* Washington, DC: National Academy Press.

Norris, S. P. (1995). Learning to live with scientific expertise: Toward a theory of intellectual communalism for guiding science teaching. *Science Education, 79*(2), 201–217.

Ocvirk, O. G., Bone, R., Stinson, R., & Wigg, P. (1962). *Art fundamentals.* Dubuque, IA: W. C. Brown.

Ogawa, M. (1986). Toward a new rationale of science education in a non-Western society. *European Journal of Science Education, 8*(2), 113–119.

Ogawa, M. (1995). Science education in a multiscience perspective. *Science Education, 79*(5), 583–593.

Olson, D. (1994). *The world on paper.* Cambridge: Cambridge University Press.

Ong, W. J. (1982). *Orality and literacy: The technologizing of the word.* London: Methuen.

Oram, R. F. (1983). *Biology: Living systems* (4th ed.). Columbus, OH: Merrill.

Orpwood, G. (1976). *Analyzing curriculum prescriptions: A case study in the context of science education.* Unpublished master's thesis, University of Toronto.

Orpwood, G. (1980). Analysing arguments for objectives. In H. Munby, G. Orpwood, & T. Russell (Eds.), *Seeing curriculum in a new light: Essays from science education* (pp. 88–99). Toronto: OISE Press.

Orpwood, G. (1985). The reflective deliberator: A case study of curriculum policymaking. *Journal of Curriculum Studies, 17*(3), 293–304.

Östman, L. (1994). Rethinking science teaching as a moral act. *Journal of Nordic Educational Research, 14*(3), 141–150.

Östman, L. (1995). *Socialisation och mening: No-utbildning som politiskt och miljö-moraliskt problem* [Socialization and meaning: Science education as a political and environmental-ethical problem] (Uppsala Studies in Education 61). Stockholm: Almqvist & Wiksell.

Östman, L. (1996a). Discourses, discursive meanings and socialization in chemistry education. *Journal of Curriculum Studies, 28*(1), 37–55.

Östman, L. (1996b, April). Language, companion meaning and socialization. Paper presented at the American Educational Research Association Conference, New York.

Östman, L., & Roberts, D. A. (1994). Toward understanding the production of meaning in science education. *Journal of Nordic Educational Research, 14*(1), 2–9.

Oxford University Department of Educational Studies. (1989). *Enquiry into the attitudes of sixth-formers towards choice of science and technology courses in higher education.* Oxford: Author.

Panwar, R., & Hoddinott, J. (1995). The influence of academic scientists and technologists on Alberta's secondary science curriculum policy and programme. *International Journal of Science Education, 17*(4), 505–518.

Pella, M. O. (1976). The place and function of science for a literate citizenry. *Science Education, 60*(1), 97–101.

Pepper, S. C. (1942). *World hypotheses: A study in evidence.* Berkeley: University of California Press.

Pepper, S. C. (1945). *Basis of criticism in the arts.* Cambridge, MA: Harvard University Press.

Peters, R. S. (1967). *Authority, responsibility and education.* New York: Atherton Press.

Phelan, P., Davidson, A., & Cao, H. (1991). Students' multiple worlds: Negotiating the boundaries of family, peer, and school cultures. *Anthropology and Education Quarterly, 22*(3), 224–250.

Phenix, P. H. (1964). *Realms of meaning: A philosophy of the curriculum for general education.* New York: McGraw-Hill.

Pomeroy, D. (1994). Science education and cultural diversity: Mapping the field. *Studies in Science Education, 24,* 49–73.

Posner, G. F. (1988). Models of curriculum planning. In L. E. Beyer & M. Apple (Eds.), *The curriculum: Problems, politics, and possibilities* (pp. 77–97). Albany: State University of New York Press.

Posner, G. F. (1992). *Analyzing the curriculum.* New York: McGraw-Hill.

Prosser, M., Trigwell, K., & Taylor, P. (1994). A phenomenographic study of academics' conceptions of science learning and teaching. *Learning and Innovation, 4*(3), 217–231.

Qian, G., & Alvermann, D. (1995). Role of epistemological beliefs and learned helplessness in secondary school students' learning science concepts from text. *Journal of Educational Psychology, 87*(2), 282–292.

Ramsey, W. L., Gabriel, L. A., McGurik, J. F., Phillips, C. R., & Watenpaugh, F. M. (1986). *Holt life science. Teachers' edition.* Toronto: Holt, Rinehart & Winston.

Roberts, D. A. (1982a). Curriculum emphases: A key area for teacher decision making (the case of school science). In K. A. Leithwood (Ed.), *Studies in curriculum decision making* (pp. 211–227). Toronto: OISE Press.

Roberts, D. A. (1982b). Developing the concept of "curriculum emphases" in science education. *Science Education, 66*(2), 243–260.

Roberts, D. A. (1982c). The place of qualitative research in science education. *Journal of Research in Science Teaching, 19*(4), 277–292.

Roberts, D. A. (1988). What counts as science education? In P. J. Fensham (Ed.), *Development and dilemmas in science education* (pp. 27–54). New York: Falmer Press.

Roberts, D. A. (1995a). Building companion meanings into school science programs: Keeping the logic straight about curriculum emphases. *Journal of Nordic Educational Research, 15*(2), 108–124.

Roberts, D. A. (1995b). Scientific literacy: The importance of multiple "curriculum emphases" in science education standards. In R. W. Bybee & J. D. McInerney (Eds.),

Rethinking the science curriculum: A report on the implications of standards and benchmarks for science education (pp. 75–80). Colorado Springs: BSCS.

Robottom, I. (1983). Science: A limited vehicle for environmental education. *Australian Science Teachers Journal, 29*(1), 27–31.

Roman, L. (1993). White is a color! White defensiveness, postmodernism, and antiracist pedagogy. In C. McCarthy & W. Chrichlow (Eds.), *Race, identity, and representation in education* (pp. 71–88). New York: Routledge.

Rorty, R. (1982). *Consequences of pragmatism*. Minneapolis: University of Minnesota Press.

Rosenthal, D. B., & Bybee, R. W. (1987). Emergence of the biology curriculum: A science of life or a science of living? In T. S. Popkewitz (Ed.), *The formation of the school subjects: The struggle for creating an American institution* (pp. 123–144). New York: Falmer Press.

Rowe, P. G. (1992). *Design thinking*. Cambridge, MA: MIT Press.

Rushton, J. P. (1991). Do r-K strategies underlie human race differences? A reply to Weizmann et al. *Canadian Psychology, 32*(1), 29–42.

Russell, T. L. (1983). Analyzing arguments in science classroom discourse: Can teachers' questions distort scientific authority? *Journal of Research in Science Teaching, 20*(1), 27–45.

Ryan, A. G., & Aikenhead, G. S. (1992). Students' preconceptions about the epistemology of science. *Science Education, 76*(6), 559–580.

Rydell, R. W. (1993). *World of fairs: The century-of-progress expositions*. Chicago: University of Chicago Press.

Säfström, C. (1994). *Makt och mening. Förutsättningar för en innehållsfokuserad pedagogisk forskning* [Power and meaning. The prior conditions for content-focused educational research] (Uppsala Studies in Education 53). Stockholm: Almqvist & Wiksell.

Säfström, C. (1996). Education as a science within a scientific rational discourse. *Journal of Curriculum Studies, 28*(1), 57–71.

Säljö, R. (1990). Språk och institution: Den institutionaliserade inlärningens metaforer [Language and institution: The metaphors of institutionalized learning]. *Forskning om Utbildning, 17*(4), 5–17.

Säljö, R. (1992a). Human growth and the complex society: The monocultural bias of theories of learning. *Cultural Dynamics, 5*(1), 43–56.

Säljö, R. (1992b). Kontext och mänskliga samspel. Ett sociokulturellt perspektiv på lärande [Context and human interaction. A sociocultural perspective on learning]. *Utbildning och demokrati, 1*(2), 21–36.

Säljö, R. (1995). Begreppsbildning som pedagogisk drog [Concept formation as pedagogic drug]. *Utbildning och demokrati, 4*(1), 5–22.

Säljö, R. (1996a, April). *Concepts, learning, and the constitution of objects and events in discursive practices*. Paper presented at the American Educational Research Association Conference, New York.

Säljö, R. (1996b). Mental and physical artifacts in cognitive practices. In P. Reimann & H. Spada (Eds.), *Learning in humans and machines: Towards an interdisciplinary learning science* (pp. 83–96). Oxford: Pergamon.

Säljö, R., & Wyndhamn, J. (1988). A week has seven days. Or does it? On bridging linguistic openness and mathematical precision. *For the Learning of Mathematics, 8*(3), 16–19.

Scheffler, I. (1965a). *Conditions of knowledge: An introduction to epistemology and education.* Glenview, IL: Scott, Foresman.

Scheffler, I. (1965b). Philosophical models of teaching. *Harvard Educational Review, 35,* 131–143.

Schilling, M. (1986). Knowledge and liberal education. *Journal of Curriculum Studies, 18*(1), 1–16.

Schutz, A., & Luckmann, T. (1973). *Structures of the life world.* London: Heinemann.

Schwab, J. J. (1962). The teaching of science as enquiry. In J. J. Schwab & P. F. Brandwein, *The teaching of science* (pp. 3–103). Cambridge, MA: Harvard University Press.

Schwab, J. J. (1970). *The practical: A language for curriculum.* Washington, DC: National Education Association.

Schwab, J. J. (1974). Decision and choice: The coming duty of science teaching. *Journal of Research in Science Teaching, 11,* 309–317.

Science Council of Canada. (1984). *Science for every student: Educating Canadians for tomorrow's world.* Hull, PQ: Canadian Government Publishing Centre.

Seymour, E. (1992). Undergraduate problems in teaching and advising in S.M.E. majors: Explaining gender differences in attrition rates. *Journal of College Science Teaching, 21*(5), 284–298.

Shapiro, B. (1992). A life of science learning: An approach to the study of personal, social and cultural features in the initiation to school science. In G. L. C. Hills (Ed.), *History and philosophy of science in science education* (Vol. II, pp. 429–447). Kingston, ON: Faculty of Education, Queen's University.

Shipman, P. (1994). *The evolution of racism: Human differences and the use and abuse of science.* New York: Simon & Schuster.

Shotter, J. (1992). *Conversational realities.* London: Sage.

Simonelli, R. (1994). Sustainable science: A look at science through historic eyes and through the eyes of indigenous peoples. *Bulletin of Science, Technology & Society, 14*(1), 1–12.

Slesnick, I. L., Balzer, L., McCormack, A. J., Newton, D. E., & Rasmussen, F. A. (1985). *Scott, Foresman biology.* Glenview, IL: Scott, Foresman.

Snow, C. P. (1964). *The two cultures.* New York: Menton Books.

Snow, C. P. (1965). *The two cultures: And a second look.* Cambridge: Cambridge University Press.

Solomon, J. (1984). Prompts, cues and discrimination: The utilization of two separate knowledge systems. *European Journal of Science Education, 6*(3), 277–284.

Solomon, J. (1987). Social influences on the construction of pupils' understanding of science. *Studies in Science Education, 14,* 63–82.

Solomon, J. (1988). Science technology and society courses: Tools for thinking about social issues. *International Journal of Science Education, 10*(4), 379–387.

Solomon, J. (1994a). Knowledge, values and the public choice of science knowledge. In J. Solomon & G. Aikenhead (Eds.), *STS education: International perspectives on reform* (pp. 99–110). New York: Teachers College Press.

Solomon, J. (1994b). Towards a notion of home culture. *British Education Resource Journal, 20*(5), 565–577.

Solomon, J., & Aikenhead, G. (Eds.). (1994). *STS education: International perspectives on reform.* New York: Teachers College Press.

Songer, N. B., & Linn, M. C. (1991). How do students' views of science influence knowledge integration? *Journal of Research in Science Teaching, 28*(9), 761–784.

Sonidsson, G., & Hörnqvist, A. (1984). *Undersökande kemi. Grundskolans högstadium* [Investigative chemistry. Lower secondary school]. Stockholm: Natur och Kultur.

Steedman, P. H. (1988). Curriculum and knowledge selection. In L. E. Beyer & M. W. Apple (Eds.), *The curriculum: Problems, politics, and possibilities* (pp. 119–139). Albany: State University of New York Press.

Stepan, N. L. (1982). *The idea of race in science: Great Britain, 1800–1960.* London: Macmillan.

Stepan, N. L. (1993). Race and gender: The role of analogy in science. In S. Harding (Ed.), *The racial economy of science: Toward a democratic future* (pp. 359–376). Bloomington: Indiana University Press.

Swerdlow, J. L. (1995). Quiet miracles of the brain. *National Geographic, 187*(6), 2–41.

Thomas, I. (1987). Assessing understanding of science, technology and society interactions in a public examination. In D. Waddington (Ed.), *Education, industry and technology: Vol. 3. Science and technology education and future needs* (pp. 199–220). Oxford: ICSU–ST and Pergamon.

Thorp, S. (1991). *Race, equality and science teaching.* London: Association for Science Education.

Tobias, S. (1990). *They're not dumb, they're different: Stalking the second tier.* Tucson, AZ: Research Corporation.

Toulmin, S. E. (1958). *The uses of argument.* Cambridge: Cambridge University Press.

Tyler, R. W. (1949). *Basic principles of curriculum and instruction.* Chicago: University of Chicago Press.

Uno, G. E., & Bybee, R. W. (1994, September). Understanding the dimensions of biological literacy. *BioScience, 44*(8), 553–557.

van Berkel, B. S. (1994). A conceptual structure of school chemistry. In P. Janich & N. Psarros (Eds.), *Proceedings of the Second Erlenmeyer colloquy* (Vol. 1, pp. 141–157). Würzburg, Germany: Verlag Königshausen und Neumann GmbH.

Vickers, G. (1965). *The art of judgment: A study of policymaking.* London: Chapman & Hall.

Victoria Curriculum and Assessment Board. (1990, February). *Provisional science study design.* Melbourne: Author.

Voloshinov, V. N. (1973). *Marxism and the philosophy of language* (L. Matejka & I. R. Titunik, Trans.). New York: Seminar Press. (Original work published 1930)

von Wright, G. H. (1991). *Vetenskapen och förnuftet* [Science and reason]. Stockholm: Månpocket.

Vygotsky, L. S. (1986). *Thought and language* (A. Kozulin, Trans.). Cambridge, MA: MIT Press.

Walker, D. F. (1971). A naturalistic model for curriculum development. *School Review, 80*(1), 51–65.

Walker, D., & Soltis, J. (1986). *Curriculum and aims*. New York: Teachers College Press.

Wason, P. C., & Johnson-Laird, P. N. (1972). *Psychology of reasoning: Structure and content*. London: Batsford.

Watson, F. G. (1967). Why do we need more physics courses? *The Physics Teacher, 5*, 212–214.

Webster, V. R., Fichter, G. S., Coble, C. R., & Rice, D. R. (1980). *Prentice-Hall life science. Teachers' annotated edition*. Englewood Cliffs, NJ: Prentice-Hall.

Weizmann, F., Wiener, N., Wiesenthal, D., & Ziegler, M. (1991). Discussion. Eggs, eggplants and eggheads: A rejoinder to Rushton. *Canadian Psychology, 32*(1), 43–50.

Wertsch, J. V. (1985). *Vygotsky and the social formation of mind*. Cambridge, MA: Harvard University Press.

Wertsch, J. V. (1991). *Voices of the mind: A sociocultural approach to mediated action*. Cambridge, MA: Harvard University Press.

West, L. H. T., & Pines, A. L. (Eds.). (1985). *Cognitive structure and conceptual change*. New York: Academic Press.

Westbury, I. (1995). Didaktik and curriculum theory: Are they the two sides of the same coin? In S. Hopmann & K. Riquarts (Eds.), *Didaktik and/or curriculum* (pp. 233–263). Kiel: Institut für die Pädagogik der Naturwissenschaften an der Universität Kiel.

Whitty, G. (1985). *Sociology and school knowledge*. London: Methuen.

Willinsky, J. (1998). *Learning to divide the world: Education at empire's end*. Minneapolis: University of Minnesota Press.

Wittgenstein, L. (1995). *Philosophical investigations* (G. E. M. Anscombe, Trans.). Oxford: Blackwell. (Original work published 1953)

Wittrock, M. C. (1994). Generative science teaching. In P. J. Fensham, R. F. Gunstone, & R. T. White (Eds.), *The content of science: A constructivist approach to its teaching and learning* (pp. 29–38). New York: Falmer Press.

Wolcott, H. F. (1991). Propriospect and the acquisition of culture. *Anthropology and Education Quarterly, 22*(3), 251–273.

Wong, W. (1993). *Principles of form and design*. New York: Van Nostrand Reinhold.

Worster, D. (1985). *Nature's economy: A history of ecological ideas*. Cambridge: Cambridge University Press.

Wynne, B. (1991). Knowledge in context. *Science, Technology and Human values, 16*(1), 111–121.

Young, R. E. (1980). The controlling curriculum and the practical ideology of teachers. *Australian and New Zealand Journal of Sociology, 16*(2), 62–70.

Zacharias, J. R., & White, S. (1964). The requirements for major curriculum revision. In R. W. Heath (Ed.), *New curricula* (pp. 68–81). New York: Harper & Row.

Ziegler, M., Weizmann, F., Wiener, N., & Wiesenthal, D. (1989). Phillipe Rushton and the growing acceptance of "race-science." *Canadian Forum, 68*(781), 19–22.

Ziman, J. (1980). *Teaching and learning about science and society*. New York: Cambridge University Press.

About the Editors and the Contributors

Glen S. Aikenhead is a Professor in the College of Education, University of Saskatchewan, Saskatoon, Canada. A humanistic perspective on science has guided his research into student assessment, classroom instruction, curriculum policy, and classroom materials. Dr. Aikenhead has published books, monographs, and articles in all four of the above areas, including *Science: A Way of Knowing, Science in Social Issues: Implications for Teaching, Teaching Science Through an STSE Approach*, and *Logical Reasoning in Science and Technology*. He has served as chairperson of the International Organization for Science and Technology Education, as Special Section Editor for *Science Education*, and most recently as co-editor (with Joan Solomon) and contributor to *STS Education: International Perspectives on Reform*.

Rodger W. Bybee is Executive Director of the Center for Science, Mathematics, and Engineering Education at the National Research Council, Washington, DC. For 10 years prior to that appointment he worked at Biological Sciences Curriculum Study (BSCS). The author and editor of many publications about science curriculum, especially in biology, he recently published *Reforming Science Education: Social Perspectives and Personal Reflections*.

Tomas Englund is a Professor of Education at the Department of Education, Uppsala University, and also at the University of Örebro, Sweden. His research interests center on curriculum theory/didactics, curriculum history, political socialization/citizenship education, and philosophical aspects of education. Among his publications are *Curriculum as a Political Problem, Citizenship Education in Swedish Schools in the Twentieth Century* (in Swedish), and *The Educational Policy Shift in Sweden* (in Swedish), as well as chapters in books and articles in various journals, such as *Journal of Curriculum Studies, Scandinavian Journal of Educational Research*, and *Curriculum Studies*.

Peter J. Fensham is Professor Emeritus of Science Education, School of Graduate Studies, Faculty of Education, Monash University, Australia, where he held a chair in Science Education from 1967 until his retirement in 1992. Professor

Fensham's interests include science education (curriculum issues), environmental and technology education, and equity in education. His significant publications include *Science for All, Development and Dilemmas in Science Education*, "Science and Technology" in the *Handbook of Research on Curriculum*, and *The Content of Science: A Constructivist Approach to Its Teaching and Learning*.

Arthur N. Geddis is an Associate Professor in the Faculty of Education at the University of Western Ontario, London, Canada. He teaches graduate courses in science education and curriculum studies and works with preservice science teachers. His research interest in the improvement of teaching is a natural outgrowth of the 24 years he spent teaching science in schools. Since 1990, he has conducted and published research with the "Learning About Teaching Group," which is examining preservice teacher education with a focus on the practice of teacher educators.

Brent Kilbourn is an Associate Professor at The Ontario Institute for Studies in Education, University of Toronto, Canada, where he also holds an appointment in the Department of Curriculum, Teaching, and Learning and in the Centre for Teacher Development. In addition to numerous articles on science education and the analysis of teaching, he is the author of *Constructive Feedback: Learning the Art*.

Hugh Munby is a Professor in the Faculty of Education, Queen's University, Kingston, Canada, where he has taught in the graduate and preservice programs since 1971. In 1996, Dr. Munby received the Whitworth Award for Educational Research from the Canadian Education Association, recognizing his research contributions to fields such as science education and teachers' knowledge.

Graham Orpwood is an Associate Professor in the Faculty of Education at York University, Toronto, Canada. A former teacher in England, Ontario, and New York, he was also Director of the Science Council of Canada study on science education in Canadian schools in the 1980s and science coordinator of the Third International Mathematics and Science Study (TIMSS) in the 1990s. His present interests include science curriculum and assessment policy in the service of educational reform and the assessment of scientific literacy.

Leif Östman (Editor) is a Lecturer in the Department of Teacher Training at Uppsala University, Sweden. His research interests include curriculum theory, curriculum history, communication theory, social epistemology, political and moral socialization, and science education. In addition to articles in journals such as *Journal of Curriculum Studies* and *Journal of Nordic Educational Research*, he has published *Socialization and Meaning: Science Education as a Political and Environmental-Ethical Problem* (in Swedish).

Douglas A. Roberts (Editor) is a Professor in the Faculty of Education at the University of Calgary, Canada. His research interests include curriculum policy and implementation, science curriculum history, and science teacher thinking as it relates to teacher preparation and classroom practice. Dr. Roberts has published articles, monographs, and classroom materials in these areas, including *Scientific Literacy: Toward Balance in Setting Goals for School Science Programs* and a 7-volume set of *Science and Society Teacher Manuals*. In 1992 he received an Award for Distinguished Contribution to Curriculum in Canada, from the Canadian Association for Curriculum Studies.

Roger Säljö is a Professor of Educational Psychology at Göteborg University. For the previous 15 years, he was Professor of Behavioural Sciences at Linköping University, Sweden. His research interests include human learning, development, and interaction from a sociocultural and discursive perspective, areas in which he has published widely. He is also the editor of *Learning and Instruction*, the journal of the European Association for Research on Learning.

Joan Solomon is Professor of Science Education at the Open University, Milton Keynes, and Visiting Professor at King's College, London. For the previous 14 years, she was Lecturer in Research at the Oxford University Department of Educational Studies. She was the National Coordinator of the Science in a Social Context (SISCON) Project. Dr. Solomon has carried out substantial research on many aspects of science education. She is the author of *Teaching Children in the Laboratory*, *SISCON-in-Schools*, *Explaining the Nature of Science*, *Getting to Know About Energy*, and *Teaching Science, Technology & Society*. She is a co-editor (with Glen Aikenhead) and contributor to *STS Education: International Perspectives on Reform*.

John Willinsky is a Professor of Language Education at the University of British Columbia, Vancouver, Canada. He recently published *Learning to Divide the World: Education at Empire's End,* and currently he is spending a year as Wm. Allen Visiting Professor of Education at Seattle University.

Index